"At last, an analysis that gives thorough att[...] history! Nijay Gupta's *Tell Her Story* une[...] women and their allies. It may be the final nail in the co[...]"
Mimi Haddad, president of CBE International

"A first-rate introduction to the place of women in the earliest churches. With care and sensitivity to the ancient context, Nijay Gupta skillfully uncovers the stories of a range of female leaders, teachers, and missionaries, and highlights their relevance for today. If you think that only men held leadership roles in the first-century church, you need to read this book! Highly recommended for students and church groups alike."
Helen K. Bond, chair of Christian Origins and head of the School of Divinity at the University of Edinburgh

"Oh, what we can learn when we tell her story! Wherever you stand on women in the church, *Tell Her Story* will enrich you. This book shows that we still have a lot of work to do in making women visible. What do the stories of women in Scripture teach us about our God, discipleship, and ministry? How we listen to these stories can reveal what we value. Nijay Gupta gives witness to God's work in the unfolding of the prominence of women in the Scriptures, which also makes visible the overarching story and our location in it as the bride of Christ."
Aimee Byrd, author of *The Sexual Reformation*

"This book is a significant contribution to the ongoing conversations about women in leadership in the early church. Nijay Gupta takes the reader on an important journey throughout the New Testament and demonstrates that 'wherever men were doing ministry, women were there doing it as well,' leading, teaching, and ministering not as second-class citizens but as equals bearing witness to the power of the gospel to transform lives."
Lisa Bowens, associate professor of New Testament at Princeton Theological Seminary

"The history of Christianity is filled with untold, even hidden stories of women's contributions to the ministry of the church from Scripture and beyond. That's why it's my pleasure to recommend biblical scholar Nijay Gupta's most recent book, which features the stories of prominent women from Scripture and the early church based on the most current scholarship. In a readable, informed, vulnerable, and engaging way, Gupta sets the record straight that women could and did serve in significant roles in ministry leadership from Christianity's inception."
Jennifer McNutt, Franklin S. Dyrness Associate Professor of Biblical and Theological Studies at Wheaton College

"In *Tell Her Story*, Nijay Gupta brings to the topic of early Christian women (and some of their foremothers) a mastery of New Testament texts and backgrounds. Combining academic expertise with approachable prose, Gupta takes a fresh look at stories, people, and contexts—from judge Deborah leading Israel, to deacon-patron Phoebe delivering the epistle to the Romans, to apostle Junia doing prison time. In exploring the prominent place of women in the history of our faith, the author recovers lost meanings and casts a vision for men and women partnering to serve God's people."

Sandra Glahn, seminary professor and general editor of *Vindicating the Vixens*

Tell Her Story

How Women Led, Taught, and
Ministered in the Early Church

Nijay K. Gupta

Academic

An imprint of InterVarsity Press
Downers Grove, Illinois

InterVarsity Press
P.O. Box 1400 | Downers Grove, IL 60515-1426
ivpress.com | email@ivpress.com

©2023 by Nijay Kumar Gupta

InterVarsity Press® is the publishing division of InterVarsity Christian Fellowship/USA®. For more information, visit intervarsity.org.

Figure 1: Archivio Fotografico del Parco Archeologico di Ostia Antica. Used by permission.
Figure 2: Everett Ferguson Photo Collection, Brown Library, Abilene Christian University. Creative Commons License CC BY 4.0.

The publisher cannot verify the accuracy or functionality of website URLs used in this book beyond the date of publication.

Cover design and image composite: David Fassett
Interior design: Jeanna Wiggins

ISBN 978-1-5140-0074-8 (print) | ISBN 978-1-5140-0075-5 (digital)

Printed in the United States of America ♾

Library of Congress Cataloging-in-Publication Data
Names: Gupta, Nijay K., author.
Title: Tell her story : how women led, taught, and ministered in the early church / Nijay K. Gupta ; foreword by IVP Academic.
Description: Downers Grove, IL : InterVarsity Press, 2023. | Includes bibliographical references and index.
Identifiers: LCCN 2022046015 (print) | LCCN 2022046016 (ebook) | ISBN 9781514000748 (print) |
   ISBN 9781514000755 (digital)
Subjects: LCSH: Women in the Bible. | Bible. New Testament—Biography.
Classification: LCC BS2445 .G87 2023 (print) | LCC BS2445 (ebook) | DDC 220.9/2082–dc23/eng/20221115
LC record available at https://lccn.loc.gov/2022046015
LC ebook record available at https://lccn.loc.gov/2022046016

29   28   27   26   25   24   23 | 13   12   11   10   9   8   7   6

To Amy

Contents

Foreword

Beth Allison Barr

Wind gusted through the streets of Salisbury that morning, rushing past in an audible swirl as the door closed behind me. An abrupt silence followed, ringing almost as loud as the wind. For the first time I stood inside the parish church of St. Thomas and St. Edmund. It was founded in the thirteenth century to provide the workers building Salisbury Cathedral a place to worship, but the current church dates mostly from the fifteenth century.

What I had come to see was one of the fifteenth-century additions: the "Doom" (Last Judgment) mural stretched high above the chancel arch. Sometime between 1470 and 1500 a local artist painted the resurrected Christ sitting on a double rainbow in judgment over the saved and the damned. Vibrant robes of red, blue, gold, and green drape the twelve disciples lined up at his feet; angels with trumpets and wings welcome the blessed into the streets of heaven; and scaly demons drag unrepentant sinners into the jaws of hell. The words *Nulla est Redemptio* (There is no escape for the wicked) made sure viewers understood their fate.

It is a stunning sight.

I don't remember how long I stood there, just staring at the image. I finally looked away because I was short on time and there was more to see. Tucked away to the right of the Doom mural, three more late-fifteenth-century paintings grace the interior of the stone arches separating the nave from the Lady chapel. Although less well restored and much smaller than the depiction of the Final Judgment, they show scenes just as significant to medieval Christians: the annunciation by the angel Gabriel to the Virgin Mary, the visitation of Mary to Elizabeth, and the adoration of the Magi.

Again, I stood transfixed, looking mostly at the center image in which Mary—her visibly pregnant body juxtaposed with her long flowing hair, the symbol of her virginity—greeted her also visibly pregnant cousin. The faded colors of the image do not dull the women's joy as they each touch the swollen belly of the other. Not only do they see the miracle God has wrought within their bodies, but the fifteenth-century artist who painted them made sure that all who visited the church would see that miracle too.

Except that, for more than two hundred years, no one did.

For more than two hundred years, no one knew these medieval paintings existed.

According to the official church guide, the walls were whitewashed during the Reformation—hiding the striking medieval Catholic scenes behind a drab coat of Protestant white. For generations worshipers came and went through this church, not much more than a stone's throw from the soaring spire of Salisbury Cathedral. They listened to sermons, sang hymns, celebrated weddings, and buried their friends. Their eyes would have wandered across the wood beamed ceiling and stone walls around them. Yet, until 1819 when someone investigated the traces of color in the chancel arch above, no one who had been inside the church of St. Thomas after the sixteenth century had seen the medieval paintings that were (and had always been) right before their eyes.

As I read Nijay Gupta's *Tell Her Story,* it struck me how much women in the early church are like these medieval paintings in St. Thomas. Just as Deborah was called by God to lead Israel and did so successfully, with wisdom and integrity, Jewish women served their synagogues in leadership roles, even as synagogue rulers. Should it surprise us, then, that women in the early church led in similar ways? From women disciples like Mary Magdalene and Joanna the wife of Chuza, who traveled with Jesus and learned from him, showing up, as Gupta writes, "when the men were nowhere to be found," to ministry couples like Priscilla and Aquila in which the wife took the foremost role, to Lydia of Philippi who led a house church, *diakonoi* like Phoebe of Cenchreae, coworkers like Euodia and Syntyche, and even apostles like Junia imprisoned for her ministry work—women in the early church led with the approval and support of men around them.

Like the fifteenth-century painter who rounded Mary's belly with his brush and lit her face with a smile as she welcomed her cousin, Nijay Gupta breathes historical life into the dry bones of these biblical women— showing us the vivid reality of their leadership. Just like the Doom painting soaring about the nave in St. Thomas, women led in the early church. The problem has never been their existence. The problem has only been our ability to see them.

This is the brilliance of *Tell Her Story*. It does not tell a new story; it just helps us see the story as it has always been. The modern restorations in the parish church of St. Thomas and St. Edmund did not paint the scene of the Last Judgment or the visitation between Mary and Elizabeth; the restorations only helped us see what the medieval artist had already done. In the same way, *Tell Her Story* helps us see biblical women as they have always been—faithful leaders called by God and recognized by the early church. What Nijay Gupta has done for us is simply, brilliantly, to remove the whitewash.

God has always seen women.

I'm so thankful for Nijay Gupta because, in *Tell Her Story*, he helps us see them too.

Acknowledgments

I have been thinking and teaching about the women leaders of the early church for over fifteen years, so this book has been a long time coming. Special thanks are owed to Anna Gissing, one of the finest editors in the business and also a good friend, and to Jon Boyd, who stepped in to see this book to completion with skill and enthusiasm. A number of colleagues generously offered resources, advice, and feedback along the way: Lynn Cohick, Katya Covrett, Beverly Gaventa, Kimberly Majeski, Scot McKnight, Marg Mowczko, Margaret Mitchell, Peter Oakes, and Cindy Westfall. I was able to test out some of my ideas in the fall of 2021 when I gave Anderson University's Newell Lectures on women in the New Testament. Also in 2021 I taught a seminar on women and the New Testament at Northern Seminary, a memorable course full of rich and rewarding conversations with my students.

Introduction

Hidden Figures

In 2016, Margot Lee Shetterly's book *Hidden Figures* made a big splash in nonfiction literature. Shetterly pushed into the public spotlight the lives of three Black women in the 1950s who made major achievements in mathematics and engineering in their work for NASA. We should have grown up knowing the names and accomplishments of Katherine Johnson, Dorothy Vaughan, and Mary Jackson—but we didn't. We are more acquainted with the men who went into space, whom we remember in textbooks and for whom we build statues and monuments. But some of the great American space-flight achievements would not have been possible without these brilliant and brave women, eager to make scientific breakthroughs in spite of the sexism and racism they faced.

In the summer of 2020, NASA announced that its Washington, DC, headquarters would be renamed the Mary W. Jackson building in honor of its first African American female engineer. This is a reminder to me that we can all benefit from telling the stories of women who have done great things. The problem of unknown changemakers is not just a 1950s phenomenon, or 1850s, or 1750s. As I learned about these three Black women, I couldn't help but wonder what leadership contributions made by ancient women have been "lost to history" and obscured by cultural dynamics and the myopia of our history tellers. More specifically related to Christian history, what do we really know about women leaders in the early church?

Most of us are familiar with a few names. Mary, the mother of Jesus, was clearly an important figure, not only in the life of Jesus as mother, disciple, *and* mentor of the Messiah, but also after Jesus' ascension, when she was still centrally involved in the gospel mission (Acts 1:14).[1] Prisca (a.k.a. Priscilla) is another notable figure; she was an artisan and business-woman, and she and her husband, Aquila, were a traveling missionary couple who were frontline gospel-mission leaders. But were there others?

In the early years of my Christian faith, my knowledge of the contri-bution of early women leaders pretty much ended with these two women. I had the impression that ministry was a man's job—after all, patriarchy ruled the day (more on that in chapter three). But historians like Shet-terly have left me wondering, *What stories have not been told, perhaps once known, but later lost and forgotten?* I have come to learn over the past twenty years that the New Testament *does* testify to the roles and impact of many women, if only we pay attention. But I didn't always think that way.

When I began reading the Bible as a teenager, I attended a church where men stood up front and led the church service, only men served as elders, and only men could preach the Word of God. In college, I participated in parachurch ministries that had male-only campus di-rectors (in some cases as a policy). I took for granted that this is the way things should be in the church and that this reflects what is in the Bible—men are leaders, women are followers and supporters. At first, I didn't really question any of this, because it was so deeply ingrained in the church and ministry cultures I was in at the time, and also because it could be reinforced by appealing to the fact that Jesus was a man, the disciples were all men, and the Bible said women couldn't teach or have authority in the church (didn't it?). So, for about the first decade of my Christian faith, I was content with the assumption that the church is for everyone to attend and participate in, but should be led by men, because that's the way it has always been according to the Good Book. Then I went to seminary.

---

[1]See chapter four in this book for more on Mary, the mother of Jesus.

No, seminary didn't turn me "liberal." I learned the biblical languages (Greek, Hebrew, Aramaic), and I was trained and challenged to study the Bible and its world in depth, and it opened up a three-dimensional world, where I had experienced before only a two-dimensional one. Before, I had been *unconsciously* constructing a theology of gender (where men lead, women support) on the basis of a handful of biblical texts and a few observable patterns (male Israelite priests, male disciples), but the tools I acquired in seminary equipped me to look more *comprehensively* at the Bible in its time, culture, and environment. And I began to see the women that were there all along (just like the women of NASA in the twentieth century) but to whom I hadn't paid much attention. These women leaders of the early church are more than just extras on the set of the gospel drama. They are often key characters. I was not taught their importance in my early years, but I know better now. And now more than ever, their presence and work deserve our attention, our thorough examination, and also our admiration.

This book, to be clear, is *not* an attempt at some form of revisionist history. Our goal is not to upend everything said or written before about the history of the early church. It is an exercise in *amplification*. For centuries, the church has focused its interest on the male leaders of the early church—as if women weren't even there. In fact, some seem to think women *weren't* there in the rooms where important things happened. But there is ample evidence inside and outside the New Testament that women *were* actively involved in ministry, at the frontier of the gospel mission, as respected leaders in the church, and even as primary leaders of household congregations. Does what I am saying sound unbelievable? Women leaders of the earliest Christian churches? That is precisely why a book like this is necessary.

Part of the problem is that we often bring to the New Testament what I call a "Little House on the Prairie" perspective on the world of Jesus and the apostles. When we think about "the ancient world," we might imagine a place where mama and sister are sewing in the house while soup begins to boil in the pot. Father is out hunting, and brother is chopping wood. That image of the family might resemble rural life throughout time, but we need a more diverse, complex, and sophisticated imagination to conceive of life in the many-cultures world of the Roman Empire, which is the historical, social, political, religious, and cultural environment of the New Testament, and the home of the birth of the early Jesus communities. Patriarchy was the dominant cultural infrastructure of the Roman world, but that system did not mean that women were resigned to only "domesticated" duties, or that they never exercised leadership or power related to civic life, religion, or business.

Let's briefly look at a case study: Romans 16:1-15 (we will discuss this passage in much more detail in chapter six). This is a greetings and commendation list from Paul to the churches in Rome. It's the kind of thing we might just skip over when reading this weighty letter, like the closing credits of a movie. But this is precisely the kind of stuff that historians pay attention to. There is a gold mine of information embedded in these verses that tells us a lot about the lives of the early Christians.

There are, in total, twenty-six people mentioned in this list. (That may not seem like an interesting phenomenon, but think about it like this: Apart from the genealogies in Matthew and Luke, do you know of another long list of names in the New Testament?) The fact of Paul's greeting implies that he knew these people, either in person or perhaps in some cases by reputation. His comments, titles, and descriptions are all positive, so he was honoring each of them publicly, praising them as model leaders. Ten of them are women. Ponder that for a moment: more than a third of Paul's list was model Christian women, many of them recognized Roman leaders: Phoebe (vv. 1-2), Priscilla (v. 3), Mary (v. 6), Junia (v. 7), Tryphena and Tryphosa (v. 12), Persis (v. 12), the mother of Rufus (v. 13), Julia (v. 15), and the sister of Nereus (v. 15). This is nothing short of astounding. First, it is unusual in any piece of literature to have such a long list of commendations of women (most of whom are mentioned without reference to a husband). Second, none of Paul's comments are focused on their domestic duties. The most common commendation Paul gives is for their "hard work" on behalf of the Lord. Paul doesn't make explicit what this work is. But it is unlikely that he had in mind household work. Why? You have to ask yourself, *How does*

Paul know these ten women? Keep in mind, he says to the Romans that he had not visited them before, so Paul did not meet the people he greeted in Rome. So where did he meet them? How exactly does he know so much about them? He could have met them anywhere they traveled for ministry, as he did with his friends Priscilla and Aquila, but travel many of them did and that tells us something about their independence and mobility. Some of these women of Romans 16 were apparently out and about doing ministry, participating in the gospel mission. Our goal in this book is to know them better and to create a more complete picture of the first-century beginnings of the people of Jesus. To achieve this goal we will listen to their stories, stories about their many inspiring contributions to the planting, growth, and health of the earliest Christian churches.

This is not a comprehensive handbook detailing the lives of all the women mentioned in the New Testament. Our discussion will be selective, focusing on the most important figures. Also, it will become clear that the writings of Paul are the main sources we will use for studying women leaders in the early churches. That is for two reasons: first, Paul is our earliest witness to early Christianity, having written his letters around the middle of the first century; second, Paul happens to mention numerous women *by name* and with some descriptions of their social status, location, social identity, and relationships. And that is extremely helpful in the historical task of reconstructing social history as best we can.

The book is broken up into two main parts plus a bonus section. In part one, I will offer the background to the main discussion of early Christian women leaders. It begins with Deborah (Judg 4–5) because of the important role she played in Israel's history. Then we will go back to Genesis 1–3 to consider Scripture's vision for man and woman, and how sin unraveled the harmony that God had created. The next chapter paints a picture of the Greco-Roman world of the first century, especially the lives of women. There are a lot of popular misconceptions about how women navigated a world of Roman patriarchy, and I think you might be surprised to learn about some of the accomplishments and positions of power associated with certain women in the Roman world. Getting some of this "scene setting" information clear as a first step is important for processing what women could and did do in those early Christian communities. That is not to say there were no legal, social, or cultural barriers for women. There were, and we will discuss that as well. But a major point of this book is to look not just at laws and generalities but at actual women who held positions of authority and power, whose faces were on coins, and who found ways to circumvent certain cultural rules and expectations. The final chapter of part one examines the women who were in the life and ministry of Jesus, according to the Gospels.

The second part of the book focuses on the women of the early churches. We will look at the many named women leaders that are discussed in the New Testament (e.g., Phoebe, Prisca, Junia). After these five chapters, we have a bonus "What About . . . ?" section. Here I address hot topics like Paul's prohibition texts (1 Tim 2:11-15) and the household codes that use submission language for women (e.g., Col 3:18–4:1).

My hope is that when we really understand the world in which Jesus and his followers lived and what the New Testament *actually* attests about women leaders in the churches, it will become clear that women were there; they were welcomed and supported by apostles like Paul, they were equipped and trained for ministry leadership, they ministered *to* leaders, they served on the frontline of the gospel mission and faced hardships because of it—and some became heroes and legends. Their stories are amazing and inspiring, and it is my honor to help tell them.

Part One

Before the
Women Leaders of
the Early Churches

1

Deborah

Prophet, Judge, Mother over Israel

When I was in the early years of my Christian faith, the idea of a woman leader among God's people with any kind of executive power or high office was, frankly, unfathomable. I never felt that women were lesser people or bad leaders as a matter of fact. It just seemed to add up that men were meant to lead, women to follow and support. But I am sure back then, some twenty-five years ago, I never read through the book of Judges. If there is one figure in this book that stands out, it is Deborah. Deborah is not the only impressive woman of faith and courage in the Old Testament—Miriam, Ruth, and Esther come to mind as well—but I find Deborah the most remarkable. Israel had many, many leaders throughout its long history before Jesus showed up. Some leaders were good, men like Jehoshaphat and Josiah. But by and large, Israel's kings and military leaders were dismissive of Torah and unfaithful to God and to their duty of leading the people of God toward covenantal faithfulness.

Deborah appears in a brief period before the monarchy of Israel—its pre-royal days, if you will. She is not mentioned in the rest of the Old Testament. She is not mentioned by name in the New Testament either, for that matter. But she certainly had an impact on the great story that the Bible tells. In her own time, her wise leadership and responsiveness to God's giftings and calling led to forty years of peace in the land (Judg 5:31). Beyond that, Deborah's warrior song of victory and praise for

God may have inspired Mary's own Song of Praise (Lk 1:46-55).[1] And surely Deborah deserves a special spot in the book of Hebrews' "Hall of Faith Heroes" (Heb 11:4-32), where many patriarchs and leaders are presented as models of perseverance in suffering. Some are named, but Hebrews gives tribute to many more heroes who "conquered kingdoms, administered justice, . . . and who became powerful in battle and routed foreign armies" (Heb 11:33-34). Judges celebrates Deborah as just such a hero of faith, so Hebrews surely has leaders like her in mind too.[2]

The reason I wanted to start this book off with Deborah is that she defies so many gender stereotypes, then and now, as she led Israel with confidence and courage. Whatever terms we might use to describe femininity and "ladylike" behavior from days of old, she does not seem to fit that mold. Whenever we might be tempted to say, "Women can't perform such and such a role in ministry because they are too . . ."—I wonder, if we can't say that about Deborah, ought we to say it about anyone?

I honestly don't know what I would have thought if someone had sat me down when I was sixteen and explained to me all the amazing things God did through this woman for the faith and glory of Israel. But about a decade ago, I was assigned to teach a college course on Judges. As I learned more about her leadership in a man's world, I was immediately struck by this leader: prophet, judge, and "mother over Israel."

THE ERA OF THE JUDGES

To fully appreciate how Deborah stands out as a courageous, wise, and effective leader in the history of Israel, we need to understand the moment in history that she found herself. The era of the "judges" was a major transition period after Israel's slavery and before the monarchy. As the Old Testament story goes, God rescued Israel from Egypt and the heavy and cruel hand of Pharaoh (Exodus). God reclaimed Israel as his own and gave them a covenantal constitution (the law of Moses) and a

---

[1]For more on this, see chapter four in this book.

[2]It is a curiosity to me that Hebrews mentions Barak but not Deborah (Heb 11:33). I can only assume that Hebrews was especially identifying warriors trained for battle (like Jephthah).

mission to become a priestly kingdom and holy nation (Ex 19:6). The plan was to settle them in a special land as a base of operations for their ministry as a light to the nations.[3] One problem (actually, more than one problem, but this one is a major focus of Joshua and Judges): there were people in the Promised Land. God would drive these people out of the land, but as the Israelites encountered any of them, they must not be tempted to worship false gods and live in the people's wicked ways (Deut 7:1-6). But by and large, Israel *failed* to conquer them and set them to flight and had to put up with the consequences: the Israelites were constantly at war with Canaanites and struggled to maintain a pure devotion to the God who freed them and made them his special possession. This "war" was not just a battle of swords and bloodshed. That happened a lot, of course. But it was also a war *within* the hearts and minds and wills of the Israelites as they struggled with divided allegiances without and temptations within.

The narrator of Judges makes it clear that this was a particularly dark era for Israel because they lacked clear and sustained leadership. This retrospective line is repeated several times: "In those days Israel had no king" (Judg 17:6; 18:1; 19:1). Looking back (from the monarchy period), the narrator recognizes that Israel wrestled in this period with living and behaving as a unified people. Instead of moving forward with their mission and ministry, they were "dragged away . . . and enticed," as James puts it (Jas 1:14), by their own evil desires, which constantly got them into situations they could not get themselves out of. Two haunting refrains are repeated in Judges: "The Israelites did what was evil in the sight of the LORD" (Judg 2:11; 3:7, 12; 4:1; 6:1; 10:6; 13:1 NRSV) and "All the people did what was right in their own eyes" (Judg 17:6; 21:25 NRSV).

So Judges narrates a seemingly hopeless cycle of ups and downs for this wayward people: (1) they cry out in suffering at the hands of the Canaanites (due in part, of course, to their failure to put them to flight);

---

[3]For helpful studies that explain the story of Israel, see Sandra L. Richter, *The Epic of Eden: A Christian Entry into the Old Testament* (Downers Grove, IL: IVP Academic, 2008); Craig G. Bartholomew and Michael W. Goheen, *The Drama of Scripture: Finding Our Place in the Biblical Story* (Grand Rapids, MI: Baker Academic, 2014).

(2) God has compassion on them and sends to them an Israelite "judge" to deliver them; (3) they experience a season of peace and rest; (4) they settle back into old wicked ways of idolatry and irresponsible intermixing with their enemies, and the trouble starts all over again.

Here is where the Israelite judges come in. First, they are not "judges" in the sense of a gavel, a robe, and a courtroom. The majority of them functioned as temporary warrior-leaders raised up by God to get Israel out of the mess that they got themselves into. But it is helpful to know that, by and large, the judges were not role models. (Remember, the book of Judges points ahead to the ideal of the Davidic monarchy.) Gideon, for example, struggled with faith and courage. Samson was pretty much an antitype to the righteous Israelite leader. Deborah is the only judge given extensive narration of whom nothing negative is said or implied. In fact, her narrative episode ends with a beautiful song of triumph and praise of God sung together with her military partner, Barak. In one of the darkest eras of Israel's history, Deborah stands as a singular, but intensely bright, luminary.

JUDGES 4:1-24: INTRODUCING DEBORAH

The story of Deborah appears in Judges 4–5. Judges begins with the death of Joshua (Judg 1:1) and the emergence of a whole new generation who did not know the Lord (Judg 2:10). They forgot their redemption from Egypt, broke the covenant, and followed the "Baals" (locally venerated idols). God gave them into the hands of their enemies: "Whenever Israel went out to fight, the hand of the LORD was against them to defeat them, just as he had sworn to them. They were in great distress" (Judg 2:15).

But the Lord raised up for them judges who served the purpose of rescuing them from their enemies (Judg 2:16). The narrator explains the cycle that repeats throughout this period: "Whenever the LORD raised up a judge for them, he was with the judge and saved them out of the hands of their enemies as long as the judge lived. . . . But when the judge died, the people returned to ways even more corrupt than those of their ancestors, following other gods and serving and worshiping them" (Judg 2:18-20).

Before getting to Deborah, let's start with a critical question for understanding this book: What is a "judge"? The Hebrew word *shophet* can
mean a judge, as in someone who decides legal cases. But in the context
of the book of Judges, the purpose of their divine calling was to rescue
Israel from hostile enemies. Thus, it makes better sense to understand
the term as "governor," as in national leader. Indeed, throughout the
book, the "judge" is also referred to as "deliverer."[4] These individuals
were called on by God, for a period of time, to lead and deliver God's
people from hostile enemies. So there was Othniel (Judg 3:9), then Ehud
(Judg 3:15), and then Deborah. In some ways, she fits the pattern of the
judge-deliverer. For example, after Ehud was gone, the Lord allowed the
Canaanites to menace Israel and treat them cruelly for twenty years.
They cried out to the Lord, and God blessed them with the wisdom and
leadership of Deborah.

But there are a couple of peculiarities in her story that break from the
pattern. First, Deborah was not "raised up" as a deliverer; she was already
"judging" Israel (Judg 4:4).[5] Also, she was not a trained warrior. (But
neither was Gideon, the judge who came after her.) Deborah is described
as a prophet and a magistrate who arbitrated disputes among the Israelites (Judg 4:4-5). This didn't make her less of a judge-deliverer; it made
her a different kind of judge, and certainly not less effective since her
ministry brought the cyclical forty years of peace (Judg 5:31).

It is worth reflecting on her ministry of settling disputes among her
people. This seems to parallel Moses' activity when he "took his seat
to serve as judge for the people" (Ex 18:13).[6] Similarly, Deborah's legal
adjudication may have intentionally foreshadowed that of Samuel,
who "judged Israel all the days of his life" (1 Sam 7:15 NRSV).[7] As
Barry Webb explains, "In many ways, Deborah's 'judging' of Israel

---

[4]The Septuagint (Greek) text of Judges renders this as *sōtēr*, "savior."
[5]Sometimes it is pointed out that Deborah is never called a "judge," but this role is assumed by
the use of the verb in Judges 4:4: "she judged [*shaphat*] Israel at that time" (my translation).
[6]See Rebecca G. Idestrom, "Deborah: A Role Model for Christian Public Ministry," in *Women,
Ministry and the Gospel: Exploring New Paradigms*, ed. Mark Husbands and Timothy Larsen
(Downers Grove, IL: IVP Academic, 2007), 17-31, at 23-24.
[7]The locations Ramah and Bethel are mentioned in Deborah's and Samuel's stories.

anticipates that of Samuel; she is a kind of female counterpart of the Samuel who is to come."[8]

What about her husband, Lappidoth? What role does he play in the leadership of Israel? This is a mystery since he is never mentioned again, and we can only assume he did not play a functional leadership role at all.[9] Deborah judged cases on her own authority, she alone counseled Barak, and she was called "mother in Israel" (Judg 5:7).

Now, it becomes clear that Deborah does not do the fighting that rescues Israel. She calls for the Israelite commander Barak and gives to him a prophetic word to conquer Sisera and Jabin's army (Judg 4:6-7). Barak asks for Deborah to go (presumably as God's spokesperson). She agrees but pronounces that the victory will happen through a woman (Judg 4:9). As the story unfolds, Deborah continues to advise Barak and his ten thousand men (Judg 4:14-15). Deborah's prophecy comes true as Sisera dies at the hand of Jael the Kenite (Judg 4:17). Jael kills Sisera with a clever trick before Barak could get to him (Judg 4:22).

Sometimes the question is raised whether God used Deborah only because there were no men available, or because Barak had weak faith.[10] But if we look at the judges as a whole, especially Gideon and Samson, it is clear that they were not chosen for their virtue or strong faith. In fact, Deborah appears to be the most faithful, the most prophetically tuned into God, and the wisest of them all. This is even more clearly pronounced in the victory song that appears in Judges 5 (see below). There is only one such song in Judges, and had Barak been the real hero, it would have been fitting for him to sing that all by himself. The fact that Deborah and Barak sing together a victory

---

[8]Barry Webb, *The Book of Judges*, New International Commentary on the Old Testament (Grand Rapids, MI: Eerdmans, 2013), 148.

[9]The Hebrew name Lappidoth means "torches," so it may be that the writer was making a spiritual point that Deborah was committed to being "a brilliant light" in those dark days; see Daniel Block, *Judges, Ruth*, New American Commentary (Nashville: Broadman & Holman, 2007); Joy Schroeder, *Deborah's Daughters* (Oxford: Oxford University Press, 2014), 236-37.

[10]For an extended engagement with this question, see Ron Pierce, "Deborah: Only When a Good Man Is Hard to Find?," in *Vindicating the Vixens*, ed. Sandra Glahn (Grand Rapids, MI: Kregel, 2017), 191-212.

hymn is extraordinary and testifies to her status as a model judge, securing peace for Israel.[11]

JUDGES 5:1-31: THE SONG OF DEBORAH AND BARAK

That brings us to the thirty-verse duet in chapter five. Deborah and Barak call Israel to recognize the faithfulness of God and his care for his people. It is a bit odd that even though they sing the song together, the song uses the language of "I" and not "we" (Judg 5:3, 9). Israel feared the Canaanites; they dared not travel on highways, and they would not fight the enemy: "they held back until I, Deborah, arose, / until I arose, a mother in Israel" (Judg 5:7). Later on, both Deborah and Barak are invoked (Judg 5:12); they are presented as a dynamic duo at war. The heavenly stars are credited with aiding in the victory, divine intervention to secure the victory for Israel (Judg 5:20); the river Kishon joined in as well (Judg 5:21). Jael is celebrated as an unassuming but intrepid ally (Judg 5:24-27). Sisera is mocked as a failed and shamed opponent (Judg 5:28-31). The song imagines Sisera's mother waiting for her son to return in victory; she can only imagine that what has delayed him is a long victory celebration and the time it takes to count his spoils.

For a warrior song in Scripture, Judges 5 spends a remarkable amount of time thinking about the stories of women: Deborah, of course, but also Jael and the mother of Sisera. The song begins with a call for "princes" and "kings" to take notice and listen (Judg 5:2-3). Normally these kinds of war tales are from men talking about men to men. Here Deborah and Barak sing about a hero woman Deborah and a hero ally Jael, and about the sad and false hopes of a foreign mother waiting for the return of a son who is never coming back. The book of Judges in many ways is very formulaic (but no less entertaining for it) because of its overt narrative patterns; however, the story and song of Deborah, the judge-deliverer, is anything but predictable.

---

[11]It is worth adding that Deborah is named first in the introduction to the song *and* she is named without reference to a male figure (father or husband), while Barak is associated with his father: "On that day Deborah and Barak son of Abinoam sang this song" (Judg 5:1).

WAS DEBORAH A SPIRITUAL LEADER IN ISRAEL?

In this phase of salvation history, God's people did not have pastors and apostles; technically the priesthood was established for Israel, but without a constructed temple they had no permanent base of operations. The people would have looked to the governing leaders and tribal elders for covenantal guidance. Moses was the primary leader to free Israel from Egypt and to bring them to Sinai. He was responsible for leading them to the Promised Land, Canaan, but his story concluded before they entered the land. His mantle was passed on to Joshua. Joshua was a crucial military leader for Israel, but he also led them toward obedience to God. This is climactically represented in Joshua's final words to his people in his old age (Josh 23). Joshua exhorts the people to obey the law of Moses, to avoid intermixing with the Canaanites, and to reject idols (Josh 23:6-8). Then he turns his attention to the elders. With a prophetic word, he recounts God's history thus far with this people: the calling of the patriarchs, the exodus, the new land. God has been faithful in all these things, and Israel has covenanted with God to return loyalty. Joshua famously challenges them with this word: "If serving the LORD seems undesirable to you, then choose for yourselves this day whom you will serve, whether the gods your ancestors served beyond the Euphrates, or the gods of the Amorites, in whose land you are living. But as for me and my household, we will serve the LORD" (Josh 24:15).

When we look at Deborah, as judge-deliverer and prophet, she plays the same basic role as Joshua. As an adjudicating judge, she was responsible for keeping the people in line with the standards of righteousness established in the law of Moses. As a leader against the Canaanites, she was responsible for repelling them and helping the Israelites to be free from idolatry. We also see Deborah's spiritual leadership in her battle hymn duet. Just as Joshua recounted and interpreted the history of Israel, so too Deborah and Barak frame the success over Sisera as a divine triumph. God entrusts Deborah as prophet and governor, as one who can and should speak on God's behalf. For all intents and purposes, for a certain period of time, God called Deborah to be his people's executive, judicial, and spiritual leader. As "mother" over Israel, she safeguarded Israel's life, not just physically, but also in relationship to God.

Deborah Throughout the Centuries

How is Deborah remembered in the Jewish and Christian traditions? One might say she is not, simply because her name does not appear in the rest of the Old or New Testament, as already mentioned. But we have Jewish writers from around the time of Jesus and Paul who did occasionally reflect on Deborah's role in the history of Israel. For example, one writer we refer to as Pseudo-Philo (writing sometime in the first century AD) produced a text called Book of Biblical Antiquities. He makes reference to a woman who ruled over Israel and gave them rest for forty years.[12] Pseudo-Philo offers an imaginative rendition of how Deborah may have spoken to the people in her last days. She calls the whole people of Israel (men and women) to hear her final exhortations: "Only direct your heart to the Lord your God in the time of your life, for after your death you will not be able to repent of those things."[13]

According to Pseudo-Philo, when Deborah breathed her last, the people wept and mourned her as they would for any beloved ruler, man or woman.[14] They remembered her, saying, "Behold, a mother is gone from Israel, and a holy one that ruled in the house of Jacob, which secured a fence around her generation, and her generation shall follow after her."[15]

The Jewish historian Josephus (ca. AD 37–100) also recounts Israel's history in his book *Jewish Antiquities*. He discusses Deborah and Barak at length and presents her as a wise prophet and a governing leader.[16] God spoke through Deborah to lead Barak. Josephus explains not only that Deborah went into war with Barak but that when the Israelite warriors wanted to retreat, she "retained them, and commanded them to fight the enemy that very day that they should conquer them, and God would be

[12]Book of Biblical Antiquities 30.2; 33.1.
[13]Book of Biblical Antiquities 33.2-3 (my translation).
[14]Book of Biblical Antiquities 33.6.
[15]Book of Biblical Antiquities 33.6 (my translation).
[16]Josephus, *Jewish Antiquities* 5.200-202.

their assistance."[17] Deborah was also discussed by the rabbis. In one text, a certain rabbi proclaims that the quintessential judges were Barak and Deborah, while another rabbi gives that distinction to Shamgar and Ehud.[18]

In the early Christian tradition, Theodoret of Cyrus (393–457) briefly mentions Deborah in reference to his study of the book of Judges. He seems to be at pains to explain how she would be the top prophet, as a woman, representing God in this time. He explains this with reference to Galatians 3:28: "Men and women have the same nature. As you know, the woman was formed from Adam and, like him, possessed the faculty of reason. Hence, the apostle says, 'In Christ Jesus there is neither male nor female.' Thus, Moses was called a 'prophet,' and Miriam a 'prophetess.'"[19] About a millennium later John Calvin was also at a bit of a loss for words as he pondered the leadership of Deborah (and it is exceptionally difficult to render Calvin speechless): "It was an extraordinary thing, when God gave authority to a woman."[20]

DEBORAH AND LEADERSHIP TODAY

In 2013 Deana Porterfield (now president of Roberts Wesleyan College) conducted a fascinating study of the (then) six female presidents of Christian colleges and how they arrived in those positions.[21] At that time, there were 118 member institutions of the Council for Christian Colleges and Universities. Porterfield made a number of interesting discoveries in the course of her research; one was that several of these women didn't originally aspire to the highest office of the college. They were already in some form of cabinet leadership (e.g., VP level), and during a period of institutional crisis they were elevated and promoted into the presidential role. Perhaps it began as an interim presidency or involved absorbing some presidential functions during a vacancy, and then it became clear

---

[17]Josephus, *Jewish Antiquities* 5.204.

[18]Ruth Rabbah 1.1.

[19]Theodoret of Cyrus, *Questions on the Octateuch, On Leviticus, Numbers, Deuteronomy, Joshua, Judges, Ruth*, trans. Robert C. Hill (Washington, DC: Catholic University of America Press, 2007), 329.

[20]John Calvin, *On Micah* 6.4. English Translation from David M. Gunn, *Judges*, Blackwell Bible Commentaries (Malden, MA: Blackwell, 2005), 59.

[21]Deana Porterfield, "Presidents of the Council for Christian Colleges & Universities: A Study of the Successful Attainment of Six Female Presidents" (EdD diss., University of La Verne, 2013).

to them and others that it was a fit. But again, a common denominator among many of these women's stories is that they stepped up to higher leadership during a time of crisis.

These stories, in some ways, fit that of Deborah. Israel was in an (admittedly long-term) period of crisis, in need of judge-deliverers. As a Spirit-led prophet of God, as a sharply competent decision maker, as an adroit strategist, Deborah was the right person to lead Israel through a major crisis. Unlike Samson, she had no selfish bone in her body. Moment after moment, she acted carefully and only for the glory of God and in concern for her people. Unlike Gideon, Deborah demonstrated incredible faith in God, acting as an effective conductor of the divine voice in her prophetic power.

I am inspired by Deborah in many ways, but two are prominent. First, she was the singular supreme court justice of the people. I wonder how many people were upset with her verdicts. In court cases, there are often winners and losers, and the losers almost never think they were wrong. How often did they shout at her? Call her names? Gossip about her? (Remember, these weren't Israel's most holy years.) This inevitable set of challenges did not seem to weaken her resolve to answer God's call for her to "mother" Israel.

Second, Deborah was willing to boldly speak the truth of God. She had some very hard words for Barak. Given the times and her cultural world, it must have been difficult for a woman to give the leading warrior the hard news that he would not seal the victory for Israel. Furthermore, as you can imagine, the battlefield was not a common place for women. Deborah willingly accompanied Barak in his campaign, but I have to imagine that there were few women who traveled with their army. If I were in her shoes, I might be intimidated, even scared. Whatever the case, the victory song reflects her successful leadership at the end of it all.

Deborah is an important answer to the question "Can a woman . . . ?" or "Is a woman allowed to . . . ?" Deborah could. Deborah was. God was behind it; he filled her with prophetic wisdom, and her sung words became part of the Word of God, testifying to the brave and wise woman who brought God's peace to a troubled people.

2

Going Back to the Beginning

Genesis 1–3

That the Bible should speak of the beginning provokes the world,
provokes us. For we cannot speak of the beginning. Where the beginning
begins, there our thinking stops; there it comes to an end. Yet the desire to
ask after the beginning is the innermost passion of our thinking; it is
what in the end imparts reality to every genuine question we ask.

DIETRICH BONHOEFFER

A Christian leader, man or woman, inevitably finds him- or herself asking, *Who am I? Who am I that I should lead? Why should people listen to me? Why should they follow me?* I wonder if women leaders in the early church looked back to Deborah to help them answer some of those questions. But eventually our minds wander further back, back to the beginning, back to Adam and Eve. What does it mean to be man? What does it mean to be woman? To be human? To be one image of God together? What role does sin play in frustrating God's plans for us? What was the ideal relationship between man and woman before sin brought strife? And how did God's punishments and pronouncements for Adam and Eve change their relationship?

In this book we will not dwell at length on women in the Old Testament; our primary focus will be on women in the early church. But the Bible's beginning stories of creation and fall (as tradition has come to call them) play a crucial role in shaping a Christian understanding of anthropology (what does it mean to be human?), sex and gender (what does it mean to be man and woman?), and vocation and ministry (what ought man and woman to do in God's world and God's church?).

GETTING ORIENTED TO GENESIS 1–3

The keen reader of Genesis 1 and 2 will note that this is not really one continuous narrative but two tellings of creation. Put another way (to use language from Tremper Longman), these chapters are not "sequential" but "synoptic." If we draw from the analogy of the fourfold Gospel testimony of Jesus, Genesis 1 and 2 could be described as complementary perspectives on the singular divine act of creation.[1] But why, we inevitably wonder, does the creation story need two separate perspectives, and how are they different? Genesis 1 takes a sweeping perspective of the whole of creation, all creatures and material phenomena. In the seven-day sequence, God forms all things good and beautiful, and then rests and enjoys his handiwork. The second, "synoptic" vantage point (Gen 2) offers a more intimate, personal, relational perspective on creation. Together these two stories reflect the paradox of a great Creator God much higher than and far beyond us, who desires to walk with us and have a deep interpersonal relationship with us. But that trajectory is thrown off by sin—we will get to that in a bit. First things first, Genesis 1.

GENESIS 1: MAN AND WOMAN IN THE IMAGE OF GOD

The Old Testament begins at the beginning—not of Israel, but of the cosmos. Its opening chapters move from the morning of the universe to the ordering of families and nations to the birthing of the fathers and mothers of Israel. God was there "in the beginning,"

---

[1] See Tremper Longman III, *Genesis*, Story of God Bible Commentary (Grand Rapids, MI: Zondervan Academic, 2016), 47.

but this is a new day for God, too. Given the divine commitment to
relationships with the creation, God will never be the same again.

BRUCE C. BIRCH ET AL., *A THEOLOGICAL INTRODUCTION*
TO THE OLD TESTAMENT

This is a grand narrative of the incredible act of God who desired to
fashion a good and beautiful world: light, day and night, waters, sky, land
and greenery, sun and moon and stars, sea creatures and birds
(Gen 1:1-20), and the command for all things to produce abundance
(Gen 1:21-25). The "days" of creation do not reflect specific hours and
minutes. They mark a careful divine ordering of God's work, climaxing
with the formation of his greatest creation—humanity.

In Genesis 1:26, the Hebrew word *adam* (human) does not mean
"Adam," nor does it mean "man/male." We know that because it switches
immediately from *adam* (singular) to "they" (plural), implying that
adam stands for humanity as a category. This seems somewhat ambiguous in 1:26 but becomes clearer in 1:27 when they are defined as
"male and female." Man and woman (they are not technically referred to
by name until Genesis 2) are created in God's own image, which means
they are like him in special ways that are not true of other creatures.

The most obvious feature of this "imaging of God" is their calling to
rule over the earth (Gen 1:28).[2] The destiny of humanity is to "subdue"
the earth. As Terence Fretheim and others explain, "subdue" does not
refer to coercive exploitation, certainly not destruction. Rather, in the
"pre-sin" context of Genesis 1, it implies cultivating creation so that it
may thrive.[3] Good rulers don't plunder their resources; they utilize
them responsibly with a view toward sustainability and the promotion
of abundance.

What do we learn about man and woman in Genesis 1? Here they are
not treated as differentiated beings in terms of status or function. Both

---

[2]For a helpful study, see J. Richard Middleton, *The Liberating Image: The* Imago Dei *in Genesis 1*
(Grand Rapids, MI: Brazos, 2005); also Middleton, "The Liberating Image? Interpreting the
Imago Dei in Context," *Christian Scholars Review* 24, no. 1 (1994): 8-25.
[3]See Terence E. Fretheim, *Creation Untamed: The Bible, God, and Natural Disasters* (Grand Rapids,
MI: Baker Academic, 2010), 14, 33, 41.

are fashioned in the image of God (Gen 1:26-27); not Adam, then Eve, but both together reflect God. Both are blessed and are given the responsibility of ruling the earth (Gen 1:26, 28). Both are given the fruit of the earth for food and enjoyment (Gen 1:29-30). While they are distinguished according to two types, male and female, nothing in Genesis 1 distinguishes the two in their God-given identity, calling, and relationship to other parts of creation. If all we knew of creation came from this chapter, we would conceive of man and woman as equals, partners and co-rulers on earth as the image of God. There is no statement of first-made privilege, headship, or gender roles. Now, of course, there *is* a second telling of the forming of humanity (Gen 2), but it is worth letting the portrayal of humanity in the first chapter have its moment before moving on. According to the opening chapter of the Bible, humanity was created in two forms, male and female; together they are called to administer God's own life-giving rulership to the earth.

GENESIS 2: THE PURSUIT OF A PARTNER

This second account of creation goes back and retells parts of the world's story in a different way. Genesis 1 is a sweeping overview story of God creating all the major features of the world as we know it. It's like a skycam or blimp view. You don't see details from that far; you see the big picture, the whole and the basic contours of that whole. Genesis 2, then, is the ground view, the helmet cam, or footage from the GoPro. This chapter is more of a personal story. It begins with God making man, in this case the male "Adam" (Gen 2:7). The forming of Adam has the feel of a potter forming mud into something with shape and purpose.[4] Adam is given the breath of God and then comes to life. First, Adam is given life, then he is given a home (Gen 2:8). God provides plentiful resources and work for Adam to do as a caretaker of the Eden garden (Gen 2:9-17).

Then we are told that Adam ought not to be alone (Gen 2:18). Take note, though, that Adam does not say he is *lonely*. Perhaps he was, we don't know, but I take God's statement and God's gift of a life partner as

---

[4]See R. W. L. Moberly, *The Theology of the Book of Genesis*, Old Testament Theology (Cambridge: Cambridge University Press, 2013), 43

a more holistic partnership. Adam is incomplete in how he fits into the world without a partner.

Genesis 2 patiently narrates Adam's search for this perfect partner. The quest begins with the animals. We are not told that Adam wandered around studying each animal to discern his true partner. Rather, *God* brings them to Adam and lets him name them (Gen 2:19-20). God could have just told Adam, "You aren't going to find what you are looking for here." But Adam must go through a process of discovery, one that involves *disappointment*. No other creature is fit to participate in Adam's life and work at the peer level. So God puts Adam into a deep sleep and fashions woman out of his body (Gen 2:20-22).

Let's go back to 2:18 to acquaint ourselves with what role this special creature is meant to play in God's plan for humanity. Man cannot be alone (Gen 2:18), so he must have a "helper." "Helper" is the term most often used in English translations for the Hebrew *'ezer*. But in English this is a somewhat ambiguous term. It is easy for us to take the word *helper* as "assistant," as in the proverbial magician's assistant (or assistant *to* the regional manager). But *'ezer* is a generic term that refers to someone who contributes to completing a task or accomplishing a goal. The objective here is for the *'ezer* to partner in tending the Eden garden. Genesis does not comment one way or another on whether woman is a minor partner (contributing less than Adam), a major partner (contributing more), or an equal partner. The point of the animal discernment process is to rule out the suitability of lesser creatures.

It is often pointed out, and for good reason, that *'ezer* is often used in the Old Testament to refer to *God* as "helper" and protector of Israel. When Israel is in trouble, they can count on God to "help."[5]

> He is your shield and *helper*
> and your glorious sword. (Deut 33:29)

> You are destroyed, Israel,
> because you are against me, against your *helper*. (Hos 13:9)

---

[5]See Alice Mathews, *Gender Roles and the People of God: Rethinking What We Were Taught about Men and Women in the Church* (Grand Rapids, MI: Zondervan, 2017), 50.

But as for me, I am poor and needy;
    come quickly to me, O God.
You are my *help* and my deliverer. (Ps 70:5)

I lift my eyes to the mountains—
    where does my *help* come from?
My *help* comes from the LORD,
    the Maker of heaven and earth. (Ps 121:1)[6]

Now, Eve is not Adam's savior (like God), nor is she Adam's servant. The task given to Adam by God to complete in the garden is something he cannot do alone. The animals will no doubt help (as they do today!), but Adam needed a partner, an equal to share the work. Reading from Genesis 1:27-28 to Genesis 2:24, we are compelled to see Eve as a natural counterpart to Adam, their callings and their fates intertwined.

Regarding Genesis 2, the question sometimes comes up: Does Adam have a higher creation status than Eve because he was made first? This relates to the ancient principle of "primogeniture," special privileges marked out for the firstborn. This does not seem to be implied in the creation story and is certainly not stated. First of all, Adam is not born, and neither is Eve. Each are formed uniquely by God. And Eve is not fashioned as a kind of younger sibling, to be mentored by and apprenticed to Adam. She is created as an equal to Adam, to partner with him in taking care of the created world. Nothing in Genesis 2 clearly establishes headship, female submission, or unique male ruling authority. In fact, quite the opposite, man is not commanded to lead or guide woman; he is "united" with her (Gen 2:24), and they become one. When it comes to primogeniture, though it is true that ancient cultures tended to favor the oldest, this is not always the case in the biblical story. Isaac, Jacob, and David were all *younger* brothers given special blessing and privilege by God. This should caution readers against making assumptions about age and order.

---

[6]The Greek word *boēthos* is used in the Septuagint as a corresponding term to the Hebrew *'ezer*. In the Jewish text called Judith, God is referred to as the "helper" (*boēthos*) of the weak (Jdt 9:11).

PUTTING TOGETHER GENESIS 1 AND 2

When we read Genesis 1 and 2 together as a "synoptic" account of creation, here is what we learn about the formation of humanity and their role in the world:

- *A unified species*: The first mention of human(s) is in 1:26, and they are treated as one thing, a unified species, made in the image of God and created to co-rule.

- *Two types*: In 1:27 the clear addition is that there are two types, male and female.

- *Man needs help*: In 2:18 it is made clear Adam can't do this work alone; he needs help.

- *Woman helps man*: The animals cannot suffice, so woman is created *from man* to show her fitness for helping him.

There are no clear prerogatives that man is given special command to rule or serve as leader over or above woman. On the contrary, *he* is seen as incomplete and lacking without *her*. That doesn't make her superior; presumably she needs him as much as he needs her. But all in all everything is considered "very good" because there is the possibility of these two being united as one. The sum is greater than the parts, and together they have the potential to unlock the full vitality of God's creation on earth. By the end of Genesis 2, the one "problem" presented in the story so far—Adam's need of a partner—is resolved, and everything is on track in terms of the creation project moving in a fruitful direction.

GENESIS 3: THE UNRAVELING

Genesis 3 tells the story of what is popularly known as "the fall." While this language is conventional, I find it insufficient to describe the situation in "Genesis-ian" terms. Looking at the narrative flow and the momentum that is built as we transition from Genesis 1–2 to Genesis 3, I prefer to label it the "unraveling" or "undoing" of God's good work in creation. All that beauty and innocence is marred; the unity and harmony is undone.

The first thing to notice with Genesis 3:1 is that the "problem" seems to come out of nowhere. The cunning serpent appears on the scene with a dastardly agenda. He succeeds in sowing the seed of doubt in the mind of Eve (Gen 3:3-4). What is worse, Eve gives in to temptation and seeks to "be like God" (Gen 3:5) in her knowledge of good and evil. She believed it would give her special insight or divine wisdom such that she could be independent of God (Gen 3:6). Adam is not absent but is there next to her, as Genesis points out, so he joins in this rebellion and is equally culpable (Gen 3:6). They hide and are ashamed when their eyes are finally opened (Gen 3:7-9).

Their reaction isn't to revel in their newfound wisdom. When they are confronted by God, they immediately cast blame. Man blames woman (Gen 3:12), and woman blames the serpent (Gen 3:13). Conscience and integrity are betrayed. All this backstabbing and division jeopardizes God's work of establishing unity and abundance. And God's words of judgment underscore the frustration of creation's fecundity.

A key verse here in terms of the "gender roles" conversation is Genesis 3:16, where God says, "Thy desire shall be to thy husband, and he shall rule over thee" (JPS). This is a "literal" translation of the Hebrew text, but what does it mean? It seems obvious to most interpreters that man's "ruling" over woman is a problem, not a blessing. This verb is about absolute authority over someone, like a king ruling a subject (Gen 4:7; 37:8). The creation accounts do not call for man to rule over woman; he lacks the capability of fulfilling his mandate without her; she partners with him, and they care for the garden together. One human ruling the other—that is not an ideal of the garden but an intrusion and an undoing.[7]

A more difficult interpretive issue is what it means that her "desire" will be toward her husband. What kind of desire? The Hebrew word *teshuqah* means "passions" or "longings." It could identify good desire, like deep love. But it can also be destructive yearnings, lusts that can overtake rational thought. The use of this word later in Genesis is

---

[7]See Mary L. Conway, "Gender in Creation and Fall: Genesis 1–3," in *Discovering Biblical Equality: Biblical, Theological, Cultural & Practical Perspectives*, ed. Ronald W. Pierce, Cynthia Westfall, and Christa L. McKirland, 3rd ed. (Downers Grove, IL: IVP Academic, 2021), 35-52, at 46-48

instructive. The Lord confronts Cain in his anger and warns him, "If you do not do what is right, sin is crouching at your door; it *desires* to have you, but you must rule over it" (Gen 4:7). This is clearly a devious desire on the part of sin, "to control and dominate."[8] How does this relate to the woman's desire in Genesis 3:16? Just as sin "desires" to take advantage of Cain in his anger, so God pronounces the corruption of harmony where the woman will "desire to break the relationship of equality and turn it into a relationship of servitude and domination [and the] sinful husband will try to be a tyrant over his wife."[9] As Richard Hess poignantly summarizes, "The emphasis here is on the terrible effects of sin, and the destruction of a harmonious relationship that once existed. In its place comes a harmful struggle of wills."[10]

So, does Genesis 3 teach that men must lead and women must follow? Not at all. We see hope in Adam and Eve joining together as one flesh, and it is Eve who has the final word as she praises God for blessing them with a child. The ultimate redemptive hopes of Scripture and the gospel are not that man will find his rightful place as head over woman. It is the good news that man and woman can be restored to a healthy partnership where each one is given dignity and respect, and where each brings their gifts and wisdom toward a cooperative tending of God's world.[11]

GENESIS AND WOMEN IN MINISTRY: BACK TO DEBORAH

What does Genesis 1–3 have to say about women in leadership? To put a sharper point on the question, what would Deborah have learned from these chapters about her own ministry in leading Israel into deeper faithfulness to God?

According to the opening chapter of the Bible, humanity (man and woman) is created as God's image to govern wisely over the earth.

---

[8]Victor Hamilton, *The Book of Genesis*, New International Commentary on the Old Testament (Grand Rapids, MI: Eerdmans, 1990), 201.

[9]Hamilton, *Genesis*, 201.

[10]Richard Hess, "Evidence for Equality in Genesis 1–3," *E-Quality* 7, no. 3 (2008): 8-11, https://www.cbeinternational.org/sites/default/files/Hess.pdf.

[11]Lucy Peppiatt offers a compelling "mutualist" reading of the Genesis accounts; see *Rediscovering Scripture's Vision for Women: Fresh Perspectives on Disputed Texts* (Downers Grove, IL: IVP Academic, 2019), 47-55.

Deborah took this responsibility seriously. She did not seem to need to find a man to back up her decisions. While the ideal was partnership, nations in Deborah's time were in the habit of relying on a single leader. Deborah, especially as an experienced judge and inspired prophet, was perhaps capable of leading on her own, but she joined efforts with the military leader Barak to bring peace to Israel.

Deborah was married at some point. If Lappidoth, her husband, was dead, apparently Deborah did not remarry during her reign as judge-deliverer. If Lappidoth was alive in that period, he did not play a functional role in Israel's rulership or deliverance. Therefore, it is unclear how Deborah would have processed the curses of the first father and first mother. What we do know from her story is that, while distorted relationships certainly did emerge in humanity (just look at Samson and Delilah!), we see glimpses of healthy relationships as well. In the case of Deborah, she did not have any clear desires to subvert, control, or trick other men (like Barak). She carried out the work of her leadership role with focus, transparency, and integrity. The Genesis curses may have predicted a dark pattern for men and women, but this disunity was not an absolute inevitability for everyone.

Going back to the beginning is important. We long to understand where we came from, as Bonhoeffer so passionately describes in our opening epigraph. We cannot blame our forefather and foremother for all of our problems. But we can learn a lot from what came before us. Some have tried to paint a picture of creation as a hierarchy that has been threatened by sin. But I have argued here for a faithful reading of the creation story as a tale of harmonious partnership unraveled and frustrated by sin. The way back is unity and harmony through Jesus Christ, not hierarchy. In the next chapter, we will jump forward in time to the world Jesus stepped into. It is a world still reflecting the male effort to rule over woman, a patriarchal social economy. But a closer look will reveal that not all women fit the profile of the quiet, domestic wife. How did Jesus engage such social dynamics? How did the apostles and the early churches? We will address these fascinating and important questions after properly setting the scene.

3

Women in the New Testament World

The ancient world was a man's world. Men had more power on just about every level compared to women. The rulers were men, the politicians, certainly the military leaders. Wealth was predominantly in the hands of men, and so was the judicial system. Much of this relates to the concept and structure of patriarchy, which we will come back to in a minute. Suffice it to say for now, men held power and exercised leadership, and women didn't.

It is no surprise, then, to see some scholars propose that women were not leaders in the apostolic period. Thomas Schreiner argues, for example, that Christian women would not have been present at elders' meetings of early churches in any official or recognized way, and probably did not give feedback directly to the elders.[1] Basically, in the patriarchal world, men exercised power and leadership; women weren't even in the room. As we think about the early Christians in the Greco-Roman world,

---

[1]Tweet from Thomas Schreiner (@DrTomSchreiner), June 3, 2019: "I don't think it makes sense for women to be present in any regular way at elders' meeting as advisors, as those who give feedback on the spot to the elders." Tweets are generally not treated as academic statements, but Schreiner, I am sure, would agree that this statement is in keeping with his scholarship on this subject; see Schreiner, "An Interpretation of 1 Timothy 2:9-15," in *Women in the Church: An Interpretation and Application of 1 Timothy 2:9-15*, ed. Andreas J. Köstenberger and Thomas R. Schreiner, 3rd ed. (Wheaton, IL: Crossway, 2016), 163-226; Schreiner, "Women in Ministry: Another Complementarian Perspective," in *Two Views on Women in Ministry*, ed. James R. Beck (Grand Rapids, MI: Zondervan Academic, 2005), 263-322. See also this blog post where Schreiner talks about his views on biblical eldership: Denny Burk, "Can Broad and Narrow Complementarians Coexist in the SBC?," *Denny Burk* (blog), June 3, 2019, https://www.dennyburk.com/can-broad-and-narrow -complementarians-coexist-in-the-sbc/.

I have these questions: (1) If women were not present at such meetings, where were they and what were they doing? (My answer will be, they were everywhere and were doing everything the men were doing.) (2) Was gender the only categorical index of influence in a patriarchal culture? (My answer to this is no, social class also played a massive role in the Roman world and affected drastically what women could and did do—and this factored into *who* got into those meetings and how their words were received.)

First things first, what is patriarchy and how did it work in the first-century Roman world?

ROMAN PATRIARCHY

Patriarchy refers to a system of male power and dominance.[2] The fact that it is called *patri*-archy (rule of the father) and not *andri*-archy (rule of the man) attests to a history of male power in the household, which extends outward to the male ruler as the "father" of the state. Case in point: Roman sovereign Caesar Augustus was given the title "father of the fatherlands" to represent his total authority over the empire.[3] In the Roman world, the standard operating principle was that the father was the pillar of the household, bearing economic, legal, social, and even religious authority. Hence, the "household codes" of the Greco-Roman world revolved around the competent, confident, and just leadership of the paterfamilias, the "father of the family," the governor of the household. The man's place in society was to act according to the classic virtues of good judgment and wisdom, courage and resilience, self-mastery and discipline, and justice.

Women were expected to be wise and just, but there were common stereotypes about women that they were simple-minded, overly emotional, unable to control their passions, gossipy, and backstabbing.[4]

---

[2]For an academic discussion of the terminology of patriarchy, see Carol P. Christ, "A New Definition of Patriarchy: Control of Women's Sexuality, Private Property, and War," *Feminist Theology* 24, no. 3 (2016): 214-25.

[3]Suetonius, *Augustus* 58; *Res Gestae Divi Augusti* 35.1.

[4]See Judith Evans Grubbs, *Women and the Law in the Roman Empire: A Sourcebook on Marriage, Divorce, and Widowhood* (London: Routledge, 2002), 46-59.

Women ought not to be leaders, it was thought, because they would steer society in the wrong direction.

Now, that does not mean that women were never praised. Women were viewed as important contributors to Roman society. What was encouraged and celebrated regarding women were their roles as supportive wife and nurturing mother.[5] Susan Hylen refers to three feminine virtues that were projected onto the "good woman" in Roman life. She was expected to be modest (we might say humble, meek, unassuming), industrious (contributing positively to society), and loyal (especially to husband and family).[6] We see this illustrated in a Roman son's eulogy for his mother. After commenting that he does not have much to say because women's lives are unremarkable, he celebrates his mother, Murdia, with these words: "My dearest mother deserved greater praise than all others, since in modesty, propriety, chastity, obedience, woolworking, industry, and loyalty she was on an equal level with other good women."[7]

Now, when we talk about women in the ancient world, we tend to imagine social dynamics as they have just been described, because that is the message sent to us from public inscriptions (the ancient equivalents of billboards and neon signs) as well as etiquette textbooks, imperially sponsored statues, and "idealized" novels and dramas. If we take that image of a patriarchal Roman world into our reading of the New Testament, no wonder we couldn't possibly imagine a woman in the elders' meeting. Women should be at home working wool and tending to the children. They ought to be living quiet and predictable lives away from the "action" of war, politics, business, and professional religion.

I will admit that when I went to seminary, I brought with me to the study of the New Testament just this sort of flat, imperially curated view of the Roman patriarchal world. I am going to challenge that

---

[5]See Elaine Fantham et al., *Women in the Classical World: Image and Text* (Oxford: Oxford University Press, 1995), 315.

[6]See Susan Hylen, *Women in the New Testament World* (Oxford: Oxford University Press, 2019), 42–64.

[7]*Corpus Inscriptionum Latinarum* [*CIL*] 6:10230, cited in Mary R. Lefkowitz and Maureen B. Fant, *Women's Life in Greece and Rome: A Sourcebook in Translation* (London: Bloomsbury, 2016), 318.

perspective—but not because I am trying to be sensationalistic or revisionist for the sake of finding something "new." I will not be telling you that the Roman world was *really* feminist or egalitarian. It wasn't. It was patriarchal from top to bottom, literally. And when it comes to sociology, we are used to thinking in terms of one dimension—gender. But especially in the *Romanized* world of the apostles, in order to account for a more complete understanding of society, we must also attend to the dynamic of *class*.

SOCIAL CLASS AND STATUS IN THE ROMAN WORLD

Roman people prized social class.[8] At the top of the pyramid you had the emperor, of course, the highest person in the land. Below that you had the senatorial class, a tier of nobles with considerable wealth and political power. Then the equestrian class, a rank of wealth, men hoping to rise up into the senatorial echelon. Underneath that you had commoners, then foreigners, then freedpersons (ex-slaves), and last of all slaves. For the nobility classes especially, membership was tied to men; women enjoyed the privileges of high status through their father or their husbands. We cannot overestimate the social importance of class and its cultural power. As Tim Parkin and Arthur Pomeroy explain, "Those privileged few [in the Roman nobility classes]—probably less than 0.1 per cent of the population—dominated the vast majority beneath them."[9] What does this mean for our discussion of women in the Roman world? One might say that men were more powerful and more privileged than women, all things being equal, but here's the catch: *things weren't always equal.* Yes, by and large, if we *only* looked at commoners, we could say that patriarchy typically meant "men lead, women follow." But people were often interacting *between* classes, and this adds a layer of complexity to how one lives their public life. So, when we talk about the New Testament world as the world of Roman patriarchy, we

---

[8]From here on out, when I refer to "Romans" or "Roman people," I am not necessarily talking about ethnicity; I am referring to people (of any ethnicity) who are shaped by Roman culture—Romanized people.

[9]Tim G. Parkin and Arthur J. Pomeroy, *Roman Social History: A Sourcebook* (London: Routledge, 2009), 3.

aren't viewing a complete picture. We do better to talk about Roman *class* patriarchy. The male power over the female was not an inflexible or immutable social construct.

Richard Ascough offers this helpful analogy: "Women from the senatorial class would have been accorded much more social status than a man of a lower rank. For example, if walking toward one another on the street, a freedman would be required to give way to an upper-ranking woman, in recognition of her higher status."[10] A good case study, along these lines, is found in Apuleius's famous tale *Metamorphoses*. A certain man called Lucius is visiting the Greek city Thessaly and finds himself in the city market. He happens on a long-lost aunt, Byrrhena, who is a woman of high class and of great influence in Thessaly. She compels him to visit her home and enjoy her lavish hospitality; he agrees. Byrrhena seems to be married, but she is clearly the one calling the shots. Roman historian Emily Hemelrijk describes her social status this way: "Byrrhena is presented as a prominent figure in local society; as the 'first lady' (*primas femina*) of her town, she was very much in the public eye, even in her own home."[11] *Metamorphoses* is a work of fiction, but it accurately reflects social dynamics in the Greco-Roman world. Social class played an essential part in the lives of both men and women, and it was a means of influence, power, and upward mobility in society. Now we will look at women who wielded influence in various areas of society, thanks to class, grit, or shrewdness.

PATRONAGE AND SOCIAL POWER

MANLIA GNOME FREEDWOMAN OF TITUS
This is a woman who always lived with an excellent disposition.
I [Manlia Gnome] had many clients.
I obtained this one place for myself,

---

[10]Richard S. Ascough, "What Kind of World Did Paul's Communities Live In?," in *The New Cambridge Companion to St. Paul*, ed. Bruce W. Longenecker (Cambridge: Cambridge University Press, 2020), 48-68, at 52.

[11]See Emily Hemelrijk, *Hidden Lives, Public Personae: Women and Civic Life in the Roman West* (Oxford: Oxford University Press, 2015), 7.

And so in this spot I wanted to live out my life.
I never was in debt to anyone. I lived in good faith.
I gave my bones to the earth, I gave my body to the fires of Vulcan,
So it was I who carried out the last injunction, that of death.

CIL 6:21975

The Roman world depended on social reciprocity through "patronage." In this system, patrons (more privileged parties) bestowed gifts and benefits on clients (socially lower parties) in exchange for the clients' devotion and public praise. Patronage was deeply woven into the fabric of society; it was everywhere and existed on every level of society from slaves all the way up to the emperor. Women were certainly involved in patronage as well, though evidence for one-to-one patronage is limited (versus euergetism and civic patronage, which we will address below). Nevertheless, you see women as patrons and clients of other women.[12] Less common, but not absent, is evidence of a female patron and a male client. Women of high class and influence *did* offer benefaction to men who wanted to move up in the world.

Most women received their influential positions as patrons through their own husbands (e.g., Livia, wife of Caesar Augustus), but not always. The Rome-situated Vestal Virgins, venerated priestesses of Vesta (goddess of the hearth), played a key role in securing the favor of the gods in the capital city. As should be obvious from their title, they were not tethered to particular men, so in some sense they maintained independent status—a cultural anomaly, to be sure, but extremely powerful by virtue of their religious functions. We have evidence that, because of their connection to imperial rituals, they had major political sway. One priestess, Campia Severina, was publicly praised by Quintus Veturius Callistratus for helping him gain an imperial post through her

---

[12]A woman named Cratia (the wife of Fronto, tutor of the emperor Marcus Aurelius) was a client of Domitia Lucilla, the emperor's mother; see *Marcus Cornelius Fronto*, trans. C. R. Haines, Loeb Classical Library (Cambridge, MA: Harvard University Press, 1962), 145-51, cited in Carolyn Osiek, "Roman and Christian Burial Practices and the Patronage of Women," in *Commemorating the Dead: Texts and Artifacts in Context*, ed. Laurie Brink and Deborah Green (New York: de Gruyter, 2008), 243-73, at 258.

commendation;[13] he was made *procurator* in charge of the finances of
the imperial libraries.[14]

Fulvia offers an interesting case study. She was a Roman noblewoman
whose first two husbands (both politicians) were killed. She eventually
married Mark Antony and became influential in Roman politics. While
Antony went into battle in Egypt, Fulvia was at home in Rome publicly
advocating for his policies. It's hard to overestimate her social power; as
Judith Hallett explains, she was "staging summit conferences, commanding armies, implementing political proscriptions, and thereby con-
trolling men's affairs."[15] Antony had her likeness put on coinage as the
"face" of Victory (the goddess representing triumph in war); some historians consider this the first portrait coin of a historical Roman woman.[16]
Eventually the city of Eumenia (Phrygia) was renamed Fulviana.[17]

A similar story can be told of the empress Livia. She met with ambas-
sadors and foreign dignitaries in Augustus's absence. And, according to
ancient historian Suetonius, Augustus himself recorded Livia's advice in
his personal notebook.[18] When Livia died, her son Tiberius forbade her
deification (the granting of divine status and honors). Later on, her
grandson, Caligula, allowed it, and she became *Diva Augusta* (divine
wife of Augustus). Veneration of Livia was formally established in more
than a dozen cities.[19]

Going back to a wider point I have been trying to make in this chapter,
we must disabuse ourselves of a rigid and flat understanding of the
Roman world in which early Christianity originated. Yes, it was thor-
oughly patriarchal: men dominated the world; women were widely

---

[13]*CIL* 6:2132.
[14]*CIL* 6:32418.
[15]Judith P. Hallett, "The Paradox of Elite Roman Women: Patriarchal Society and Female Formi-
dability," in *Fathers and Daughters in Roman Society: Women and the Elite Family* (Princeton, NJ:
Princeton University Press, 1984), 3-34, at 9.
[16]T. Corey Brennan, "Perceptions of Women's Power in the Late Republic: Terentia, Fulvia, and
the Generation of 63 BCE," in *A Companion to Women in the Ancient World*, ed. Sharon L. James
and Sheila Dillon (Chichester: Wiley-Blackwell, 2015), 354-65, at 358.
[17]Brennan, "Perceptions of Women's Power," 358.
[18]Suetonius, *Augustus* 84.2.
[19]See Gertrude Grether, "Livia and the Roman Imperial Cult," *American Journal of Philology* 67,
no. 3 (1946): 222-52, at 249.

marginalized, ignored, abused, and taken advantage of. But that does not tell the whole story. The social reality is well stated by Carolyn Osiek and Margaret MacDonald: "We are accustomed to thinking systemically about women in this [Roman] society in terms of gender dichotomies in a gender-based hierarchical structure. But in face of the evidence, we can only conclude that women of sufficient social status in the Roman world exercised a great deal of freedom and power with regard to business and social activities."[20] Exactly right, and women could bear significant influence in politics, business, and religious life as well.

WOMEN IN THE ROMAN HOUSEHOLD

The forum was the male world par excellence, whereas the women were closely associated with the domus, the home and family.

EMILY HEMELRIJK, *HIDDEN LIVES, PUBLIC PERSONAE*

It would be misleading for me to say that the primary role of women in the Roman world was that of wielding political influence or social power. These things did happen sometimes, as we have seen, but Roman social ideology emphasized the woman's role in the family, particularly as wife, mother, and caretaker of the household. As a wife, the good Roman woman was meant to be honorable, pious, sweet, dutiful, loyal, and chaste.[21] As a mother, she was meant to raise her children with Roman values, honoring the gods and state leaders, and learning to contribute to the commonwealth. These funerary inscriptions reflect these values:

> Friend, I have not much to say; stop and read it. This tomb, which is not fair, is for a fair woman. Her parents gave her the name Claudia. She loved her husband in her heart. She bore two sons, one of whom she left on earth, the other beneath it. She was pleasant to talk with, and she

---

[20]Carolyn Osiek and Margaret Y. MacDonald, with Janet H. Tulloch, *A Woman's Place: House Churches in Earliest Christianity* (Minneapolis: Fortress, 2006), 209.

[21]These are common terms found on funeral inscriptions honoring Roman wives; see Susan Treggiari, *Roman Marriage: Iusti Coniuges from the Time of Cicero to the Time of Ulpian* (Oxford: Oxford University Press, 1991), 204-25.

walked with grace. She kept the house and worked in wool. That is all. You may go.[22]

Here lies Amymone, wife of Marcus, best and most beautiful, worker in wool, pious, chaste, thrifty, faithful, a stayer-at-home [*domiseda*].[23]

In an interesting inscription from Nicaea, both husband (Sacerdos) and wife (Severa) are praised after their deaths. The wife's inscription is as follows: "Sacerdos, your rituals and your manly work proclaim your life for all time to come. But for me, Severa, my husband, my child, my character, and my beauty have made me more renowned than Penelope, who lived before."[24]

Women could be given in marriage at a very young age, early teenage years. But our best evidence points to a more common marriage age of early twenties for women, late twenties for men.[25] Teenage marriage, though, was not necessarily frowned on. One inscription from the Roman city of Thasos refers to a girl betrothed at fifteen years to a man of eighteen years, and they celebrated fifty years of marriage in their life together, an extraordinarily long lifetime when the average age of death was thirty years old.[26] Speaking of family and households, I think it would be beneficial to clear up some common misconceptions about women in the families of the Roman world.[27]

Myth 1: Wives were always under the legal authority of their husbands. The classic Roman family had a paterfamilias, a father of the household, and that man held *patria potestas* (the legal powers of the father). In that case, he had legal authority over everyone in the household, including wife, children, and slaves. But this "default" setting for the household had exceptions. It was possible for a wife to have a *sine manu* marriage where she was *not* in the hands (authority) of her husband but

[22]*CIL* 1²:1211.
[23]*CIL* 6:11602.
[24]*Steinepigramme aus dem griechischen Osten* (*SGO*) 09/05/08. G.
[25]See Richard P. Saller, *Patriarchy, Property and Death in the Roman Family* (Cambridge: Cambridge University Press, 1995), 26-32.
[26]Lefkowitz and Fant, *Women's Life*, 29.
[27]At the end of this book, a "What About . . . ?" section offers more information about Roman households and the New Testament household codes.

remained under the legal supervision of her father.[28] While she was not "independent," it did mean that she was not obligated to go along with her husband in legal matters, and sometimes she kept her finances separate from him. In the first century AD, the New Testament period, manus marriage (with the wife in the legal hands of the husband) was a rarity, not the norm.[29] That fact and phenomenon complicates the ancient standard of the "loyal" wife.

Myth 2: Women could not own property. It is a commonly repeated misconception that women at that time could not own property. This is not technically accurate. The paterfamilias did carry the power of passing on the family's patrimony—that is, heirlooms, estate, and wealth. But this did not make it impossible for women to have and sell or gift property and goods. Tax records from the Roman world show women as owners of property.[30] We also have last wills and testaments from women.[31] From the remains of Pompeii, we learn that Emperor Nero's wife, Poppaea Sabina, owned property there, as did two sisters, Marcia and Rufina Metilia.[32] If a woman was not under a paterfamilias (usually because he died), she was assigned a male guardian to help oversee her assets. But in practice, these guardians were often in name only. Richard Saller explains that in the first century AD, "Roman women, whether married or not, enjoyed independent property rights nearly the equal of men's and the concomitant social power that wealth granted within the household and in broader society."[33] Saller goes so far as to say that at this time there

---

[28]*Sine* means "without" and *manu* means "hand," thus "not in the hand of the husband."
[29]See Grubbs, *Women and the Law*, 21; Saller, *Patriarchy*, 76.
[30]See Osiek and MacDonald, *Woman's Place*, 156.
[31]See Lefkowitz and Fant, *Women's Life*, 149. For example, a certain mother, Tamystha, willed to her daughter Toarsenouphis a house, a courtyard, and assets in the village of Talei. In this case, Toarsenouphis would receive property despite the fact that Tamystha had a male heir (Heron, who received a small amount of money, twenty silver drachmas); see Teresa J. Calpino, *Women, Work and Leadership in Acts* (Tübingen: Mohr Siebeck, 2014), 85-86.
[32]Fantham et al., *Women in the Classical World*, 331.
[33]Richard P. Saller, "The Roman Family as Productive Unit," in *A Companion to Families in the Greek and Roman Worlds*, ed. Beryl Rawson (Malden, MA: Wiley-Blackwell, 2011), 116-28, at 120. Gardner backs this up: "The consent of tutors . . . could be compelled; thus probably most freeborn women had virtually free capacity of testamentary disposal"; Jane F. Gardner, *Women in Law and Roman Society* (London: Routledge, 2015), 168; see Herculaneum Tablet 13 and 14; 149.6.2.2650, 7468; Cicero, *Pro Cluentio* 178, 179, 171.

were so many widows who received wealth from their fathers or husbands such that they owned up to one-third of all the property in the
Roman Empire.[34]

Myth 3: Women lived private lives in the home. We saw above that
the popular-culture perspective was that the home was the woman's
place and the forum (the public square for commerce and exchange) was
the man's. This is true, though exceptions were not uncommon. But even
when we are talking about the home, the Roman home was not a private
space in the way many modern homes are. Hemelrijk explains that patrons who wanted to increase their social status would receive clients and
visitors in their atrium; "a grand mansion thronged by visitors was sought
after as a sign of dignity and prestige."[35] She talks about houses having
different types of rooms, some for family only and others that functioned
more like public spaces. One could tell the room's usage by decor like
columns and art.[36] Hemelrijk sums up the situation aptly: for a woman
of means, "the ideal of female domesticity did not imply privacy or a life
of seclusion. On the contrary, the reception of numerous clients and
visitors put her in the public eye even within her own house."[37]

This seems to be true for Jewish communities in the Greco-Roman
world. As Eric Meyers explains, male Jews who were interested especially
in the business world did not prevent their wives from working and participating in professional commerce. If work was done at home, it might
naturally be done by both husband and wife; indeed, physical spaces
within the house do not appear to be gendered. There were no split female/
male quarters, and no part of the house seems to have been off limits as
a matter of fact.[38] We must be careful not to retroject modern house-use

[34]Saller, "Productive Unit," 120. This is obviously difficult to prove given the large scale of the
empire, but village records from Fayum (Roman Egypt) attest to women owning approximately
one-third of the property in that region; see D. W. Hobson, "Women as Property Owners in
Roman Egypt," *Transactions of the American Philological Association* 113 (1983): 311-21.
[35]Hemelrijk, *Hidden Lives*, 10.
[36]Hemelrijk, *Hidden Lives*, 10.
[37]Hemelrijk, *Hidden Lives*, 11.
[38]Eric Meyers, "The Problems of Gendered Space in Syro-Palestinian Architecture," *Early Christian Families in Context: An Interdisciplinary Dialogue*, ed. David L. Balch and Carolyn Osiek
(Grand Rapids, MI: Eerdmans, 2003), 44-69, esp. 68-69; cf. Monika Trümpter, "Space and Social

or gender-territory assumptions onto that time period. For example, because of the common use of slaves in domestic work, "the kitchen was not the feminine preserve it became in modern times."[39] The same goes for house decorations. We simply cannot say women were responsible for the art, furniture, and aesthetic appearance of the house and its rooms.[40]

The book of Tobit, an early Jewish text, offers an insightful look into a fictionalized but realistic Jewish household. Tobit, narrating in the first person, explains that his wife, Hanna, earned money in "women's works" (Tob 2:11). She had employers outside her family; it would seem Tobit himself was not directly involved in this business. Hanna sent her weaving work to her employers, and they would pay her wages (Tob 2:12). We know that Tobit was not a middleman in this business, because the employers gave Hanna a goat apparently as a bonus for her work, and when Tobit saw it, he said, "Where is this kid from? It is not stolen, is it?" (Tob 2:13).[41] A fight ensues, and Tobit says a long prayer (we never find out what happens to the goat). Still, it is fascinating to me that the book of Tobit treats as normal a wife and mother working independently of her husband for an outside business. We will return to women in business again in a bit.

MAJOR INSTITUTIONS OF THE GRECO-ROMAN WORLD

I have tried to paint a picture of a complex social world of the Roman period. On the one hand, women were expected to focus their energies on being good wives and mothers and helping to maintain an honorable household. On the other hand, this did not exclude female engagement in many of the major social, commercial, and civic institutions of society. Women did not have equal power or presence, but neither were they excluded.

Politics and civic benefaction.[42] It is often said that women could not hold political office in the Roman Empire. That's true. Women could not obtain

---

Relationships in the Greek Oikos of the Classical and Hellenistic Periods," in Rawson, *Companion to Families*, 32-52.

[39]Fantham et al., *Women in the Classical World*, 339.

[40]Fantham et al., *Women in the Classical World*, 341.

[41]Albert Pietersma and Benjamin G. Wright, eds., "Tobit," in *A New English Translation of the Septuagint (Primary Texts)*, trans. Alexander A. Di Lella (Oxford: Oxford University Press, 2007), Tob 2:13.

[42]"Civic benefaction" refers to the use of one's money, energy, and resources to support the local community; today we might think of this as philanthropic activity for the benefit of one's city.

an elected position, nor could they vote. But they did participate in civic leadership through appointed positions and civic benefaction. For example, Lalla of Arnae was a gymnasiarch, an administrator of local athletics.[43] Phile was a *stephanephorus*, a "crown-bearing" processional leader in public cult practices.[44] Pedia Secunda was an *epimelētēs* (overseer) in Eucarpia.[45]

We have several interesting case studies from the remains of Pompeii. Eumachia held the honor of priestess of the cult of Ceres, and she financially supported the city fullers;[46] in turn, they erected a public statue in her honor.[47] From Pompeii we also know of Julia Felix, who was heavily invested in the financial and political affairs of the city.[48]

The most interesting example from the Roman world of a female civic patron is Plancia Magna.[49] She was hailed "daughter of the city" and a magistrate.[50] She built a new city gate for Perge and had it decorated with images of the many founders and major patrons of the city, including the emperors Trajan and Hadrian and their wives. We do know from other records that Plancia Magna was a widow when the gate was installed, but her deceased husband is not a point of focus in the gate inscriptions.[51] There are a couple of peculiarities here. First, when relatives of Plancia Magna are mentioned, they are described in relationship to *her* ("father of Plancia Magna," "brother of Plancia Magna"), not vice versa. Second, as Eve D'Ambra explains, the statues of women outnumber those of men, extraordinary for a visual representation of the history and values of the city.[52]

---

[43]See Lefkowitz and Fant, *Women's Life*, 190.

[44]Lefkowitz and Fant, *Women's Life*, 190.

[45]Ramsay MacMullen, "Women in Public in the Roman Empire," in *Changes in the Roman Empire: Essays in the Ordinary* (Princeton, NJ: Princeton University Press, 1990), 162-68, at 165.

[46]A fuller works in cleaning or dying wool or other textiles.

[47]*CIL* 10:811; see Fantham et al., *Women in the Classical World*, 334.

[48]*CIL* 4:1136; see Fantham et al., *Women in the Classical World*, 334.

[49]She lived in Perge, Turkey, in the second century AD. See Mary T. Boatwright, "Plancia Magna of Perge: Women's Role and Status in Roman Asia Minor," in *Women's History and Ancient History*, ed. Sarah B. Pomeroy (Chapel Hill: University of North Carolina Press, 1991) 249-72.

[50]As the city's magistrate (*dēmiourgos*), not only did she have status and power, but in that position "her name . . . would be used to date all public documents for the year of her magistracy." Boatwright, "Plancia Magna of Perge," 254.

[51]See Barbara F. Caceres-Cerda, "The Exceptional Case of Plancia Magna: (Re)analyzing the Role of a Roman Benefactress" (MA thesis, City University of New York, 2018), 46-47.

[52]Eve D'Ambra, *Roman Women* (Cambridge: Cambridge University Press, 2007), 22; Boatwright, "Plancia Magna of Perge," 252.

How could such a woman exist in a patriarchal society? However we answer that question, we must accept the reality that women like Plancia Magna did exist and held social and political power normally only wielded by men.[53]

Business. Saller examined the evidence for the business sector of the Roman world and identified about two hundred occupations held by men. Women, he explains, were also sometimes involved in business but occupied only about thirty-five positions. The most common business activities of Roman women were in the areas of food production and service, crafts (especially textiles), hairdressing, and wet-nursing and nannying.[54] A variety of other non-domestic professions are also attested. A certain Secunda was a doctor.[55] A woman named Aufria gave lectures at a public festival of the Pythian games.[56] There were, however, certain types of jobs that women never participated in. Saller mentions banking, construction, and transportation.[57]

Figure 1. Relief of woman shopkeeper from Ostia Antica

[53]So Boatwright's concluding statement: "Plancia Magna and a significant number of other elite women crossed over into traditionally male roles, public ones, and achieved status and prominence equal to that of many men." "Plancia Magna of Perge," 263.

[54]See Saller, "Productive Unit," 35.

[55]*CIL* 4:8711.

[56]Lefkowitz and Fant, *Women's Life*, 190.

[57]Saller, "Productive Unit," 123.

Voluntary associations. Roman society valued social groups referred to in scholarship today as "voluntary associations."[58] There were basically three types of associations. Business associations brought together members of the same occupation, like a leather-workers guild. Burial associations had members pay dues so that each person could be assured a proper burial when the time came. Some associations were squarely focused on venerating a local deity (though all associations observed religious rituals). We know that women were sometimes honored for helping to fund association buildings or activities. For example, of 147 association inscriptions from Italy, twelve mention women as *patrona* or *mater* (honored female benefactor).[59] In terms of association leadership, a woman named Sergia Paulina hosted a burial meeting in her house in Rome.[60] The elite (senatorial class) Pompeia Agrippinilla was priestess and patron of a large association dedicated to Dionysius.[61] All in all, we know that women were very active in religious associations, much less so in business ones.

Cults and priesthoods. We have already noted briefly the Vestal Virgins of Rome, women who held privileged religious positions without gaining them through marriage. Women also served as priestesses for local cults, as with the case of Pompeian Eumachia. Now, you have to get out of your mind the image of the Jewish male priest who had a meager living and whose priesthood was assumed by birthright. In the Roman cult system, city priesthoods were positions sought after by the upper crust of society. They performed religious rites, of course, but it was also seen as community patronage, maintaining peace with the gods for the good of one's community. This is one sector of life where women enjoyed privileges closer to that of their male counterparts. Meghan DiLuzio states, "The Romans employed a surprisingly egalitarian approach to managing the community's relations with the divine."[62]

---

[58]See John S. Kloppenborg and Stephen G. Wilson, eds., *Voluntary Associations in the Graeco-Roman World* (London: Routledge, 1996).

[59]Hemelrijk, *Hidden Lives*, 184.

[60]*CIL* 6:9148; Osiek and MacDonald, *Woman's Place*, 208.

[61]*L'Année épigraphique* (*AE*) 1933.4.

[62]Meghan DiLuzio, *A Place at the Altar: Priestesses in Republican Rome* (Princeton, NJ: Princeton University Press, 2017), 10.

One of the highest privileges in the cultic context was serving as a priest for the imperial cult, as was the case with Licinia Flavilla, priestess in Nimes.[63] Another high honor went to the *flamen Dialis* (male priest) and *flaminica Dialis* (female priest) who served the high god Jupiter. Civic priests and priestesses across the Roman Empire held coveted positions of status and influence. They were treated along the lines of royalty or dignitary in their communities. They were given special seats of honor in theaters and sports arenas. "In sum, a civic priesthood offered wealthy women, both within and outside the elite, an opportunity to fulfil a prestigious public role that did not conflict with traditional ideals of femininity."[64]

JEWISH WOMEN IN THE GRECO-ROMAN WORLD

Jews in the Greco-Roman world did not form one culturally homogeneous group. Some Jews and Jewish communities assimilated to their wider environment, and others did less so.[65] Therefore, it is difficult to explain the lifestyles of Jewish women in summary. We can imagine that many Jewish women were expected to embody the traditional roles of the chaste, holy, and faithful wife. Jewish sage Ben Sira encouraged husbands to cherish their wives (Sir 7:19). The best wives are virtuous, he writes, courageous (literally "manly"!), loyal (Sir 26:1), modest, and self-disciplined (Sir 26:14-15). But he also warned men not to become slaves to their wives (Sir 25:8). Wives ought not to be the breadwinners in the family, and a wife should be treated as wicked if she does not seek to make her husband happy (Sir 25:22-23). She should be a silent partner in the relationship, and if she steps out of line, the husband should exercise his right to discipline her (Sir 26:14; 42:6).

From this perspective, Jewish women were marginalized in the family and society. At the same time, several Jewish writings produced

---

[63]Imperial family members Antonia (niece of Caesar Augustus) and Agrippina the Younger (granddaughter of Antonia) also both served as priestesses of the Augustan imperial cult; see Mary T. Boatwright, *The Imperial Women of Rome* (Oxford: Oxford University Press, 2021), 156.
[64]Hemelrijk, *Hidden Lives*, 101.
[65]John M. G. Barclay, *Jews in the Mediterranean Diaspora* (Berkeley: University of California Press, 2010).

in this era featured the lives and virtues of women, giving some of them higher profiles and opportunities for a greater positive impact on society. The book of Susanna, set in the Babylonian exile (597–538 BC), was written in the Greco-Roman period and focuses on a pious Jewish woman (Susanna) and her husband, Joakim. Two visitors to their house admire Susanna's beauty and try to compel her to sleep with them, or else they would spread rumors that she was an unfaithful wife. She refuses to accept their proposal, and they follow through with their threat and put her on trial for adultery. She cries out for justice, and Daniel steps in to demand a retrial. He questions the testimonies of the two elders separately and uncovers their lies. This is a fictional story but demonstrates Jewish virtues including justice, piety, and chastity. Daniel is clearly the hero of the story, and in some ways Susanna is the proverbial damsel in distress, but she models deep faith in God and respect for the covenant.

We also have the fictional story from the book of Judith, this time retelling the story of Israel engaging the superpower Assyria (set in the eighth century BC). When the Assyrians attack Israel, the beautiful widow Judith seduces and kills enemy leader Holofernes. Her actions on behalf of her people protect her country and the sanctity of the Jerusalem temple. Judith's character differs from Susanna in the sense that the former is a widow and is the heroine versus a victim. But, like Susanna, Judith is pure and pious (Jdt 8:8).

Tal Ilan has studied extensively the portrayal and lives of Jewish women in the Greco-Roman period, and she finds the books of Susanna and Judith illuminating in terms of spotlighting the world of women. However, she urges that "[these] books do not openly promote women's leadership, nor are they revolutionary in nature."[66] That is, they are not modern feminist texts, and we ought not to treat them that way. Yet, she argues, they do upset classic Jewish cultural views that men make the best models of piety and courage. Ilan proposes an interesting theory. Alexandra Salome was a queen ruling over Judea from 76 to 67 BC, and

---

[66]Tal Ilan, *Jewish Women in Greco-Roman Palestine* (Peabody, MA: Hendrickson, 1996), 153.

it was probably around this time that these women-focused works were written. Ilan considers the possibility that the books of Susanna and Judith were written as literature to support her reign.[67]

An energetic scholarly conversation involves the participation and leadership of women in ancient Jewish synagogues. We have little knowledge of how Jewish women engaged in religious services. What we *do* know is that they sometimes served as benefactors (i.e., donors) of synagogues. For the Jewish community in Phocaea, a woman named Tation funded the entire building. In return, they erected an honorary inscription and gave her a golden crown and a privileged front seat in the synagogue.[68] From inscriptional evidence, we also know that women sometimes held leadership titles in the synagogue. Women were called "synagogue ruler" (*archisynagōgos/archisynagōgissa*) in places like Smyrna, Crete, and Myndos; "ruler" (*archēgissa*) in Thessaly; "elder" (*presbytera*) in Crete, Thrace, Venosa, Tripolitania, Rome, and Malta; "mother" (*mater*) of the synagogue in Rome, Venosa, and Venetia; "female-father" (*pateressa*) of the synagogue in Venosa; and priestess of the synagogue in places like Egypt, Rome, and Jerusalem.[69] For the longest time, these titles were interpreted by modern scholars as "honorific," as in name only and obtained through these women's husbands or male relatives. Bernadette Brooten challenges this "honorific only" argument in her important book *Women Leaders in the Ancient Synagogue*. She notes that only in a few inscriptions about these women are their husbands mentioned.[70] As a key piece of evidence, she appeals to the inscription mentioning Rufina.

> Rufina, a Jewess, head of the synagogue (*archisynagōgos*), built this tomb for her freed slaves and the slaves raised in her house. No one else has the right to bury anyone (here). If someone should dare to do, he or she will pay 1500 denars to the sacred treasury and 1000 denars to

---

[67]Ilan, *Jewish Women*, 21-23, 153.

[68]See Paul Trebilco, *Jewish Communities in Asia Minor* (Cambridge: Cambridge University Press, 1991), 110-11.

[69]See Lee I. Levine, *The Ancient Synagogue: The First Thousand Years* (New Haven, CT: Yale University Press, 2005), 499-518.

[70]Bernadette Brooten, *Women Leaders in the Ancient Synagogue* (Atlanta: Scholars Press, 1982), 9-10.

the Jewish people. A copy of this inscription has been placed in the (public) archives.[71]

Brooten is quick to point out that no husband or father is mentioned here, and she is the only figure of prominence connected to the slaves and freedpersons of her household.[72] Furthermore, Brooten notes that in the Roman cults, women served as functional priestesses in their own right, even when their husbands were priests. With terms like "mother" or "elder," it is *possible* these are honorific titles that reflect respect for these women among the people in the community. But "synagogue ruler" (*archisynagōgos*) carries the assumption of leadership and authority. The exact same term is used in the New Testament for Jairus (Mk 5:22), a synagogue ruler who read from the Law and the Prophets (Acts 13:15); Crispus, a synagogue ruler who believed the gospel (Acts 18:8); and another synagogue ruler named Sosthenes (Acts 18:17).

EARLY CHRISTIANITY AND WOMEN IN THE ROMAN WORLD

In the discussion above, I sketched the lives of women in the Roman world. While the Roman world was a patriarchal society in structure, that did not mean women were not seen or heard or did not exercise power, influence, or leadership. Though misogyny and destructive genderized stereotypes were widespread in society, Roman people were also "class-conscious" and very pragmatic when it came to advancement in power, money, and glory. The net effect socially is that women could and did slip or maneuver through the cracks of the patriarchal infrastructure (via tools like class, shrewdness, popularity, industry, and success) to be able to exercise influence and power.

What can we say, then, about early Christianity and the women in Jesus communities of the first century? Despite some of our impressions about the motivations or effects of the "prohibition" passages (1 Cor 11:2-16; 14:33-36; 1 Tim 2:11-15; see the "What About . . . ?" section

---

[71]*Corpus Inscriptionum Iudaicarum* 741 (Smyrna). Similarly, "Sophia of Gortyn, elder and head of the synagogue (lies) here. The memory of the righteous one forever. Amen" (Crete), as translated by Brooten, *Women Leaders*, 11-12.
[72]Brooten, *Women Leaders*, 7-8.

of this book), the women we actually *meet* in Acts and the Pauline letters demonstrate that the ministry world was not a "man's domain." Women in positions of influence and leadership appear across numerous texts (as will become clear in part two). Important leaders like the apostle Paul not only acknowledged women leaders in Christian communities but also commended and praised them for their work. All that to say, people like Paul did not seek to restrict women in terms of leadership or the wielding of power. At the end of the day, Paul appears to have been a ministry pragmatist: those gifted by God and ready to serve with a willing heart are needed for the gospel mission.

I don't think it is the case that the apostles blindly followed "culture" when it came to sexual anthropology. Just as we are today, the early churches were constantly asking themselves whether the things affirmed in society could be affirmed by the people of God in Christ. As Paul engaged with Lydia of Philippi, an independent businesswoman (Acts 16:11-40), what did he think of her? It is not reasonable to imagine that he pressured her, after her baptism, to find a husband and follow his lead. Or that she could not lead a house-church community unless she had a male partner. The impression we get from Luke's account is that she immediately presents herself to Paul and Silas as a capable person, fully devoted to God, and that when Paul and Silas finally depart from Philippi, they leave the fledgling church in her hands (Acts 16:40).

CONCLUSION

In this chapter we have looked carefully at the lives of women in the Roman world, imagining a more realistic picture of their struggles, barriers, opportunities, and accomplishments. There was a time when I had a wrong notion that the "ancient world" was neatly constructed into leaders (men) and followers (women). It is true that in most ancient societies men held the privileges of authority, power, comfort, and safety, which they protected through intimidation and sometimes violence. But a simplistic, "snow-globe" image of patriarchy clearly does not tell us the whole story, and there is a lot more in the picture as we look at life in the Roman Empire. Yes, women were wives and mothers, but there were many high-class widows, and a good number of them independently managed households like small estates.

Women were encouraged to focus on the home, but this did not prevent women from running businesses or acting as patrons and bene-factors to clients (female and male). It is true that there were no female Roman senators, but a shrewd priestess of a powerful religious cult could wield social power on a similar level. And what about Christian women? I used to assume they were at home, sewing up tattered clothes and minding the children. Surely, many women did that—and there's nothing wrong with that! But when it comes to the many named women in the New Testament, we know their names precisely *because* they were out and about doing ministry. They traveled long distances, sometimes without a husband. They wound up in prison because of their dangerous frontline ministry. They trained and instructed other leaders. They helped their churches make strategic decisions. In the following chapters, I am excited to introduce and discuss these women by name. The apostles and other New Testament writers tell their stories—and it is important that we retell them again and again.

4

The Women in Jesus' Life and Ministry

On the face of it, the Gospels seem to be stories about the lives of men. Jesus was a man sent from God to bring the good news. The twelve apostles were men. Jesus argued with male leaders among the Pharisees, Sadducees, scribes, and priests. Men arrested Jesus. Men sentenced Jesus to death. Men executed Jesus. All these things are true, but when we look at the Gospels more carefully, women are not absent; in fact, the story of Jesus can't be told without them. Now, it is true that women are rarely addressed in speech, far less do they speak, but they are *there* and often modeling and performing ministry faithfully, if sometimes quietly. Christian history has been too quick to ignore the women of the Gospels, dismissing them as backdrop characters. But when we study these women, what they say and do, and the roles they play in the story of God, we clearly see that they were instrumental agents of the beginning of the gospel and the birth of the church.

MARY, THE MOTHER OF JESUS

A handful of years ago, I was engaged in an argument with an old friend from high school. He was arguing that women do not have authority to teach theology to men. I asked, "What about when women speak in Scripture? Is that not God blessing the teaching voice of women?" He responded, "Yes, women are given voice in the Bible, but they do not say anything 'new' or more important than what men teach on important theological issues." Basically, he was saying that the words of women could be ignored or removed from Scripture and the truth would still remain in the words of men. I disagreed, but the conversation led me to look at the speech of women in the Bible more carefully. I went on an expedition to find the most powerful testimonies of women present in Scripture. It didn't take me long to become enamored with the Magnificat, Mary's Song of Praise (Lk 1:46-55).[1]

Each Gospel begins differently; each one frames the story of Jesus in its own unique way.[2] Luke commences with the story of the miraculous pregnancies of Elizabeth and Mary. It would be odd for *any* story from the first-century Greco-Roman world to begin with a spotlight on the lives of two humble women. Luke gives these women the first two major agenda-setting speeches in his Gospel. After Mary finds out she is with child, she travels to the hill country of Judea to be with Elizabeth. This becomes a special occasion to voice her thoughts and feelings. The Lukan scene here has the feeling of a modern-day musical, where the drama is seemingly interrupted by a song and dance sequence:

My soul glorifies the Lord
    and my spirit rejoices in God my Savior,
for he has been mindful
    of the humble state of his servant.
From now on all generations will call me blessed,
    for the Mighty One has done great things for me—
    holy is his name.
His mercy extends to those who fear him,
    from generation to generation.
He has performed mighty deeds with his arm;
    he has scattered those who are proud in their inmost thoughts.
He has brought down rulers from their thrones
    but has lifted up the humble.

---

[1] As a result, I published the following: "Teach Us, Mary: The Authority of Women Teachers in the Church in Light of the Magnificat," *Priscilla Papers* 29, no. 3 (2015): 11-14, https://www.cbeinternational.org/resource/article/priscilla-papers-academic-journal/teach-us-mary-authority-women-teachers-church.
[2] See Morna D. Hooker, *Beginnings: Keys That Open the Gospels* (London: SCM Press, 1997).

He has filled the hungry with good things
    but has sent the rich away empty.
He has helped his servant Israel,
    remembering to be merciful
to Abraham and his descendants forever,
    just as he promised our ancestors. (Lk 1:46-55)

Mary's song is not just a reflection on her feelings of joy. After the first statement about her exuberance, she looks back on a long history of God's faithfulness to his people, and then she looks ahead to the fulfillment of his covenantal promises of the redemption of her people.[3] The style of Mary's song resembles Old Testament hymns of divine victory. There are clear parallels to the Psalms.[4] But there are even *more* resonances with faith-filled songs of faithful and inspired women, like Miriam (Ex 15:1-21), Hannah (1 Sam 2:1-10), and Deborah (Judg 5:1-31). What these songs have in common with Mary's is the celebration of God fighting on behalf of his people, acting in conformity to his covenant love, and overturning what may have seemed like impossible odds. In the words of Barbara Reid, "These songs are not sweet lullabies; they are militant songs that exult in the saving power of God that has brought defeat to those who had subjugated God's people."[5] The singers of these kinds of songs—many of them women—interpret current events with a view toward the divine perspective. Humans see with fleshly eyes, but prophets see beyond the flesh to a great work of God on earth.[6]

As far as Luke the storyteller is concerned, Mary's song is not just another dialogue snippet in his Jesus story. Mary plays the role of a kind of character-narrator, singing to Elizabeth (and hoping her voice will echo

---

[3]Joel B. Green, *The Gospel of Luke*, New International Commentary on the New Testament (Grand Rapids, MI: Eerdmans, 1997), 98.

[4]R. T. France, *Luke*, Teach the Text (Grand Rapids, MI: Baker Books, 2013), 20-21.

[5]Barbara Reid, "An Overture to the Gospel of Luke," *Currents in Theology and Mission* 39 (2012): 428-34, at 429.

[6]For the idea that Mary sings with prophetic insight, see Beverly Gaventa, *Mary, Glimpses of the Mother of God* (Minneapolis: Fortress, 1999), 58; Deirdre Good, *Mariam, the Magdalen, and the Mother* (Bloomington: Indiana University Press, 2005), 64; F. Scott Spencer, *Salty Wives, Spirited Mothers, and Savvy Widows: Capable Women of Purpose and Persistence in Luke's Gospel* (Grand Rapids, MI: Eerdmans, 2012), 76-77; Barbara Reid, *Wisdom's Feast: An Invitation to Feminist Interpretation to the Scriptures* (Grand Rapids, MI: Eerdmans, 2016), 52-56.

out to all Israel) but with a wink to us, the reader of Luke's Gospel. She is granted spiritual insight into the "covenantal purpose of God."[7] She describes the redemptive and justice-seeking work of God as a great upheaval and reversal of the fortune of her weary people. As John Carroll explains, "It is a hymn of praise to God, whose ways challenge and subvert the way things are in the world. It is about God, who keeps promises and cares for the lowly and powerless. Singing her faith in God, Mary models authentic response to divine initiative: joyful praise and bold proclamation."[8]

Brittany Wilson shows how Mary's song trains the reader of Luke to see this upending divine activity throughout Luke, in Simeon's prediction of "the falling and rising of many" (Lk 2:33-35), the welcoming of the poor and lame at the great banquet (Lk 14:12-24), the afterlife blessing of the beggar Lazarus and the rich man's consignment to Hades (Lk 16:19-31), and justice for the lowly widow (Lk 18:1-8). Mary's song warns the reader to look for signs of life overpowering death and to anticipate the greatest of reversals, the resurrection of Jesus.[9]

Mary's Song of Praise amplifies how God's singular act in the life of a Jewish woman has cosmic repercussions. By raising her voice in song, Mary harmonizes her own story with the story of Israel; by speaking out of her own situation, she speaks on behalf of Israel and draws from Israel's scriptural songbook to do so. In the story of Jesus' birth, Mary is a spokesperson for Israel and for Luke's larger theme of reversal.[10]

At nearly ten verses, Mary's song is one of the longest speeches in the Gospels by a person other than Jesus. And that phenomenon becomes even more extraordinary when we think of an ancient biographer (Luke) giving voice to the experiences and hopes of a woman. But what does the rest of the Jesus story hold for Mary?

---

[7] Green, *Gospel of Luke*, 98.

[8] John T. Carroll, *Luke*, New Testament Library (Louisville, KY: Westminster John Knox, 2012) 47; see also Amy Smith Carman, "*Ave Maria*: Old Testament Allusions in the Magnificat," *Priscilla Papers* 31, no. 2 (2017): 14-18, at 14.

[9] Brittany Wilson, "Luke 1:46-55," *Interpretation* 71, no. 1 (2017): 80-82, at 81.

[10] Wilson, "Luke 1:46-55," 82. Similarly, Spencer, *Salty Wives*, 80: "Mary's Magnificat functions as a paradigmatic agenda of Jesus' messianic activity throughout Luke's Gospel. As such, this young virgin and village girl of twelve, let us say, demonstrates remarkable vision, insight, and boldness—and yes, *agency*—to proclaim the reordering of society under God's rule."

Pretty quickly after the early years of Jesus' incarnate life, Joseph disappears from the picture without a trace. His name is mentioned a few times when Jesus begins his adult ministry (Lk 3:23-24; 4:22), but the last time we see Joseph in action is when Jesus is twelve years old (Lk 2:41). After that, for all intents and purposes, Joseph is out of the picture. In Luke's Gospel, Mary doesn't play a prominent role either, but according to the other Gospels, she is very much present (Mt 13:55). She stays close by during his ministry (Mt 12:46), and it is interesting that *she*, not an uncle or grandfather, continues to be his closest family member. From this we can safely postulate that there was no more formative mentor in Jesus' life than his mother. In the famous episode of the wedding in Cana, Mary turns to Jesus for help when the wine runs out, and though he questions her, he ultimately responds positively to her concerns (Jn 2:1-5). Their back-and-forth feels very much like a close relationship between mother and (adult) son.

When Jesus was crucified, Mary again was there—we get the impression she had been in Jesus' traveling entourage all along, but John specifically mentions her presence at the cross (Jn 19:25). Jesus is recorded as uttering a few statements in his agony on the cross, such as the famous Cry of Dereliction (Mt 27:46; Mk 15:34) and the decisive "It is finished" (Jn 19:30). But according to John, among Jesus' final thoughts before his death was his concern for his mother. When he saw his mother there on the ground below, he was struck with concern and requested that the Beloved Disciple "adopt" Mary as his mother and give her a safe home (Jn 19:27).

To Jesus, Mary was far more than just the woman that birthed him. She was caregiver, teacher, companion, disciple, mourner, and eventually church leader (more on that last role at the end of this chapter). She was with him through thick and thin, and she may have been the last person Jesus looked in the eyes when he breathed his last. As a kind of prophet, she witnessed the fulfillment of her divinely inspired word; as a mother, she suffered through the agony and death of her own son.

JESUS AND WOMEN

What was Jesus' attitude toward women in general? Keep in mind that the popular stereotypes of women at the time portrayed them as nagging and unintelligent. Most ancient literature gave women very minor roles and flat characterization; sometimes writers left women out altogether. Remember from the previous chapter the son eulogizing his mother, with the preface that he won't have much to say because women lead colorless lives. Well, we encounter a different sort of story when we read the Gospels, especially the Gospel of Luke. From the testimony of the four Jesus biographers, Jesus engaged with the lives of women in deeply meaningful ways.

Women paved the way for Jesus. We have already begun to identify how Luke in particular demonstrates how women played strategic roles in Jesus' life.[11] Mary, a young maiden, took bold steps to protect and nurture the wombed Savior of Israel. In parallel, Elizabeth, a woman "righteous in the sight of God" and obedient to the law (Lk 1:5-7), is also blessed with a miracle baby in her old age. Like Mary, Elizabeth is given divine insight into what God is up to: "The Lord has done this for me. . . . In these days he has shown his favor and taken away my disgrace among the people" (Lk 1:25). Later on, when Elizabeth greets Mary, two pregnant women full of joy, she perceives the work of God in Mary: "Blessed are you among women, and blessed is the child you will bear! . . . Blessed is she who has believed that the Lord would fulfill his promises to her!" (Lk 1:42-45).

We know that Mary stayed with Elizabeth for three months (Lk 1:56). No doubt they spent many hours talking about what the Lord was doing. Elizabeth may have been several decades older than Mary and perhaps gave her life wisdom and advice.

Sometimes Luke's Gospel is called the "Gospel for Women," because his story pays attention to the lives of women from beginning to end. But it might more appropriately be considered the "Gospel for Women and

---

[11]See Derek Tidball and Dianne Tidball, *The Message of Women* (Downers Grove, IL: InterVarsity Press, 2012), 151-60; Jaime Clark-Soles, "Magnificent Mary and Her Magnificat," in *Women in the Bible*, Interpretation (Louisville, KY: Westminster John Knox, 2020), 147-86.

Men Together." Luke likes to show the parallel or paired lives of men and women. So, we see Mary and Joseph, Zechariah and Elizabeth, and when it is time for Jesus' dedication at the temple, we read of the ministries of Simeon and Anna. Simeon held the child and praised God (Lk 2:29-35). Likewise, Anna, the elderly prophet, was what we would call a prayer warrior (Lk 2:37). She approached the holy family, praised God, and proclaimed to all that this child would fulfill Israel's redemptive hopes (Lk 2:38). Throughout these first few chapters of his Gospel, Luke seems to be saying, *Yes, men had something to do with preparing the people for the Messiah, but in quiet faith women like Elizabeth did hard work to pave the way as well (imagine having a baby when you are old). And other women, like Mary and Anna, contributed important things in not-so-quiet ways.*

Jesus addressed the lives of women. As we have noted, Luke especially emphasizes that Jesus "saw" the lives of women. Luke tends to present stories and events related to Jesus in men and women pairs.[12] Jesus teaches that the kingdom is like a man planting a mustard seed and like a woman adding yeast to dough (Lk 13:18-21). In Luke 15, he talks about a (male) shepherd searching for the one lost sheep and then rejoicing when it is found (Lk 15:4-7). Then he adds an image of a woman searching for and finding a lost coin (Lk 15:8-10).[13] We already talked about the early chapters of Luke, but to reiterate, there you find parallel angelic encounters involving Zechariah (Lk 1) and Mary (Lk 2). To bookend the Gospel, men and women visit the tomb (Lk 23:50-56) and learn of the resurrection (Lk 24:1-12). In Luke 4:31-39 the healing of a possessed man is followed by the healing of Peter's mother-in-law. A few chapters later, the healing of the widow of Nain is paired with the healing of the

---

[12]See Barbara Reid, *Choosing the Better Part? Women in the Gospel of Luke* (Collegeville, MN: Liturgical Press, 1996), 2-3.

[13]One might think this is a net loss for women, as the image of the woman is that of a domestic wife who sweeps the house; but if you read this short parable carefully, she doesn't quite fit that stereotype. The money that is lost appears to be owned by her, she does not enlist a man's help in finding it, and she initiates the subsequent neighborhood party to celebrate. When we look at the paired parables, what we know about the man is that he has sheep, and what we know about the woman is that she has money.

Centurion's slave (Lk 7:1-17). And, again, a crippled woman is restored, and then a crippled man (Lk 13:10-17; 14:1-6).

Sometimes Luke gives more focused attention to the lives of women, such as those of widows. He shares a longer parable about a persistent widow who sought out a judge for justice. She is a model of tenacious pursuit of righteousness, and in some way, too, she is the model of faith in Jesus' concluding rhetorical question, "When the Son of Man comes, will he find faith on earth"? (Lk 18:8). In chapter 21, Luke recounts Jesus' attentiveness to a "poor widow" at the temple, who gave up her two precious copper coins (Lk 21:1-4).

Jesus cared about women. We have already observed how Jesus cared for women he encountered, especially in his healing ministry (Lk 4:38; 8:41-42, 49-56; 13:10-17). We also have the story of Jesus and the woman caught in adultery in John (Jn 7:53-8:11). Now, it is unclear whether this was an original part of John's Gospel or a story added later by an editor or scribe.[14] In any case, it rings true of the Jesus attested by the four Gospels, radically compassionate and forgiving, and critical of leaders who point the finger of judgment but don't look in the mirror. Assuming this story is true, Jesus protected the woman, possibly saving her from mob execution. He speaks to her tenderly and restores her value and dignity (Jn 8:10-11). We find a similar compassion and sensitivity when Jesus responds to Mary and Martha's grief over the death of their brother Lazarus (Jn 11; see below).

Jesus had meaningful conversations with women. Jesus talked to women about the important things in life. He didn't just treat women as sinners to be saved, or weaklings in need of rescue or healing; he conversed and respected their intelligence.[15] In Matthew and Mark we have record of Jesus' engagement with the Canaanite woman (Mt 15:21-28; Mk 7:24-30). I don't know how to explain the seemingly impudent comment on Jesus' part (comparing her to a dog). All I can say is that I

---

[14]See the short but insightful reflection on this passage (and its canonical status) by Mickey Klink III, "Does This Passage Belong in the Bible? The Woman Caught in Adultery (John 7:53-8:11)," *The Good Book Blog*, September 27, 2012, https://www.biola.edu/blogs/good-book-blog/2012/does-the-passage-belong-in-the-bible-the-woman-caught-in-adultery-john-7-53-8-11.

[15]Clark-Soles, *Women in the Bible*, 209-16.

sense in this encounter Jesus continuing to play his role as parabolist and riddler, pricking at her faith and seeing how she responds. We undoubtedly still have questions about Jesus using offensive speech,[16] but I want to suggest that Jesus is engaging in a bit of a test of wits here. Jesus doesn't brush her away, dismiss her concerns. He seems to have been probing her will: *How much does she want to pursue me?* After she responds to Jesus' satisfaction, he commends her faith and grants her request for him to heal her demon-possessed daughter (Mt 15:28). "And her daughter was healed at that moment" (Mt 15:28). It is hard for us not to see this as a contrast to the dull understanding of the disciples who, earlier in that same chapter in Matthew, could not make heads or tails of Jesus' parable about defilement (Mt 15:16-20).

Another important conversation Jesus has with a woman happens at the Sycharian well in Samaria (Jn 4:4-38).[17] In popular modern reflections on this story, this unnamed Samaritan woman is often depicted as a sexually immoral person that Jesus calls out (Jn 4:18). But that is read *into* the text; nothing like that is ever stated in John. First things first. The fact that this conversation happens at a well linked to the Jewish patriarch Jacob sets the reader up for a kind of romance scene. In the Old Testament, the well was a type-scene where people fell in love or where a betrothal was initiated (Gen 24:10-27; 29:1-11; Ex 2:15-22; 1 Sam 9:3-12). Now, Jesus was not looking for a wife in Sychar, but this well type-scene does predispose the reader to expect a warm and intimate conversation to take place.

The first thing Jesus does is ask her for a drink of water (Jn 4:7). He is tired and thirsty, and he does not have a bucket. She can provide care for him; she can meet a need. They engage in a back-and-forth. Jesus asks for a drink, but then offers her living water (Jn 4:13). They get into the topic of her family life. She has had five husbands and now does not live with a husband (Jn 4:18). In our modern minds, we quickly jump to her having a string of divorces and is now shacking up with yet another man.

---

[16]See the thoughtful discussion in Reid, *Wisdom's Feast*, 69-70.
[17]Dorothy Lee, *The Ministry of Women in the New Testament: Reclaiming the Biblical Vision for Church Leadership* (Grand Rapids, MI: Baker Academic, 2021), 82-84.

But another scenario is possible, even more probable. Her husbands have died, not that uncommon in a world with high mortality, and she very well could be living with her brother or another male relative. In that case, Jesus was not calling her out on her promiscuity; he was attentive to her hard life.[18]

The woman could have ended the conversation there, but once she realizes that Jesus has prophetic knowledge and insight, she asks him some big questions about the true place for proper worship of God (Jn 4:20). She doesn't ask him about "women's issues"; she asks him what we think of as a theology question. And Jesus dignifies her good question with a direct answer, and then he reveals himself to her as the Messiah (Jn 4:21-26). Jesus' disciples return from their errand, and they are scandalized by Jesus conversing with a Samaritan woman. Again, we are meant to notice the contrast between the disciples' fog of confusion (when Jesus tells them about his spiritual food of obeying the Father, they are befuddled and say, "Could someone have brought him food?" [Jn 4:33]) and the clearheaded Samaritan woman, who promptly shares about Jesus with her village and gives compelling testimony (Jn 4:39).

Jesus was ministered to by women. Most of the Gospels highlight how Jesus performed ministry, caring for and teaching both men and women. But I want to touch on a part of these Gospels where Jesus is ministered to *by* women. This can get a bit messy in terms of sources, because I want to focus this section on the stories in which women come to Jesus and wash or anoint him. Honestly, we are not sure whether these are completely different stories or the same story told from different perspectives. I don't think those details matter too much, but for the sake of our discussion, I will treat them as different episodes.

First, we have Luke's story of the "sinful woman" who came to Jesus while he was at the home of a Pharisee (Lk 7:37-39). She brings an alabaster jar of perfume, and she washes his feet in her tears, kisses his feet, and pours perfume on them. Clearly, she is seeking his ministry and forgiveness, and he grants that to her: "Your sins are forgiven" (Lk 7:48).

---

[18]See Caryn A. Reeder, *The Samaritan Woman's Story: Reconsidering John 4 After #ChurchToo* (Downers Grove, IL: IVP Academic, 2022).

But Jesus turns this touching scene into an opportunity to rebuke the Pharisees who invited him over. They failed to show him proper respect and hospitality by greeting him warmly, washing his feet, and anointing him with oil (Lk 7:44-47). The woman was a stranger who intruded on this house, but she boldly played the role of host and treated Jesus with the respect he deserved. The Pharisee men treated Jesus with cold hospitality; this woman showed Jesus "great love" (Lk 7:47).

A similar scene occurs in Mark and Matthew when Jesus is at the home of Simon the Leper (Mk 14:3-9; Mt 26:6-13). Here we have another (?) woman coming to Jesus with an alabaster jar of perfume; but in this scenario she is not weeping, and she pours the perfume on Jesus' head. While the men rebuke her for wasting expensive perfume, Jesus commends her for anointing his body before his burial (Mk 14:8). "Truly I tell you," Jesus says, "wherever the gospel is preached throughout the world, what she has done will also be told, in memory of her" (Mk 14:9). The woman may not have known what she was doing as a prophetic testimony to his death. What Jesus was saying is that her faith and devotion to him brings her into unison with his mission and ministry, a trajectory that leads to the cross and tomb. John Nolland sums up well (with a view toward the Matthew version of the story): "The woman's good deed turns out to be a timely honouring of Jesus in a manner that fits precisely the needs of the Passion setting. Though there is something ghoulish here, we have in this anointing for burial the one really bright moment between the beginning of chap. 26 and the death of Jesus. Only this woman honours him fittingly as he faces his death."[19]

According to the Gospel of Mark, after Jesus died and was put into the tomb, some women went to anoint his dead body. They didn't find his body, but again it is worth saying that these women were seeking to care for Jesus while the men hid. Mark's Gospel ends with these women being too afraid to share with the men what the angels told them about Jesus' resurrection (Mk 16:8). But the story continues with their renewed courage and proclamation, as we learn well from the other

---

[19]John Nolland, *The Gospel of Matthew* (Grand Rapids, MI: Eerdmans, 2005), 1055.

Gospels (see Lk 24:9) and the emergence of Christianity itself. We wouldn't *have* the Gospels at all if the women did nothing—and the readers of Mark knew that.

DID JESUS HAVE WOMEN DISCIPLES?

Let's turn now to an important question regarding Jesus' ministry: Did Jesus have women disciples?[20] For many years I assumed the answer was no, because of the fact of the Twelve. (These twelve men were *the* disciples, right?) But the answer to the question is a bit more complicated than that. Yes, Jesus called twelve men to learn from him and to be sent out in mission and ministry, but that doesn't mean that only twelve people traveled with Jesus, learned from Jesus, or were sent out by Jesus. We might do better to think about Jesus' followers and disciples in tiered categories or concentric circles. The smallest circle would be the Twelve, men that Jesus selected to follow him. Then there appears to be a wider group that Jesus taught and who interacted with him on a regular basis. And the outermost circle would be the fickle crowds that come and go.

Women were not part of the Twelve, but they were certainly part of that middle group. A group of men and women followed Jesus wherever he went, received important instruction, and were taught how to do ministry. We learn some important details about some of the women in this wider group in Luke 8:1-3. Luke refers to "some women who had been cured of evil spirits and diseases: Mary (called Magdalene) from whom seven demons had come out; Joanna the wife of Chuza, the manager of Herod's household; Susanna; and many others. These women were helping to support them out of their own means." I used to think Jesus went from place to place with men, and yet Luke widens our perspective to see these (widowed?) women who were healed and set free from demons by Jesus. Not only did they travel with Jesus wherever he went, but they *funded* his ministry out of their personal wealth! My point here is that wherever Jesus was, women were there too, learning from him and also supporting

---

[20]See Lee, *Ministry of Women*, 16-21, 47-58, 75-95.

him. And it is reasonable to think that there were more than just these three named women (Mary Magdalene, Joanna, Susanna).[21]

Speaking of Luke 8, I want to say a little bit about Mary Magdalene, a key character in the Gospels but someone whose story we actually know very little about. First, she is mentioned in all four Gospels, a testimony to her impact on the story of Jesus. In terms of her background, the clue is in the name Magdalene; in actuality this is not a name but a place. It identifies this Mary, which was a very popular Jewish name, with her hometown, Magdala (between Capernaum and Tiberius by the Sea of Galilee). In three of the Gospels (Matthew, Mark, and John), she is not named until after Jesus is arrested (Mt 27:56, 61; Mk 15:40, 47; Jn 19:25). Only Luke provides background information and makes it clear that Mary Magdalene traveled with Jesus and the Twelve during his ministry. Luke comments that Jesus cast out seven demons from her (Lk 8:2).

What Mary Magdalene is most famous for is her testimony about the resurrection of Jesus. According to Matthew, Mary Magdalene and another Mary accompanied Joseph of Arimathea as he placed Jesus' dead body in the tomb (Mt 27:61). Later, these two returned again "to look at the tomb" (Mt 28:1). An angel of the Lord came down from heaven and rolled back the stone—this frightened the guards, who nearly died of dread (Mt 28:4). The angel did not speak to the male guards, according to Matthew, but instead addressed the women. He told them that Jesus had risen (as he foretold), invited them to see for themselves, and instructed them to go and tell the disciples (Mt 28:6-7). The women went quickly, with both joy and fear, but Jesus appeared to them before they reached the disciples. He encouraged them and sent them on (Mt 28:8-10). The Gospel of John picks up the story of Mary Magdalene's commission. She arrived and proclaimed, "I have seen the Lord!" (Jn 20:18). And then she reported what Jesus said to her. In Eastern Christianity, Mary Magdalene is hailed *isapostolos*, equal to the apostles (as in "another apostle"), because of her pivotal witness.[22]

---

[21]See Reid, *Wisdom's Feast*, 91-104.
[22]W. D. Davies and Dale C. Allison, *Matthew: A Shorter Commentary* (New York: T&T Clark, 2004), 531.

There is a popular myth still circulated today that Mary Magdalene was a harlot saved by Jesus. No New Testament text indicates that. What did happen is that some medieval texts tried to link Mary Magdalene to the "sinful woman" of Luke 7:36-50. But Mary is named in chapter eight (the very next chapter), so this association is unlikely, because Luke would have made that clear. Helen Bond and Joan Taylor note the bizarre but influential portrayal of Mary Magdalene in the movie *The King of Kings* (1927). In this movie depiction,

> a scantily clad Mary enjoys herself with her suitors as a wealthy courtesan. She snuggles with her pet leopard and gets around in a chariot pulled by zebras. The lush orientalism of the depiction creates an erotic, self-aggrandising aura around Mary that utterly contrasts with the depiction of the saintly, pious Mary the Mother [of Jesus]. Mary Magdalene is tamed by the eviction of seven demons, shown as the seven deadly sins, at which point she passes from autonomous waywardness to controlled devotion to her man, Christ.[23]

What Bond and Taylor are saying is that "Mary the Harlot-Turned-Christian" makes for good cinematics, but it is not the way the New Testament talks about Mary Magdalene. Her real story, as the Gospels testify, is spiritual, not sexual. Perhaps men feel the need to sexualize Mary Magdalene because of the seeming cultural oddness of a single woman traveling with Jesus.[24] But as far as the Gospel writers were concerned, this was a woman who responded well to Jesus' healing power and stuck with him to the bitter end (even after the Twelve fled, scattered, and hid). Her deep desire was to be near Jesus, even after his death (again, according to Matthew she was at the tomb twice). And we are meant to remember her obedience to the angel and to the risen Jesus, who commissioned her to testify to the good news of his living power and lordship. Jesus and the angel could have skipped the women at the tomb and appeared directly

---

[23]Helen Bond and Joan Taylor, *Women Remembered: Jesus' Female Disciples* (London: Hodder & Stoughton, 2022), 60.

[24]Bond and Taylor make the important observation that Mary Magdalene is not identified by her relationship to a man ("wife of so-and-so" or "daughter of so-and-so"), which would have been common practice at the time: "She was just Mary (the Magdalene), alone, and in Luke 8:1-3 she had her own resources" (*Women Remembered*, 72).

to the male disciples, and Jesus did so later as we know. So why did Jesus give that pep talk to Mary Magdalene? I believe that he wanted to honor the women's presence with the privilege of giving first testimony. As I have emphasized in this book, women were there, wherever the men were—and sometimes in the right place even when the men were nowhere to be found. The Gospels call her Mary of Magdala to identify her with a place. We might also call her Mary of Golgotha, because she was *there*; she showed up for Jesus when almost no one else did.

Turning our discussion back to the women followers of Jesus in general, is it fair to refer to these women as *disciples*? The Greek word *mathētēs* means "learner" or "student." This makes sense because Jesus was commonly referred to as "teacher."[25] The disciples *as learners* were meant to be taught by Jesus and to carry out ministry in his name. Mary Magdalene is a good example of a Jesus follower who was given direct instruction by Jesus and followed through. If she is not a disciple, it is hard to make a case for anyone, male or female.

Let's reflect for a moment, before concluding this chapter, on Jesus' choosing of the Twelve.[26] We might have it in our heads that Jesus chose this cadre of men because they were especially wise, brave, or faithful. But the stories told in the four Gospels don't actually bear that out. Jesus regularly calls out the disciples for their small faith and dull thinking (Mt 15:16; Mk 7:18). Peter denies Jesus (Mt 26:69-74), Judas betrays Jesus (Mt 26:48), they all abandon Jesus at his lowest point (Mt 26:31-32), and in a moment of weakness the male disciples hide and lock themselves indoors "for fear of the Jewish leaders" (Jn 20:19).[27] They were far from models of deep faith.

Now, it is true that the Twelve were chosen not only to be a special group of disciples but also to be sent out as *the apostles*. But it is important

---

[25]*Didaskalos*; e.g., Mt 9:11; 10:24; 22:16; 26:18; Mk 13:1; 14:14; Lk 6:40; 19:39; 22:11.

[26]See Joan E. Taylor, "Male-Female Missionary Pairings Among Jesus' Disciples," in *Patterns of Women's Leadership in Early Christianity*, ed. Joan E. Taylor and Ilaria L. E. Ramelli (Oxford: Oxford University Press, 2021), 11-25, esp. 13-14; cf. Aída Besançon Spencer, "Jesus's Treatment of Women in the Gospels," in *Discovering Biblical Equality*, ed. Ronald W. Pierce, Cynthia Long Westfall, and Christa L. McKirland (Downers Grove, IL: IVP Academic, 2021), 90-107.

[27]See Spencer, *Salty Wives*, 119-20.

to make two key observations. First, this group does not represent exclusive leadership—Paul becomes a bona fide apostle, even if he has to defend his inclusion on occasion. Second, Luke's Gospel recognizes the commissioning of seventy-two disciples who are sent out in gospel mission by Jesus (Lk 10:1, 17). It is very possible, even likely, that when Jesus sent them out in pairs, this refers to male-female couples.[28] The apostle Paul makes reference to the right and reality of the apostles having believing wives that accompany them in ministry (1 Cor 9:5-6). And we certainly have evidence of ministry couples in the early phases of the Christian movement: Priscilla and Aquila, and Andronicus and Junia, for example.

Before we conclude, I want to talk about Mary, the mother of Jesus, one more time. I am surprised that outside the Gospels we don't have many references in the New Testament to what we assume is one of the most important figures in early Christian history. Was she an honorary apostle? Was she treated like Christian royalty? Did she travel and do ministry? Was she ever imprisoned? Harmed? When did she die? How? I don't think we will discover the answers to these questions. But we do have a small clue about her life after the death, resurrection, and ascension of her son Jesus.

I didn't notice this clue until I paid more careful attention to paintings depicting the Pentecost event (Acts 1:12–2:13).[29] In the sixth-century Rabbula Gospels' visual depiction of Pentecost, Mary is at the center of the group of male disciples gathered in the upper room, six men on her right and six on her left.[30] There are thirteen tongues of fire, one for each disciple, and one too for Mary. And there is a descending dove above her head symbolizing the Spirit.[31] This tradition

---

[28]See Christoph Stenschke, "Married Women and the Spread of Early Christianity," *Neotestamentica* 43, no. 1 (2009): 145-94, at 150-51. Saint Ambrose makes a connection between the "pairs" (i.e., "twos") that Jesus sends out in mission and the male-female pairs of animals sent into the ark, representing complementarity; see *Exposition of the Gospel of Luke* 7.44.

[29]Christian art is not inspired in the same way the Bible is the inspired Word of God, but we can learn a lot from wise scholars, theologians, and artists throughout time and today. They can offer insight into reading the Bible well.

[30]The Rabbula Gospels is an "illuminated manuscript," a copy of a biblical text (in this case the Gospels) with ornate illustrations visually depicting biblical symbols and scenes.

[31]See Hugh Honour and John Fleming, *A World History of Art* (London: Laurence King, 2005), 318.

of "centralizing Mary" appears in Pentecost paintings by El Greco, Jean Restout II, and Peter Paul Rubens (among others). In Restout's depiction, the men in the scene are all stunned and even terrified by what is happening; in sharp contrast, Mary has a look of calm knowing. Why is Mary so prominently displayed in these scenes of Pentecost? According to Acts, there is good reason to believe she was actually *there*. When the disciples returned to Jerusalem, they went to an upper room where the disciples joined together with "*women* and *Mary* the mother of Jesus, and with his brothers" (Acts 1:14). These painters take for granted that Mary stayed there and was therefore present for the Pentecost event.

If the same person wrote both the Gospel of Luke *and* Acts (as most scholars now think), there may be a clever thematic link between Acts 1–2 and the beginning of the Gospel of Luke. In Luke 1, when the angel Gabriel appears to Mary, she is told that "the Holy Spirit will come on you, and the power of the Most High will overshadow you" (Lk 1:35). In Luke 3:22, when Jesus is baptized, the Holy Spirit descends in the form of a dove and rests on him. And in Acts 2 the empowering presence of the Spirit comes down from heaven and fills up the room (Acts 2:2-3). Mary can be seen to be a living link from the incarnation, through the life and ministry of Jesus, and into the ministry of the Spirit-empowered apostles. In these Pentecost paintings, then, she symbolizes the church, the guardian and agent of Christ's gospel, and the work of God from age to age, era to era, testified and confirmed by God's Spirit.[32] While we don't know what fate Mary faced, we do know she had some continuing presence in the life of the church after Jesus ascended into heaven. No doubt she was an important voice and bearer of tradition for some time as the apostles got their footing in their worldwide mission.

---

[32]See Heidi J. Hornik and Mikeal C. Parsons, *The Acts of the Apostles through the Centuries* (Chichester: Wiley-Blackwell, 2017), 44-46.

Figure 2. Image of Mary and the disciples at Pentecost from the Rabula Gospels

CONCLUSION

How well do we remember the women before, after, and around the Jesus who walked on earth? Women like Elizabeth and Mary paved the way for Jesus. Women like Anna proclaimed Jesus before he could speak. In his ministry, Jesus talked about women, he talked to women, he welcomed them into his ministry, he had deep conversations with women, he healed women, he received their anointing, and he invested in them the gospel witness of the resurrection. The Evangelists tell their amazing stories, if we have ears to hear.

Part Two

The Women Leaders of the Early Churches

5

The Early Churches

My earliest memories of visiting churches in grade school include the congregation rising in the pews as the ministerial team came into the room, hymns sung by the church choir, and a homily on Scripture preached by the pastor. Aside from the singing time, which I enjoyed, I was meant to be silent and well behaved. All eyes should be on the action up front.

I readily admit that it is difficult *not* to read my modern experiences back into the Bible when I read about the early churches. But many of the elements of what I experienced in my modern American church do not reflect the nature or operation of the first-century churches. The stage-audience dynamic was not reflective of the Christian assembly. Christian leaders were not yet "full-time" clergy, except perhaps for a limited group of apostles and similar leaders (see 1 Cor 9:7-12).[1] In this chapter my goal is to paint as realistic a picture as we can about what the early churches actually looked like in terms of function, structure, and leadership. That is not to say every single Christian community would have fit into some cookie-cutter mold; nevertheless, there appears to be enough apostolic instruction and homogeneity to paint with broad brushstrokes. Then we will be in the best position to see how women lived, served, and led in these spaces.

---

[1]In a text like Gal 6:6 we see signs of justification for church teachers being compensated by the recipients of the teaching.

ORIGINS OF THE EARLY CHURCHES

It is widely recognized that the only place in the Gospels that the word
"church" (*ekklēsia*) appears is in Matthew. For example, in the context of
Jesus' loaded question "Who do you say I am?"[2] Peter responds, "You
are the Messiah, the Son of the living God" (Mt 16:15-16). Jesus affirms
him, saying

> Blessed are you, Simon son of Jonah, for this was not revealed to you by
> flesh and blood, but by my Father in heaven. And I tell you that you are
> Peter, and on this rock I will build my church, and the gates of Hades will
> not overcome it. I will give you the keys of the kingdom of heaven;
> whatever you bind on earth will be bound in heaven, and whatever you
> loose on earth will be loosed in heaven. (Mt 16:17-19)

This is not a complete description of all that the church is meant to be
and become, but we do learn some key elements. The church is built on
the confession of the true identity of Jesus, Messiah and Son of God; the
church is destined to battle the work of Satan; the church carries out
Jesus' own ministry of bringing to bear the work of redemption and
restoration. This is essentially affirmed in the risen Jesus' "Great Commission" in Matthew 28:18-20: in Jesus's name, the disciples-turned-
apostles are sent to baptize, make disciples, and give formative instruction
to the nations supported by the Spirit-mediated presence of Jesus.

While Matthew's Great Commission gives direction to the future
church, we learn about the birth of the church in Luke's sequel, the Acts
of the Apostles.[3] The risen Jesus promised his apostles power by the
Holy Spirit to empower and embolden them as witnesses of Jesus and the

---

[2]Of course, just because the other Evangelists (Mark, Luke, John) don't use the word "church"
doesn't mean they have nothing to say about the origins and future of the church. Keep in mind,
by the time the four Gospels were written (or finalized), the church was several decades into its
existence, so the Gospels as a whole are not only telling the story of Jesus but also reflecting on
the identity, ethos, and mission of the church as the people of Jesus; see Markus N. Bockmuehl
and Michael B. Thompson, eds., *A Vision for the Church: Studies in Early Christian Ecclesiology*
(Edinburgh: T&T Clark, 1997), 1-94; also Michael P. Knowles, "The Least, the Lost, and the Last:
Christ's Church in the Gospels," in *The Church Then and Now*, ed. Stanley E. Porter and Cynthia
Long Westfall (Eugene, OR: Wipf & Stock), 12-40.

[3]See Arthur G. Patzia, *The Emergence of the Church: Context, Growth, Leadership and Worship*
(Downers Grove, IL: InterVarsity Press, 2001), 69-78.

gospel in all the world (Acts 1:7-8). On the day of Pentecost, they received the Spirit in power, in fulfillment of God's promises of new prophecy and a brand-new work of God to bring redemption to pass (Acts 2:1-21). Along with the believers already present, another three thousand accepted Peter's message about Jesus; they were then baptized and received the Spirit (Acts 2:40-41). This Spirit-filled group then "devoted themselves to the apostles' teaching and to fellowship, to the breaking of bread and to prayer" (Acts 2:42). God did many miraculous things in their midst through the apostles, and all the believers shared possessions and property as an expression of their solidarity and unity in Christ (Acts 2:43-44).

Despite the Lord's missional directives for the church, the apostles were not handed a full instruction manual listing all the specifications for church structure and operations. Neither did the apostles seem to make things up out of nothing. As might be expected, they appeared to have borrowed social systems from already-existing organizations and systems in their world.

STRUCTURES OF THE EARLY CHURCHES

The most obvious "affinity group" that may have inspired or influenced the structure of the early churches is the Jewish synagogue.[4] After all, Jesus attended and taught in Jewish synagogues (Mt 4:23; 9:35; Lk 4:16; Jn 18:20), as did his disciples (Mk 1:29; cf. Jn 16:2). In those early years of apostolic mission, believers were still worshiping in the Jewish synagogues (Acts 9:2), and the apostles preached Jesus as Messiah and Son of God in the synagogues (Acts 9:20; 13:5, 14; 14:1; 17:1, 17).[5] It would be quite natural, then, for the early Jesus communities to adopt and adapt features of the synagogue, such as formative instruction, singing and chanting, formal prayers, and communal

[4]See James Tunstead Burtchaell, *From Synagogues to Church: Public Services and Offices in the Earliest Christian Communities* (Cambridge: Cambridge University Press, 2004). For more general discussion of structural influences, see Wayne A. Meeks, *The First Urban Christians: The Social World of the Apostle Paul* (New Haven, CT: Yale University Press, 2003), 74-110.
[5]Luke recounts how the Christian evangelist Apollos went to the synagogue in Ephesus to proclaim Jesus; apparently Priscilla and Aquila were there too and heard Apollos preach (Acts 18:26).

meals.[6] It is possible, too, that the favored term *ekklēsia* for the church was inspired by the use of the word in the Septuagint (the Greek translation of the Old Testament) in reference to the "assembly" of the people of Israel.[7] And just as the synagogues were smaller units connected to a larger whole (i.e., the one Jerusalem temple, and the one people of God, Israel), so the churches were all a part of the one people of God through Jesus Christ.

How was the synagogue organized? We know from the Gospels and sources outside the New Testament that a synagogue commonly had a "synagogue ruler" (*archisynagōgos*), sometimes simply called a "ruler" (*archōn*).[8] It is reasonable to assume that these rulers presided over the synagogue meetings.[9] The "fathers" of the synagogue may have served as elders. A Jewish leadership council (*gerousia*) sometimes had a president (*gerousiarch*). We don't know how or how often leaders were chosen, but at least in some places it may have been by vote.[10] There were also people dubbed "fathers" and "mothers" of synagogues; scholars continue to debate whether these were functionaries (did they advise the council?) or titles of respect for honored figures in the community.

A second "affinity group" that may have inspired the structure and communal formation of the early churches is the Greco-Roman voluntary association. These were social clubs that were oriented toward business guilds (fostering networking and mutual support among professionals), cult associations (devoted to worship of a local deity), or burial societies (which collectively paid dues to ensure a proper burial for its members). All such clubs had cultic activities and communal meals. In many ways, these were the pagan counterparts to Jewish synagogues, smaller groups gathered in a local area for worship and

---

[6]See the important study by Lee I. Levine, *The Ancient Synagogue: The First Thousand Years* (New Haven, CT: Yale University Press, 2005).

[7]See the Septuagint texts of Deut 4:10; 31:30; Judg 20:2; Neh 8:17.

[8]See Andrew D. Clarke, *Serve the Community of the Church: Christians as Leaders and Ministers* (Grand Rapids, MI: Eerdmans, 2000), 127.

[9]Clarke, *Serve the Community*, 131.

[10]See Martin Goodman, *A History of Judaism* (Princeton, NJ: Princeton University Press, 2019), 290; Margaret Williams, *Jews in a Graeco-Roman Environment* (Tübingen: Mohr Siebeck, 2013), 130.

community. In fact, sometimes Gentiles referred to Jewish synagogues as if they were voluntary associations.[11] This might be helpful for understanding the early churches, because Gentiles, by and large, would not have had a working knowledge of Jewish synagogues. If an early Christian invited a Gentile neighbor to a house-church gathering, that neighbor might go home later that night with the impression that this was just like one of their own guild meetings.[12]

Voluntary associations did not have universal standards for organization and leadership. But we do get the impression that they tended to adopt terminology and structural systems from city-level political offices. So, for example, these clubs might have "magistrates" (*magister*) or "governors" (*curator*). They also frequently had priests, scribes, patrons, and elders. Occasionally, we do see the term *diakonos*, "servant/minister," which was also used by the early Christians (more on that below).[13]

A third "affinity group" would be the private household. Now, we have to think of the household less as a place simply where related people lived and more as a small, organized community, estate, or business. Especially in the age of the Roman Empire, the household played a crucial role both culturally and politically as a microcosm of the wider society and imperial order. As the household runs smoothly and efficiently, so goes the empire. Alternatively, if the household is chaotic and mismanaged, this threatens imperial peace. So householders (the household leader) had an important responsibility to properly care for all the members of the household—not just blood relatives but slaves and employees as well. And we could include in this clients of the patron household.

---

[11]See Josephus, *Jewish Antiquities* 14.216; Philo, *On Dreams* 2.127; Peter Richardson, "Early Synagogues as Collegia in the Diaspora and Palestine," in *Voluntary Associations in the Ancient World*, ed. S. G. Wilson and John Kloppenborg (London: Routledge, 1996), 90-109; Bradley Ritter, *Judeans in the Greek Cities of the Roman Empire* (Boston: Brill, 2015), 4-5. However, neither Jews nor early Christians referred to their own groups as associations (Greek *thiasoi*, Latin *collegia*), according to our available evidence; see John S. Kloppenborg, *Ptolemaic and Early Roman Egypt* (New York: de Gruyter, 2020), 4.

[12]For an important comparative study, see John S. Kloppenborg, *Christ's Associations: Connecting and Belonging in the Ancient City* (New Haven, CT: Yale University Press, 2019).

[13]For leadership terminology in associations, see John S. Kloppenborg, "Collegia and Thiasoi: Issues in Function, Taxonomy and Membership," in *Voluntary Associations in the Graeco-Roman World*, ed. Stephen G. Wilson and John S. Kloppenborg (London: Routledge, 1996), 2-28.

That the early churches were thoughtful about the house and household is obvious for two reasons. First, there was a clear preference for meeting in houses or domiciles. Second, from the evidence in Paul's letters, the household was a potent metaphor for Christian life in community, not just in references to God as Father (which occurs in non-Christian Jewish literature as well) and Jesus Christ as Son, but also in father language in relation to Paul (1 Cor 4:15; cf. Phil 2:22), the imagery of home building (Rom 14:19; 15:2, 20; 1 Cor 3:9; 8:10; 10:23; 14:3-5; 2 Cor 13:10), household management (1 Cor 4:1; 9:17), and the characterization of the church as the "family of faith" (Gal 6:10 NRSV).

The early churches were not identical to any of these organizations in the Greco-Roman world. There are some similarities, but there are also key differences. The apostles may have adopted some features and adapted others. When it comes to leadership structures and language, one thing is clear: these affinity groups maintained pyramid-like organizational structures with tiers of authority and importance, typically with a single leader at the top (i.e., some form of "ruler"). When we read the New Testament, especially Acts and the Epistles, we get the impression that the early Christians intentionally avoided the pyramid leadership system, certainly rejecting any kind of human "ruler" of churches. That is not to say the early churches were bereft of leadership or disorganized. Rather, they adapted some of the systems described above, and consciously rejected authoritarian systems that were prevalent in society.

The Ethos of Leadership in the Early Churches

When talking about leadership in the early churches, it is natural to launch into discussions of positions or "offices" (which we will get to below), but it is important first to discuss the communal ethos of the early Christians. As I have been trying to demonstrate, while Christians did not create their systems and structures ex nihilo, they did seem to consciously deviate from the cultural tendencies to establish a power and status hierarchy. Before getting into some of the more technical discussions of how the early churches were led, allow me to make a few observations about the spirit of leadership.

First, the tendency of the New Testament writers was to communicate directly to the *people*, not to a main leader of a church. Paul, Peter, James, and John placed the burden of Christian obedience on the whole community. Now, Paul *did* write individual letters to Timothy, Titus, and Philemon, but these letters provided special encouragement and specific instruction to these leaders—and in the case of Philemon, Paul still wrote expecting the whole community to take responsibility for Philemon's welcoming back of Onesimus (Philem 1-2). And the fact that Paul's letters to individuals were circulated and canonized means that they were not meant to be private correspondences for the upper echelon of leadership alone. What about Philippians' prescript note that mentions specific leadership categories: "To all God's holy people in Christ Jesus at Philippi, *together with the overseers and deacons*" (Phil 1:1)? Here it is true that Paul acknowledges the church leadership in some way, but this is not exclusionary or limiting. Paul wrote, first and foremost, to *all* God's holy people; perhaps the additional reference to leadership was a nod to the aid they sent to the imprisoned apostle, which was probably organized and dispatched by overseers and deacons.[14] We could also take the example of Paul's letter to the Galatians. Here we have a dire situation where the church was heading in a dangerous direction of relying on circumcision and "works of the law" as a necessity to be right with God; Paul's epistle is passionately corrective, but it's worth noting that Paul does not mention a single person in any of the churches in Galatians, neither a troublemaker nor a key leader. He doesn't even send greetings to particular people there in his concluding remarks. Now, that doesn't mean Paul *never* mentions leaders—he does so in 1 Corinthians, Romans, and Philemon, for example—but my point here is that he doesn't hold these leaders exclusively responsible for the well-being of the churches. His main addressees are the *people* of the churches, who have a responsibility to hear Paul out and take his instruction and teaching seriously, each and every one.

---

[14]See Michael F. Bird and Nijay K. Gupta, *Philippians*, New Cambridge Bible Commentary (Cambridge: Cambridge University Press, 2020), 33-39.

Second, Paul's tendency was to refer to leadership as giving care and oversight, not wielding power and authority. For example, in one of his earliest letters, he exhorts the Thessalonians to "acknowledge those who work hard among you, who care for you in the Lord and who admonish you. Hold them in the highest regard in love because of their work" (1 Thess 5:12-13). Paul does not refer to offices imbued with authority. At times he could reassert his own apostleship (Gal 1:1; 1 Cor 4:21), but most of the time he encouraged the people to respect and follow their leaders, because those leaders were caring, faithful, honorable, and trustworthy (1 Tim 4:12).[15]

LEADERSHIP ROLES OF THE EARLY CHURCHES

It is good and fair to ask, How were these early churches led in practice? Probably our first instinct is to point to the apostles as the most prominent and authoritative leaders in earliest Christianity (Acts 2:37, 42; 4:33, 35; 5:12; 6:6).[16] Wayne Meeks warns that we should see apostleship not as an "office" but more as a set of "functions that carried authority in the missionary activities of the Christians."[17] Also, we are accustomed to think in terms of a strict group of "Twelve" (disciples sent out as "apostles"), but these commissioned disciples of Jesus seem to have functioned as a kind of leadership of an apostolic school (composed of a much wider group of mission-oriented leaders). Note, for example, how Barnabas is called an "apostle" in Acts (14:14). And in 2 Corinthians we learn of opponents of Paul whom he calls "super-apostles" (2 Cor 11:5; 12:11; cf. 11:13). Sometimes the same Greek word (*apostolos*) is used for delegates or representatives from various churches who were sent out with a special mission (2 Cor 8:23; Phil 2:25).

The apostles (like Peter and Paul) seem to have played a strategic role in training and educating churches, and to some degree they exercised leadership over the churches in their mission or territory. But we also know that they entrusted the day-to-day leadership to local believers. It

---

[15]Andrew D. Clarke, *A Pauline Theology of Church Leadership* (London: T&T Clark, 2008), 85.
[16]See Meeks, *First Urban Christians*, 131.
[17]Meeks, *First Urban Christians*, 131.

is difficult for us today to grasp exactly how churches were led, because the evidence from the New Testament does not demonstrate uniform leadership titles, systems, or structures. Yes, leadership was important and reinforced, but often Paul generically referred to other leaders as "coworkers" or "fellow laborers," and he preferred to talk about leaders in terms of their activities rather than bequeathed titles. Wayne Meeks sums up well the situation:

> Acts and the Pauline letters make no mention of formal offices in the early Pauline congregations. This fact is striking when we compare these groups with the typical Greek or Roman private associations. The clubs' inscriptions show a positive exuberance in the awarding and holding of offices, which . . . commonly imitated those of the city government. We find nothing comparable when leading roles in the Pauline congregations are mentioned. The New Testament writers do not use the word *archē* [governor] in the sense of "office," nor its synonyms.[18]

Meeks' insight about function versus office is backed up by some of the leadership lists that appear in Paul's letters. In 1 Corinthians 12, for example, Paul talks about God giving the church apostles, prophets, teachers, workers of healing, tongue-speakers, interpreters of tongues, and so forth. This is helpful for painting a picture of how God has gifted the church, but note that this list is not comprehensive and there is no mention made of "overseers," "deacons," or "elders."[19] Ephesians 4:11 briefly mentions "pastors" (*poimēn*), but for as much as we use this terminology today in Protestant churches, it appears only in a few places in the New Testament in reference to church ministry and leadership (Acts 20:28; 1 Pet 5:2). From what we can gather, first-century churches did not have a "lead pastor" in the ways that are common today. The leadership of a church carried out "shepherding" functions in terms of guarding and caring for the people. Put another way, if you turned up to a first-century church gathering and asked to meet *the* pastor, the people would look around trying to figure out which one person you were inquiring after.

---

[18]Meeks, *First Urban Christians*, 134.
[19]See Gerald F. Hawthorne and Ralph P. Martin, *Philippians*, rev. ed. Word Biblical Commentary 43 (Grand Rapids, MI: Zondervan Academic, 2015), 8-9.

In talking about the leadership roles in the church, we must spend some time discussing three terms that are prominent in Acts and the New Testament Epistles: *diakonos* (servant, deacon, ministry provider), *episkopos* (overseer, manager), and *presbyteros* (senior leader, elder).

Diakonos *(servant, deacon, ministry provider).* When the New Testament writers talked about ministry in and by the church, they often used the term *diakonos* and its wider word group (*diakonia, diakoneō*). This terminology has to do with service. Any type of activity that helps or cares for someone else can fit this language. Slaves are "servants" in this sense, but so are soldiers and governors who "serve" the people (Rom 13:4). The main reason the church latched onto this language was Jesus' teachings about humility and a service-oriented heart of leadership: "The kings of the Gentiles lord it over them; and those in authority over them are called benefactors. But not so with you; rather the greatest among you must become like the youngest, and the leader like one who serves. For who is greater, the one who is at the table or the one who serves? Is it not the one at the table? But I am among you as one who serves" (Lk 22:25-27 NRSV). This kind of ethos set the tone for leadership in earliest Christianity. The Son of Man came not to be served but to serve through love, humility, and self-sacrifice (Mt 20:26, 28). This would predispose the church to care for the great and the least with equal passion and interest (Mt 25:44).

Servanthood was a basic concept, but this term was also sometimes used as a role title in various settings in the ancient world. Sometimes pagan religious officers were called *diakonoi* (servant, assistant).[20] Servants of these kinds played a mediatorial role, sent as secondary agents by a primary agent to support a beneficiary.[21] It was language used

---

[20]In a particular pagan cult in the Greco-Roman world (associated with Egyptian deities), we know of a college of "servants" (*diakonoi*) who were led by a cult priesthood. This cult had both male and female "servants" (*Inscriptiones Graecae* 9. 1, 486, and IV. 774). The Latin equivalent to *diakonos* is *minister*, and we see that term applied to women (*ministra*) who carried out priestly duties, conducted sacred rites, and even performed acts of healing in pagan religious cults; see John Granger Cook, "Pliny's Tortured *Ministrae*: Female Deacons in the Ancient Church?," in *Deacons and Diakonia in Early Christianity*, ed. Bart J. Koet, Edwina Murphy, and Esko Ryökäs (Tübingen: Mohr Siebeck, 2018), 133-48, at 147-48.

[21]See Anssi Voitila, "Deacons in the Texts Contemporary with the New Testament (Philo of Alexandria and Josephus)," in Koet, Murphy, and Ryökäs, *Deacons and Diakonia*, 273-83.

commonly of angels, prophetic attendants, and representatives of rulers, cult officers, and so on.[22] John N. Collins has published numerous studies on the word *diakonos* and came to the conclusion that its wider usage in the Greco-Roman world did not carry with it assumption of the accomplishment of (merely) menial tasks. He argues that the "servant" was primarily seen as a mediator or spokesperson for someone else.[23] But, as Andrew Clarke has demonstrated, the New Testament usage uniquely emphasizes the humility and "ministry" that involves suffering and hardship, and voluntary weakness rather than power and high status.[24] *Diakonoi* were not lowly "servants" in every case, but when used in the context of early Christian leadership, they were meant to imitate the service mentality and humility of Christ himself.

Was *diakonos* a leadership title in the early churches? This is hard to answer. Paul could refer to his apostleship as "service" (*diakonia*; Rom 11:13; 1 Cor 3:5; 2 Cor 3:6), but no one seems to have ever called Paul "deacon" or "minister" as a title. Jesus was a "servant" (*diakonos*) to Jews (Rom 15:8). Stephanas carried out "service" (*diakonia*) in Corinth, but again, he was not called a "minister" (1 Cor 16:15).

At the same time, on a couple of occasions we see what appears to be a more technical use: Phoebe is called a *diakonos* (Rom 16:1), and in the prescript to Philippians (as mentioned above), Paul addresses the leadership, which he calls "overseers and *diakonoi*" (Phil 1:1). What did these *diakonoi* do for the church? In all likelihood, they served under the leadership of the overseers and met the ministry needs of the church. The fact that the apostles did "ministry" (*diakonia*) should remind us that this was not menial work. And when Paul called Phoebe a *diakonos* from Cenchreae, he was commending her as a leader from the region of Corinth. For all intents and purposes, she was a key leader from a nearby city.

In 1 Timothy, Paul addresses the expectations for *diakonoi* (1 Tim 3:8-13), leaders of integrity and competence. They must meet a

---

[22]Voitila, "Deacons," 284.

[23]John N. Collins, *Diakonia: Re-interpreting the Ancient Sources* (Oxford: Oxford University Press, 1990); *Diakonia Studies: Critical Issues in Ministry* (Oxford: Oxford University Press, 2014).

[24]Clarke, *Serve the Community*, 238-42.

high standard to serve the church in this capacity (1 Tim 3:10). Paul turns to address women leaders (1 Tim 3:11); this seems to presume most *diakonoi* were men, but it shows that women were not excluded. Paul held women to the same high standards.[25]

We know that women could and did serve as *diakonoi* in churches. It is important that we let that sink in—*women were active in the ministry of the church.* Now, many women were at home caring for home and family. But the complete picture we see of Christian ministry in the first century according to the New Testament informs us that wherever men were "doing ministry," women were there doing it as well. That's what it means to be a part of the "diaconate," and women weren't treated as a secondary class of leaders.

One more consideration before we move on to talk about *episkopos*. How should *diakonos* be translated? I have used some variety in the discussion above. The problem is that there is no singular English translation that captures this word perfectly. The term "deacon" might give the wrong impression that this was some sort of formal office. Probably, the same is true if we were to translate *diakonos* as "minister." The generic meaning, "servant," can also be misleading, because writers like Paul *were* using *diakonos* sometimes in reference to a form of leadership. I want to propose a new translation that attempts to solve some of these problems: "ministry provider." "Provision" offers that sense of service that is central to *diakonos*. But in the medical world today, we call doctors and nurses "medical providers," and we naturally attribute to them respect and expertise as professionals, trustworthy people with training and experience. So "ministry provider" is meant to communicate that *diakonoi* desired to care for and serve the people, and they presumably had some experience, training, and gifting that established their authority and status to be recognized and respected.

Episkopos *(overseer, manager).* *Episkopos* is clearly one of the most formal leadership titles used in early churches, referring to one who

---

[25]It is interesting that when Paul calls Phoebe a *diakonos*, he uses the generic masculine form of the word, not the feminine form.

oversees, supervises, or manages.[26] In the wider culture, a temple manager might carry this title, or it might be used for civic officials.[27] The person who had this role was a guardian of some kind of institution, community, or trust.

In the book of Acts, Paul sends a message to the elders of the Ephesian churches and exhorts them to "keep watch over yourselves and over all the flock, of which the Holy Spirit has made you overseers [*episkopous*], to shepherd [*poimainein*] the church of God that he obtained with the blood of his own Son" (Acts 20:28 NRSV). Here the elders of the church are entrusted with oversight of the Christian flock. The connection between oversight/guardianship and shepherding is also made in 1 Peter, where Christ is presented as the self-sacrificing "shepherd and guardian" over their lives (1 Pet 2:25 NRSV). Paul does not use the language of "overseer" (*episkopos*) nearly as much as he does "ministry provider" (*diakonos*). Again, in his letter to the Philippians, Paul mentions the *episkopoi* alongside the *diakonoi* (Phil 1:1), but he doesn't make explicit exactly how these roles differ. From the evidence we have, it appears that *episkopoi* played more of an oversight or advisory function, and the *diakonoi* carried out the ministry initiatives and activity.

Did women serve as *episkopoi* in the early churches? Honestly, we don't know. No named person is called an *episkopos*, so we cannot name a female overseer, nor a male one for that matter. Now, one *could* make the case that only men served as *episkopoi* because of the instructions in 1 Timothy 3:1-7. In that passage, Paul instructs that overseers must be the "husband of one wife" (1 Tim 3:2 NET) and must manage household and children well (1 Tim 3:4). A couple of things should be said about this. First, household management was a shared duty that husband and wife carried out together in Greco-Roman homes, so by itself that doesn't restrict the role to men (see 1 Tim 5:14). Second, the emphasis on "one wife" is less about men leading (to the exclusion of women) and more about fidelity in marriage. But it is worth addressing the fact that this

---

[26]Raymond F. Collins, "Bishop," in *New Interpreter's Dictionary of the Bible* (Nashville: Abingdon, 2006), 1:472.
[27]See LXX Num 4:16; Is 60:17; 1 Macc 1:51.

passage does default to the assumption of a male overseer. There is a simple reason for this—men would have naturally comprised the majority of leaders. But it is one thing to acknowledge that men commonly held these positions and another thing altogether to take this as *excluding* women. Imagine this: a golf club with a sign by the course that says "Golfers must have their facial hair properly groomed." This statement presumes relevance for the vast majority of the golfers (who are men), but by itself it does not prohibit women from golfing. I take Paul's statements about overseers as *reflective* of the majority population of that group. If Paul wanted to forbid women from aspiring to those roles, he could have. But as it stands, I take it that only a small number of Christian women were in a position to carry out that role. So, how might have women stepped into the position of church overseer?

Now is a good place to revisit the context of the household for the life of the church. We have already addressed the fact that most churches met in private homes for worship and ministry.[28] There are many reasons for this (privacy, comfort, meals), but Roger Gehring has made the crucial observation that households would have already had a management structure that could give early Christian communities stability and leadership. It would be natural for a paterfamilias, a householder, to become the *episkopos* of the church community. Just as they gave oversight and leadership to their house (as a kind of small business or mini-corporation), so they would be set up to "manage" the church as a spiritual family. This makes sense in light of Paul's instruction that overseers of the church must be competent household managers (1 Tim 3:4).

Gehring argues that apostles like Paul had a missionary strategy of sharing the gospel with householders, knowing that they could serve as influential leaders of households.[29] So Paul baptized Stephanas and his household (1 Cor 1:14-16), and he had a strategic partnership with Philemon and his household as well. Gehring explains, "It was typical of the Pauline missional approach in any given city to target individuals from

---

[28]See Roger Gehring, *House Church and Mission: The Importance of Household Structures in Early Christianity* (Peabody, MA: Hendrickson, 2004).

[29]Gehring, *House Church and Mission*, 186.

higher social levels. In this way Paul was able to win homeowners, along with their entire households, for the gospel and to set up a base of operations in their house for local and regional mission."[30]

If this is true, then the house-church hosts (householders) would have been the most natural choices for church overseers; they would have the skills and the communal respect to carry out this form of leadership. "This means that the leadership structures of the house church did not have to be created out of nothing."[31] Householders often had some education and practical administrative skills that would have helped them serve the church.[32]

Householders were typically men, the classic paterfamilias. But there were exceptions, and we have already discussed not only that women heads of households did exist and were legally permissible but also that there is evidence in the New Testament along these lines (in some areas of the Roman world, women may have comprised up to 25 percent of the total householders). Lydia, for example, was apparently a female householder who accepted the apostles' gospel message, and *her* household was baptized (Acts 16:14-15). That her home became a hub for the Philippian church is evident in the fact that Paul and Silas accepted her hospitality at the beginning of their Philippian mission (Acts 16:15) and then went to her home again at the end when they were released from jail, looking for the assembly of believers. There they met with fellow believers for fellowship and encouragement before they departed (Acts 16:40). We don't know what came of Lydia's ministry—she is not mentioned at all in Paul's letter to the Philippians—but on the basis of the account in Acts, there was no one more qualified to serve as an overseer in Philippi than Lydia. As Gehring writes, "After [Paul's] departure and in his absence, he most likely left the householders in charge of these house churches."[33]

Presbyteros *(senior leader, elder).* Finally, in terms of leadership terms and titles, we come to the New Testament language of elders. This

---

[30]Gehring, *House Church and Mission*, 187, see 187-90.

[31]Gehring, *House Church and Mission*, 194.

[32]Gehring, *House Church and Mission*, 194.

[33]Gehring, *House Church and Mission*, 207.

is one of the most important categories of early Christian leadership, but unfortunately one that is not outlined in detail in the New Testament and also woefully misunderstood today as we seek to apply this category to our churches almost two thousand years hence. Unlike "overseer" (*episkopos*) and "ministry provider" (*diakonos*), "elder" is not primarily a functionary, so it's not really a job description. Traditionally, the elders of a clan or village were the wise, older figures who shared their wisdom and took responsibility for the well-being of the community.[34] In general, members of a community reached elder status as they grew in age and maturity; after all, the basic meaning of the term is "old person." When we look at how this language was used in the Bible, it quickly becomes clear that it didn't function as an official title, as in no one was called "Elder Markus" or "Elder Stephen" the way we say "Pastor So-and-So" today. Markus and Stephen (our imaginary ancient leaders) may very well have been elders in their community, but the term "elder" didn't quite have the formality and functionary quality of "overseer" or "ministry provider." That doesn't detract from the importance of elders in the early churches; quite the opposite, churches depended on their elders for wise guidance, direction, and leadership.

Because it is difficult to ascertain exactly how elders related to other leaders in the Christian churches, we don't fully know how they were selected and what precise roles they served. Therefore, I am going to make a proposal of my own. "Elder," I believe, was the general term for those church leaders who were responsible for taking care of the community and giving it guidance, wisdom, and direction. Overseers and ministry providers surely would have been qualified as elders (think of respected householders like Stephanas, Lydia, Aquila, and Priscilla). "Elder" would have been the most general term to describe Christians who led the churches. But when a leader had a more specific function and title, they went by that title. For example, when Paul writes to "overseers" in Philippians, these would have been qualified to be elders as well,

---

[34]See R. Alastair Campbell, *The Elders: Seniority within Earliest Christianity* (Edinburgh: T&T Clark, 1994); a helpful short version of his work is found in Campbell, "The Elders: Seniority in Earliest Christianity," *Tyndale Bulletin* 44, no. 1 (1993): 183-87.

but because they were selected specifically as "overseers," that was their titular designation. One might imagine that in theory overseers were "overseer-elders" and ministry providers were "ministry provider-elders."[35] But the broader elder category was taken for granted for those with more specific leadership functions.[36]

Now that the theory has been described, I can offer the evidence. Let's start with the Old Testament. Commonly, elders were mentioned as a broad category of Israelite leader (Ex 17:5; 19:7), sometimes with reference to a group of seventy elders (Ex 24:1; Num 11:16). Elders were to be respected by the people for their life experience and wisdom (Lev 19:32). The elders were a leadership collective that supported a main figure like Moses or Joshua (Josh 7:6). You regularly read about "Moses and the elders" or "Joshua and the elders,"[37] but it should be obvious that this does not presume Moses himself was *not* an elder, given that the Hebrew and Greek terms simply mean "old person" and carry the sense of "respected and older community leader."[38] Moses was certainly qualified to be an elder, but as prophet and spokesperson for the Lord, he had a standing above the generic group of elders.

A text like Joshua 24:1 is instructive in terms of terminology. At one point, Joshua gathered all the tribes and called for "the elders, leaders, judges and officials of Israel." It doesn't make sense that the tribal officials would not count as elders. What seems more likely is that the elders were the broadest leadership group, and specific types of leaders would go by their more specific titles. An interesting phenomenon throughout the Bible is how "the elders" are addressed collectively and speak collectively

---

[35]Edwin Hatch made the argument, over a century ago, that "elders" and "bishops/overseers" referred to the same persons, but that separate terminology was used to indicate different roles. As part of an elder council they were *presbyteroi* (elders), but in their work managing churches they were *episkopoi* (managers); see Hatch, *The Organization of the Early Christian Churches* (London: Rivingtons, 1881); see the discussion in John S. Kloppenborg, "Edwin Hatch, Churches, and *Collegia*," in *Origins and Method*, ed. B. H. McLean (Sheffield: Sheffield Academic Press, 1993), 212-38.

[36]For example, I serve on an academic board with about twenty members. Some board members have specific titles like "president" or "treasurer." But many of the board members are simply called "members at large." The president is technically a board member, but in general they are referred to by the organization as "president," not "president and board member."

[37]Ex 12:21; 19:7; 24:9; Lev 9:1; Num 11:30; Deut 27:1; 31:9; Josh 23:2; 24:31.

[38]In fact, Josh 13:1 mentions that at one point Joshua himself was old—that is, an elder.

(e.g., 1 Kings 21:7), reinforcing the argument that they were seen as a generic whole.

When we get into the period of Israel's history after they returned from Babylonian exile, this eldership pattern continues. Jewish sage Ben Sira advised good people to "stand in the company of the elders" who were wise (Sir 6:34 NRSV). He supported elders as a venerable group deserving respect (Sir 7:14; 32:3). In the text called Judith, two Jewish elders happen to be named, Chabris and Charmis (Jdt 10:6). In 2 Maccabees, Razis is named as one of Jerusalem's elders (2 Macc 14:37). A certain Eleazar was a priest, and he gave direction to the Jewish elders, but 2 Maccabees references Eleazar as an "elder" too (though this might just mean he was an old man—it's hard to tell what meaning is meant here). In 4 Maccabees, a certain faithful Jewish woman is hailed as "soldier of God in the cause of religion, elder and woman" (4 Macc 16:14 NRSV). What exactly the author meant by "elder" here we don't know, but we can say that given the high commendation for her, she would have earned great respect in the community—the exact kind of situation we would expect for someone to be recognized as an elder.

When we look at the Gospels and how Jewish leadership is described, we see much the same pattern of usage of "elder" language. Jewish elders are mentioned as those who look after the people (Lk 7:3), and they are referenced alongside figures like chief priests, scribes, and temple police (Mt 16:21).[39] In the book of Acts we start to see how elders are part of Christian communities. Luke mentions them alongside the apostles (Acts 15:4, 6, 22). In James we learn that when there are needs in the churches, the elders are responsible for responding (Jas 5:14). Peter describes himself as both elder and apostle (1 Pet 1:1; 5:1). In terms of responsibilities, we know that elders led, and some were responsible for preaching and teaching (1 Tim 5:17).

How someone became a church elder is partially clear. One can imagine that in ancient Israel elders were simply recognized by their age and community stature without an official ceremony of selection

---

[39]See also Mt 21:23; 26:3, 57; 27:1, 3; Mk 11:27; Lk 22:52.

or consecration. In early Judaism there probably developed a more formal process of appointing elders (since there were, for example, massive communities in Jerusalem and an official temple institution). In early Christianity we find reference to the appointment of elders (Acts 14:23). Along these lines, Paul called on Titus (in Crete) to appoint elders in each town who were leaders of integrity and good reputation (Titus 1:5).

What can we say about whether women served as church elders? I am often surprised to find churches today who argue that the New Testament prohibits women from eldership. This is not stated in any way in the New Testament. Now, just as with overseers, it is certainly true that most elders would have been men, because of their general status in society. But we might ask, What would disqualify Phoebe from being an elder? Priscilla? If the general indicator of worthiness was age, wisdom, and good-standing in the community, it is hard for me to imagine a male-only elder community. Take, for example, Andronicus and Junia (Rom 16:7). They were older in the faith than Paul (presumably older in age as well) and called "apostles" (see chapter nine in this book), which would put Junia in a natural position to be an elder. An apostle (*apostolos*) is a specific category of leadership, and given the pattern we saw above, it would make sense that she would also qualify as an elder.

We need to disabuse ourselves of a widespread misconception that women could not function as elders. There is a common but unsubstantiated conception that women had a lesser ranking in churches—that is, men were the elders and overseers, and women did less important ministry jobs in behind-the-scenes supportive roles. But our New Testament evidence simply does not bear that out. Take, for example, the situation of Ananias and Sapphira in Acts. As important members of the early church, this couple sold their own property and gave it to the apostles (Acts 5:1-2). Peter confronted the husband, Ananias, and after Peter called him out on lying and keeping some of the profit from the sale for himself, Ananias fell dead (5:3-6). Now, if men were really "in charge" at that time, the story would end there, but it doesn't. The wife, Sapphira, appears before Peter. He could have dismissed her as some kind of "weaker vessel" accomplice, or he could have given her a stern warning and a light punishment. Instead, he tests her with a question, which she answers with a lie, and he pronounces the *exact same* punishment on her, death (Acts 5:7-10). For as macabre as this story is, it well illustrates an "egalitarian" impulse in accountability in the church and shows the utmost seriousness with which the apostles took both Christian men *and* Christian women.

Imagine if, in the apostolic era (or now for that matter), God gave his people another Deborah. Would she be allowed to serve as an elder? If we chose to disqualify her from the role of elder (or "manager"), on the basis of what would we do this? That she should serve her husband Lappidoth? That she does not meet male standards of wisdom and decision making? That she belongs in the house? Who would dare to hinder someone that God has called into service and leadership? One can only wonder what would have happened in the era of the judges if a group of men exercised some form of community discipline on Deborah, deposing her and setting up a man to take her place. This would have robbed Israel of one of its best leaders and judges, and one of its wisest and most faithful prophets.

CONCLUSION

In this chapter we have taken a close look at the nature and forms of leadership in the early churches. There was no manual that outlined exactly what offices and positions there ought to be as a universal rule. But the language of "overseers" (*episkopoi*), "ministry providers" (*diakonoi*), and "elders" (*presbyteroi*) regularly appears. The vast majority of early Christians who were associated with these terms would have been men. But there was no explicit prohibition of women performing these roles and tasks (on 1 Tim 2:11-15, see the "What About . . . ?" section of this book). In fact, women like Phoebe (Rom 16:1) are named as *diakonoi*, and probably Euodia and/or Syntyche (Phil 4:2-3) served in this capacity. We have made the case that women were also probably elders and "managers," given the presence of householders (for example) in some of the churches.

In the next chapter we are finally ready to learn about some of the many named women leaders of the early churches recorded in the New Testament. Across the Roman world we find women working shoulder to shoulder with men in the hard work of ministry.

6

Women Co-laborers in
Ministry Leadership

If you are like me, at some point you were sent the message that there
are particular places that women should be, like the home and the children's Sunday school room at church, and places that women are not
welcome, like the business world or the church's elder boardroom. In the
ancient world as well, the "default" setting for women was the home, so
that might lead us to believe that this was reinforced by the early church.
The problem is, that's not really how things look in the New Testament
(remember Lk 8:1-3 and the women who traveled with Jesus). There were
a lot of exceptions in the Roman world inside and outside Christian
communities. Practically speaking, women were found *everywhere* men
were, and they were welcomed and invited into leadership spaces in
churches as well. In this chapter I will offer a more sweeping panoramic
image of this, from Rome to Philippi and beyond, but right now I want
to spark your historical imagination with a fascinating but often overlooked case study of a woman in a "man's" space who was remembered
in the apostolic testimony of Christian faith. I would like you to meet the
Athenian named Damaris (Acts 17:34).

According to Luke's chronicle of Paul's gospel-mission travels, Paul
made an unexpected visit to Athens after fleeing from Berea
(Acts 17:13-15). While he was there, he wasted no time sharing about Jesus,
so he went to the synagogue as was his custom. Luke tells us Paul also
preached in the marketplace to anyone who would listen (Acts 17:16-17).

Sure enough, some philosophers wanted to hear more about his foreign cult, so they invited him to the Areopagus, a kind of communal body that protected the city's well-being. Paul was not on trial; this was more of a preliminary hearing to learn more about his teachings.[1] Paul obliged and taught about his supreme Creator God who does not live in temples made with hands and has power to judge the whole world. He talked about Jesus, the unique person chosen to demonstrate God's life-giving power through resurrection. Luke notes that there were different responses to Paul's lecture: some people were dismissive and scoffing, but some were interested and sought him out to learn more. We know only two names from that Areopagus throng: Dionysius and Damaris. Dionysius, a man, is called an Areopagite, which means he was an official member of that Mars Hill assembly. But what about Damaris?[2] The only thing that Luke tells us is that this is a woman. What was she doing there? She could have been the wife of Dionysius, though Luke does not make this clear, and we can presume this was not traditionally a gathering where wives were invited or even welcome.[3] Whatever the case, the fact that she responded positively to Paul's lecture means that she could follow along pretty well, which points to some philosophical knowledge or education. Craig Keener notes that some Greek schools allowed for women philosophers, though they would have been a rarity.[4]

What I find intriguing is that Damaris is one of two named people from the Athenian converts mentioned by Luke. Luke makes reference to "others" who also began to follow Jesus and "the Way." But why does he mention Damaris by name? Perhaps it was the simple fact of a woman, probably an elite, among the throng of Areopagite men. But I

---

[1]See Bruce W. Winter, "On Introducing Gods to Athens: An Alternative Reading of Acts 17:18-20," *Tyndale Bulletin* 47 (1996): 71-90.

[2]For in-depth studies, see David E. Evans, "The First Christians of Athens," *Australian Biblical Review* 68 (2020): 40-53; Clare K. Rothschild, *Paul in Athens: The Popular Religious Context of Acts 17* (Tübingen: Mohr Siebeck, 2014), 92-93.

[3]Jipp, however, opts for this reading of Damaris as wife of Dionysius; see Joshua Jipp, "Paul's Areopagus Speech of Acts 17:16-34 as *Both* Critique *and* Propaganda," *Journal of Biblical Literature* 131, no. 3 (2012): 567-88, at 588.

[4]Craig S. Keener, *Acts: An Exegetical Commentary*, vol. 3, *15:1–23:35* (Grand Rapids, MI: Baker Academic, 2014), 2679n3814.

think there is a bit more to it than that. Richard Bauckham argues that these specific remembrances of named people in the apostolic testimony of the early church tend to reflect the fact that these women (and men) became *noteworthy* in the church[5]—as in they often became leaders and influential figures, and perhaps this was the case for the Athenian Damaris.

WOMEN LEADERS IN ROME

We have already had a chance to talk a little bit about the female Christian leaders in Rome in the introduction to this book. Here we can pick up Romans 16 again and look at it in closer detail. It is hard to overstate how eye-opening Romans 16:3-16 is for imagining what Christian communities of the first century *actually* looked like.[6] First, we will talk about where this section fits into Paul's important letter to the Romans, and then we will consider the many women Paul commends and greets.

Romans 16 has been widely neglected in the study of what many consider Paul's most important letter. It has often been brushed aside as a set of "hellos" that don't carry much theological importance. But in the past few decades it has been acknowledged that Paul carefully constructed his letters, beginning to end, and his closing remarks were anything but mundane.[7] Yes, Paul sometimes did want to send a brief word of warm wishes to a colleague here and there (2 Tim 4:19), but the extent to which Paul greets *so* many people at the end of Romans raises questions about

---

[5]Bauckham writes, "It is a good general rule, capable of explaining most occurrences of personal names in the Gospels, that when characters in the Gospels (other than public figures such as Pilate or Caiaphas) are named, it is because they were Christians well known in the early church and of whom the first readers of the Gospels in question would already have heard." *Gospel Women: Studies of the Named Women in the Gospels* (Grand Rapids, MI: Eerdmans, 2002), 211-12; see too Alice Mathews, *Gender Roles and the People of God: Rethinking What We Were Taught About Men and Women in the Church* (Grand Rapids, MI: Zondervan, 2017), 99. Evans adds that Damaris may fit the profile of a powerful (presumably widowed) woman who becomes a leader and benefactor once she enters and helps to form Christian communities, in parallel to Joanna (in Luke) and Lydia (in Acts); see "First Christians of Athens," 51.
[6]See Elisabeth Schüssler Fiorenza, "Missionaries, Apostles, Coworkers: Romans 16 and the Reconstruction of Women's Early Christian History," *Word & World* 6, no. 4 (1986): 420-33.
[7]See Mark Reasoner, "Chapter 16 in Paul's Letter to the Romans: Dispensable Tagalong or Valuable Envelope?," *Priscilla Papers* 20, no. 4 (2006): 11-16; Steve Croft, "Text Messages: The Ministry of Women and Romans 16," *Anvil* 21, no. 2 (2004): 87-94.

his rhetorical purposes. Clearly, this was more than just salutations to friends. Paul seems to have been illustrating some of his theological teachings in the first fifteen chapters of the letter, with appeal to real flesh-and-blood people in the closing chapter.[8]

Now, Romans 16 begins with Phoebe. We will discuss Phoebe in depth in chapter seven of this book. Suffice it to say here that Phoebe brought Paul's letter from Cenchreae (near Corinth) to Rome, and in Romans 16:1-2 Paul calls on the churches there to give her a warm welcome. She would be staying for a while and deserved generous hospitality.

Then Paul offers extensive greetings to friends and leaders in Rome, before likewise conveying Corinthian greetings to them (Rom 16:16). Paul lists almost thirty individuals, most of them by name, some by relationship (e.g., Nereus's sister). Some of these people were householders, and Paul was greeting their whole household community, which could include many individuals. All that to say, there are a lot of people represented in Paul's greetings. It's natural to wonder, Why would Paul go out of his way to name so many people, especially when he more commonly ended his letters with blanket closings like "Greet all God's people in Christ Jesus" (Phil 4:21; see also 1 Thess 5:26; Titus 3:15)?[9]

Scholars have hypothesized that three concerns motivated Paul to write this long section to the Roman Christians. First, it helped to communicate that Paul was already in fellowship with believers from a community in Rome he had never formally visited. Thus, when the letter arrived, they could vouch for the apostle.[10] Second, scholars have noted how Paul was not just sending his *own* greeting but also calling on the various Roman Christian communities to warmly greet *one another*,

---

[8]This kind of argument is made well by Scot McKnight, *Reading Romans Backwards* (Waco: Baylor University Press, 2019).

[9]Robert Jewett makes an insightful observation: "The combination of greetings to so large a number of persons and the use of the second person plural form in Romans is unparalleled, contributing to the establishment of a precedent that popularizes greetings in subsequent Christian letters." *Romans: A Commentary*, Hermeneia (Minneapolis: Fortress, 2006), 950-51.

[10]See Luke Timothy Johnson, *Reading Romans: A Literary and Theological Commentary* (Macon, GA: Smyth & Helwys, 2001), 232; Joseph Fitzmyer, *Romans*, Anchor Yale Bible (New Haven, CT: Yale University Press, 2008), 734; Schüssler Fiorenza, "Missionaries, Apostles, Coworkers," 428.

modeling the mutuality and respect that he promoted especially in Romans 14–15. As Frank Matera aptly states, "By using this imperative, Paul invites the Romans, who belong to different house and tenement churches, to greet one another in his name. Thus these greetings . . . encourage the Romans to overcome whatever tensions have arisen among them, especially between the strong and the weak."[11] Paul purposely chose to commend representatives from different types of house churches in order to promote respect and grace among those who might disagree and even look down on each other. Third, many scholars believe that Paul had a social agenda built into these greetings; he purposely chose to mention believers of various ethnicities and status levels to shape the Romans' attitudes toward Christian ministry and leadership. For example, according to Peter Lampe, many of the names in Paul's list reflect slave origins.[12] That is, some of the named Christians were slaves or freedpersons ("ex-slaves" who lived with a social stigma). The same could be said about Paul's mixture of greetings to Jewish and Gentile friends and coworkers. We know, for example, that Andronicus and Junia were Jewish, but people like Urbanus and Epaenetus were probably not. And, as we have already observed, Paul includes an extraordinary number of women in his greetings: Prisca, Junia, Persis, Mary, Tryphaena, Tryphosa, Julia, Nereus's sister, and Rufus's mother (and Phoebe). This is not an accident. Paul was explicitly commending women's ministry and leadership, perhaps even encouraging more Roman women to do so.[13] If we are not willing to go that far, we must at least acknowledge that Paul did not treat women differently than men when it came to

---

[11]Frank J. Matera, *Romans*, Paideia (Grand Rapids, MI: Baker Academic, 2010), 339; similarly Jewett, *Romans*, 952.

[12]See Peter Lampe, *Christians at Rome in the First Two Centuries: From Paul to Valentinus* (London: Continuum, 2006), 228; also Andrew D. Clarke, "Jew and Greek, Slave and Free, Male and Female: Paul's Theology of Ethnic, Social and Gender Inclusiveness in Romans 16," in *Rome in the Bible and the Early Church*, ed. Peter Oakes (Grand Rapids, MI: Baker Academic, 2004), 103-25, at 113. Many such believers may have been freed by the time Paul wrote to the Romans, but they would live with the social status of being former slaves. Paul was making it a point to treat such men and women with equal respect as their fellow believers who had not been slaves.

[13]Reimund Bieringer, "Women and Leadership in Romans 16: The Leading Roles of Phoebe, Prisca and Junia in Early Christianity," *East Asian Pastoral Review* 44, no. 4 (2007): 316-36, at 319; Croft, "Text Messages," 91.

church ministry and leadership. The casual intermixture of male and female names (some couples, some singles or widows), and the general terminology used to describe their ministry work, point to a nongendered conception of leadership.[14]

Next, I want to briefly address the order of the names in the list. Sometimes it is argued that this kind of list would move from more important figures to less important ones (culturally). But Paul does not do this.[15] Another option is that the list follows an order of "ecclesial" standing.[16] Formally, this is hard to prove, but what gives this theory credibility is the fact that the earlier greetings are longer and more detailed, and toward the end Paul lumps more people together with shorter comments. Whatever the exact logic of ordering, it is important to note that Paul does not begin the list with men (presuming them to be more important) and end the list with women. Women are named alongside men (often as ministry pairs or couples) and sometimes named and commended without mention of a man (like Tryphaena and Tryphosa).

Hard workers (Mary, Tryphaena, Tryphosa). It has often been noted by Romans scholars that, while Paul lists more men than women in this passage, he uses commendatory speech for more women than for men.[17] One such label is that women leaders, like Mary, Tryphaena, and Tryphosa, *work hard* in ministry. The Greek word Paul uses here, *kopiaō*, "implies honorable toil for the sake of the gospel or the Christian community."[18] This verb carries the basic meaning of toil or difficult work, as in manual labor. But Paul had a tendency to use this as a semi-technical term for the hard work *of ministry*. In fact, he often used this for his apostolic work. As Paul writes to the Colossians: "It is [Christ]

---

[14]Clarke, "Jew and Greek," 121. Wendy Cotter notes that while a highly visible and public ministry of many Christian women might have invited the suspicion of unbelieving neighbors, the privacy of the house church made it easier for Paul to invite and support women in leadership; see "Women's Authority Roles in the Church: Countercultural or Conventional?," *Novum Testamentum* 36 (1994): 350-72, at 371.

[15]Note that seemingly powerful people like Aristobulus and Herodion are not at the beginning.

[16]Bieringer, "Women and Leadership," 3; Schüssler Fiorenza, "Missionaries, Apostles, Coworkers," 428.

[17]See Clarke, "Jew and Greek," 119.

[18]Clarke, "Jew and Greek," 119.

whom we proclaim, warning everyone and teaching everyone in all wisdom, so that we may present everyone mature in Christ. For this I toil [*kopiaō*] and struggle with all the energy that he powerfully inspires within me" (Col 1:28-29 NRSV). Similarly, Paul reminds Timothy, "To this end [the goal of godliness] we toil [*kopiaō*] and struggle, because we have our hope set on the living God, who is the Savior of all people, especially of those who believe" (1 Tim 4:10 NRSV). Elsewhere, too, he refers to his apostolic ministry as labor (Gal 4:11; Phil 2:16; 1 Cor 4:12) energized by the grace of God (1 Cor 16:16). Paul also readily applied this term (toil) to local church leaders who persevere in the tiresome work of ministry (1 Thess 5:12).

Why did Paul refer to ministry as toil? If we look at Paul's speech to the Ephesian elders recorded by Luke (Acts 20:17-35), these reasons are evident:

- Ministry leaders serve the Lord with humility, because ministry life involves many trials (Acts 20:19).

- Ministry leaders do not choose their day's work but are "captive to the Spirit" (Acts 20:22 NRSV), led by God to new tasks and needs.

- Ministry leaders, as the face of public Christianity, are prime targets for persecution and punishment (Acts 20:19, 23).

- Ministry leaders work hard to protect the sheep from wolves in their midst (Acts 20:29).

- Ministry work happens through many tears shed over intramural Christian hatred (Acts 20:31).

- Ministry leaders renounce indulging in the comforts of wealth and, thus, work hard with their hands to support themselves (Acts 20:34).

- Ministry leaders work hard to support the weak in their community (Acts 20:35a).

- Ministry leaders work hard to embody Jesus' teaching: "It is more blessed to give than to receive" (Acts 20:35b).

Turning back to Paul's letters, we see this mentality borne out in some of Paul's commendations. For example, he honors the work of Stephanas in Corinth (1 Cor 16:15-18); Stephanas and his household devote themselves to ministry, and Paul urges the Corinthians to respect these leaders and "everyone who works and toils with them" (1 Cor 16:16 NRSV). What can we say, then, about Rome's "Mary"? The prominence of her being named in the early part of the list, combined with the amplifier *very* ("Mary . . . worked *very* hard"), suggests that she was a prominent church leader. Saint John Chrysostom comments on this verse that women carried out many different ministries in the apostolic age—not just Word ministry (teaching, like Priscilla) but also doing ministry in dangerous places, risking poverty, and enduring harsh travel conditions: "For the women of those days were more spirited than lions, sharing with the apostles their labors for the Gospel's sake."[19] Robert Jewett considers the possibility that Mary was one of the founding members of the Roman church.[20]

What exactly Mary did for the church is not possible to ascertain from Paul's comments. But given what we have already seen in Acts 20, it is not a stretch of the imagination to think that Mary was a leading elder in Rome. Much the same can be said about the two women Tryphaena and Tryphosa, probably sisters, and also Persis (Rom 16:12). What exactly they did for the Roman churches was known to Paul. Again, the idea of laboring for ministry implies commitment, courage, resilience, and a deep passion for the gospel. The way Paul talks about this kind of toil often implies danger (again Acts 20:28-30). These were women conducting high-level ministry with elements of risk, such that *the* apostle to the Gentiles not only knew their work but also saw fit to praise them in the presence of their peers. We could only hope to imitate the Tryphaenas and Tryphosas and Marys of today.

A mother to Paul. In the midst of the greetings in Romans, Paul mentions his appreciation for a certain Rufus as well as his mother, "a mother

---

[19]Homily 31 on Romans, English translation from Gerald Bray, ed., *Romans*, Ancient Christian Commentary on Scripture (Downers Grove, IL: IVP Academic, 1998), 372.

[20]Jewett, *Romans*, 961. Fitzmyer, who is extremely cautious about not saying more than what the text offers, still notes that Paul's description of Mary in these terms "reveals how much he thought of the work of such Christian women on behalf of the gospel" (*Romans*, 737).

to me, too" (Rom 16:13). The name Rufus is mentioned in Mark: "A certain man from Cyrene, Simon, the father of Alexander and Rufus, was passing by on his way in from the country, and they forced him to carry the cross" (Mk 15:21). Is it possible that this is the same Rufus (son of Simon of Cyrene) whom Paul greets? Many scholars think so.[21] The naming of Alexander and Rufus by Mark seems to imply that these (grown) children became well known in the church. And relocating to a major city like Rome is not that far-fetched. In any case, our interest here is on Paul's praise for Rufus's mother. What does it mean that she was a mother to Paul? The cultural image of a mother in Paul's world was that of the one who nourishes and nurtures children.[22] So, in some way, Rufus's mother took care of Paul. Given the type of commendations in Romans 16:3-16, I take this mothering to be more substantial and mission-central rather than something like cooking a meal for him. F. F. Bruce hypothesizes that Rufus's mother may have provided lodging and hospitality (in Antioch?). If she was a woman of means, she might have been a civic matron for Paul in some way, perhaps using her wealth or social connections to get him out of trouble with local authorities.[23]

It's also possible that she was a "mother" in the sense of an exemplary leader, a model of Christian faith, as parents were formative figures from a moral standpoint. For example, the Jewish Maccabean literature hails the faith, piety, and resilience of a Jewish mother facing persecution (and the martyrdom of her sons) in this way: "mother of the nation, vindicator of the law and champion of [Jewish] religion" (4 Macc 15:29 NRSV).

WOMEN LEADERS IN PHILIPPI

One might wonder whether the high number of women leaders in the Roman Christian communities was an anomaly, a one-off phenomenon.

---

[21]James D. G. Dunn, *Romans 9–16*, Word Biblical Commentary 38B (Dallas: Word Books, 1988), 2:897; Ben Witherington III and Darlene Hyatt, *Paul's Letter to the Romans: A Socio-Rhetorical Commentary* (Grand Rapids, MI: Eerdmans, 2004), 394; Jewett, *Romans*, 968; cf. Richard Bauckham, *Jesus and the Eyewitnesses: The Gospels as Eyewitness Testimony* (Grand Rapids, MI: Eerdmans, 2017), 52.

[22]See Beverly Roberts Gaventa, *Our Mother Saint Paul* (Louisville, KY: Westminster John Knox, 2007); Jaime Clark-Soles, *Women in the Bible*, Interpretation (Louisville, KY: Westminster John Knox, 2020), 63.

[23]F. F. Bruce, *Paul, Apostle of the Heart Set Free* (Grand Rapids, MI: Eerdmans, 2000), 148-49.

But as we turn to other cities and the New Testament evidence, women continue to appear in leadership roles and settings. Let us consider the situation in Philippi. From evidence we can gather from Acts (chap. 16) and Paul's letter to the Philippians, these are the Philippian Christians (men and women) that are named: Lydia, Epaphroditus, Euodia, Syntyche, and Clement. (We also know of the unnamed Philippian jailer who accepted the apostle's gospel message.) What I find fascinating in this list is that we know more names of the *women* in the Philippian church than the men.[24] Eduard Verhoef estimates that in the middle of the first century the Philippian church totaled about thirty people.[25] Given that small size, it seems beyond doubt that the named women Euodia, Syntyche, and Lydia were important leaders.

Lydia (Acts 16:11-40). According to Luke, Paul and Silas went from Neapolis to Philippi and stayed for several days (Acts 16:11-12). They went in search of a Jewish place of prayer and found a group of women. Luke's story fixates on Paul's engagement with a particular woman, Lydia. She was a "worshiper of God," as in a pagan who honored the God of Israel (Acts 16:14). She was also a businessperson, working in purple cloth. The Lord opened her heart to the gospel, and she was baptized along with her whole household. We get the immediate sense that *she* was the householder, the manager of her family and the workers (and slaves) in her household. She invited the apostles to receive hospitality at her house, and they accepted (Acts 16:15).[26] From there, the story of the apostles' adventures in Philippi carry on without mention of Lydia, but she appears again at the end of this unit. After Paul and Silas were

---

[24]Also, note that Clement is mentioned in Philippians, but it is not made clear that he is someone in their church. If Clement was a highly regarded Christian leader present in Philippi, why wasn't *he* called up to help Euodia and Syntyche with their dispute, rather than the unnamed "companion" (Phil 4:3)? He may have been a Philippian, but it is also possible he was included as an example of faith that was known to the readers.

[25]Eduard Verhoef, *Philippi: How Christianity Began in Europe; The Epistle to the Philippians and the Excavations at Philippi* (London: T&T Clark, 2013), 22; see also Lilian Portefaix, *Sisters Rejoice: Paul's Letter to the Philippians and Luke-Acts as Received by First-Century Philippian Women* (Stockholm: Almqvist & Wiksell, 1988), 178-80.

[26]See Verhoef, *Philippi*, 19-20; Lynn H. Cohick, *Women in the World of the Earliest Christians: Illuminating Ancient Ways of Life* (Grand Rapids, MI: Baker Academic, 2009), 215; Teresa J. Calpino, *Women, Work and Leadership in Acts* (Tübingen: Mohr Siebeck, 2014), 223.

released from the authorities, "they went to Lydia's house, where they met with the brothers and sisters and encouraged them. Then they left" (Acts 16:40). This is an important clue that Lydia had an immediate impact as a leader within the fledgling Christian community. She had passion, position, and means to host and lead the Christian community. As a household manager, she was a natural person to exercise oversight and care for believers, many of whom were already in her care as part of her household. Gordon Fee says it well. When Christians met in the home of a female householder,

> where they would gather in the atrium, the semipublic area where business was regularly carried on, the householder would naturally serve as the leader of the house church. That is, by the very sociology of things, it would never have occurred to them that a person from outside the household would come in and lead what was understood as simply an extension of the household. To put it plainly, the church is not likely to gather in a person's house unless the householder also functioned as its natural leader. Thus Lydia would have held the same role in the church in her house as she did as master of the household.[27]

If this is true, then the term *episkopos* (overseer, manager) would have been a natural title for the role she played in her own household and therefore also in the church community.[28]

It is a bit of a surprise to me that Lydia is not mentioned anywhere in Paul's letter to the Philippians, given her stature. But she may have been in mind as Paul wrote the prescript: "To all the saints in Christ Jesus who are in Philippi, with the overseers [*episkopoi*] and ministry providers [*diakonoi*]" (Phil 1:1, my translation). We don't know. But it is more certain that two women explicitly mentioned in Paul's letter held one or the other of these ministry titles: Euodia and Syntyche.

Euodia and Syntyche (Philippians 4:2-3). It is not until well into the second chapter of the letter that Paul mentions a specific person in the

---

[27]Gordon D. Fee, *Listening to the Spirit of the Text* (Grand Rapids, MI: Eerdmans, 2000), 73.
[28]See Cohick, *Women*, 189; F. Scott Spencer, *Salty Wives, Spirited Mothers, and Savvy Widows: Capable Women of Purpose and Persistence in Luke's Gospel* (Grand Rapids, MI: Eerdmans, 2012), 212.

Philippian church, Epaphroditus, "my brother, co-worker and fellow soldier, who is also your messenger, whom you sent to take care of my needs" (Phil 2:25). Epaphroditus was sent by the Philippian leaders with a gift for Paul while he was in prison, probably food, clothing, provisions, and perhaps money. (Ancient prisons provided "room" but not "board," if you will.)[29] Toward the end of the letter, Paul calls certain individuals in Philippi, two women, to be exact: "I plead with Euodia and I plead with Syntyche to be of the same mind in the Lord. Yes, and I ask you, my true companion, help these women since they have contended at my side in the cause of the gospel, along with Clement and the rest of my co-workers, whose names are in the book of life" (Phil 4:2-3). As is often the case, Paul tells us very little about these first-century believers. Paul already knew them (presumably, given his high commendation), and they knew each other, so we are left with lots of questions we can't answer.[30] We know they had Greek names, though that does not presume they were ethnically Greek.[31] Their names have been found to be relatively common among slave names in the Greco-Roman world. It is possible, then, they were freedwomen.[32]

While we don't know a lot of personal information about these women (marriage status, social status, occupation), the *fact* that Paul calls them out on a disagreement publicly implies that they had important stature in the community.[33] Earlier in the letter, Paul affirms the importance of unity in mission and ministry, "standing firm in one spirit, striving side by side with one mind for the faith of the gospel" (Phil 1:27 NRSV). And a bit later he exhorts the Philippians to be "like-minded, having the same

---

[29]See Brian Rapske, *The Book of Acts and Paul in Roman Custody* (Grand Rapids, MI: Eerdmans, 1994), 10-20.

[30]A helpful summary of scholarship on Euodia and Syntyche has been written in R. F. Hull, "Constructing Euodia and Syntyche," *Priscilla Papers* 30, no. 2 (2016): 3-7. Mike Bird and I have a commentary discussion of these women in *Philippians*, New Cambridge Bible Commentary (Cambridge: Cambridge University Press, 2020), 170-73.

[31]Euodia means "good journey"; Syntyche means "good luck."

[32]See Peter Oakes, *From People to Letter* (Cambridge: Cambridge University Press, 2000), 64; C. S. de Vos, *Church and Community Conflicts: The Relationships of the Thessalonian, Corinthian, and Philippian Churches with Their Wider Civic Communities* (Atlanta: Scholars Press, 1999), 252-56.

[33]We will take for granted that Paul was talking about a disagreement that these two women had *with each other*, but it is possibly that they were disagreeing *with Paul*. I am not convinced of this alternative reading, but it is a scenario worth considering.

love, being one in spirit and of one mind" (Phil 2:2). It is hard not to
think that Euodia and Syntyche were key agents for implementing—or
impeding—this apostolic vision. It is also quite possible that one or both
of these women fit the category of *episkopos* (overseer) from 1:1.[34] The
upshot to all of this would be that their disagreement was not a personal
spat but something to do with the life and direction of the church. One
interesting theory is that they were both church leaders who disagreed
about whether to continue to fund and support Paul's ministry. Let's say
Euodia said, "We don't have much to give as a community; let's not spend
it on Paul's ministry." And perhaps, then, Syntyche responded, "We've
been with Paul through thick and thin; let's not give up on him!" In the
end, we know that the church *did* send Paul a gift of supplies as a sign of
their ongoing support. The fact that Paul's acknowledgment of this gift
(Phil 4:10-20) comes (almost) right after his exhortation to Euodia and
Syntyche (Phil 4:2-3) lends some credibility to this theory.

It is interesting to me that the debated matter among these women
leaders was so dire that (1) Paul had to address it publicly in the letter
(versus in a separate private letter) and (2) their reconciliation required
a mediator. But Paul did not shame these women; he didn't use any cultural stereotypes to demean them or "put them in their place." He valued
them and showed respect. He commends them as leaders who have
"struggled" for the sake of the gospel (similar to the language of "toil" he
used in Romans 16). He labels them "co-workers" as well. Other leaders
whom Paul calls "co-workers" (*synergoi*) include Prisca and Aquila
(Rom 16:3), Urbanus (Rom 16:9), Timothy (Rom 16:21), Apollos
(1 Cor 3:5, 9), Titus (2 Cor 8:23), Epaphroditus (Phil 2:25), Justus (Col 4:11),

---

[34]See the argument made in Carolyn Osiek, *Philippians, Philemon* (Nashville: Abingdon, 2000),
230-33; see also R. F. Hull, "Constructing Euodia and Syntyche: Philippians 4:2-3 and the Informed Imaginations," in *One in Christ Jesus: Essays on Early Christianity and "All That Jazz" in
Honor of S. Scott Bartchy*, ed. David Lertis Matson and K. C. Richardson (Eugene, OR: Pickwick,
2014), 209-21, at 218. Margaret MacDonald observes that since these women are named without
mention of husbands, this opens the real possibility that they were independent householders,
like Lydia; see "Reading Real Women Through the Undisputed Letters of Paul," in *Women and
Christian Origins*, ed. Ross Shepard Kraemer and Mary Rose D'Angelo (Oxford: Oxford University Press, 1999), 199-220, at 205; L. Michael White, "Paul and *Pater Familias*," in *Paul in the
Greco-Roman World: A Handbook*, ed. J. Paul Sampley (London: Continuum, 2016), 2:171-203,
at 184.

Philemon (Philem 1), Mark, Aristarchus, Demas, and Luke (Philem 24). Quite an impressive group, and to that list we add Euodia and Syntyche, leaders in Philippi. They were not apostles (like Paul), of course, but Paul talked about them as "shoulder-to-shoulder" ministry leaders, carrying out the hard work of the gospel mission.

When he says that their names are in the book of life (Phil 4:3), that is not a mere reference to being a Christian—the Philippian readers would have already known that. It is more like Paul is saying they have a special mark, an asterisk, next to their names on account of their sacrifices and hard work in ministry. For such things, the community should honor and emulate these leaders. This seems to fit a pattern: Paul was in the habit of honoring faithful Christian women leaders, though not to the exclusion of men; but it should be noticeable how *often* Paul commends women *as* coworkers, partners in leading churches and spreading the gospel near and far.

Women Leaders in the Lycus Valley

From Philippi we travel almost a thousand kilometers southeast to Asia Minor, specifically the Lycus Valley, home to three key cities in the ancient world: Colossae, Hierapolis, and Laodicea.[35] As in the case with Rome and Philippi, we can glean scattered details about these first-century communities and their leadership in the Lycus Valley. From Colossians we learn about Onesimus (Col 4:9), Epaphras (Col 4:12), and Archippus (Col 4:17). We have some additional information about Colossian believers contained in Paul's letter to Philemon. Now, scholars are not in full agreement about exactly where Philemon lived, but Colossae is a sensible assumption. In that case, we can add to the Colossian leadership Philemon, (another?) Archippus, and a woman called Apphia (Philem 2). Finally, though we don't have a letter from Paul to the Laodiceans, we know from Colossians that he did send at least one letter

---

[35]In Paul's letter to the Colossian believers, Laodicea features in Col 2:1; 4:13-15; see also Rev 1:11; 3:14. For a detailed study of this region, see Ulrich Huttner, *Early Christianity in the Lycus Valley* (Leiden: Brill, 2013); James R. Harrison and L. L. Welborn, eds., *The First Urban Churches: Colossae, Hierapolis, and Laodicea*, vol. 5 (Atlanta: SBL Press, 2019).

there (Col 4:16). We also hear about a woman named Nympha who hosted a church in her house (Col 4:15). Again, it is hard to know exactly where she lived, certainly somewhere in the Lycus Valley, most likely Laodicea, which is mentioned in that verse. So, with this snapshot of some of the people and places as background, we will zoom in on the two named women in these texts, Apphia and Nympha.

Apphia (Philemon 2). Most Christians probably know the name Philemon, owner of the slave Onesimus, who left his household, spent time with Paul, and now was returning home to reconcile with his master. When we read Paul's letter to Philemon, we might think of this as a *personal* letter, written to one individual, and in a way it is. But the prescript reveals a wider audience.

> Paul, a prisoner of Christ Jesus, and Timothy our brother,
>   To Philemon our dear friend and fellow worker—also to Apphia our sister and Archippus our fellow soldier—and to the church that meets in your home. (Philem 1-2)

In one sense this twenty-five-verse epistle was written *for* Philemon, to ensure a warm and Christianly reception for the slave Onesimus returning home. But in another way it was like most of Paul's other letters, written to a church community, just as Paul mentions the whole house church. He makes clear that *they* are witnesses to Paul's apostolic exhortations to the one (Philemon) who presumably had a major leadership responsibility for the church community. Two other people are mentioned as addressees: Apphia and Archippus. The former, whom we will return to in a moment, is often thought of as Philemon's wife. As for Archippus, it is anyone's guess as to his formal relationship with Philemon and Apphia. Perhaps he was their son, or maybe a biological brother, or another leader in the church. The title "fellow soldier," clearly a metaphor, signals Paul's admiration for this brother's intrepid commitment to the gospel.[36]

Now, back to Apphia. It makes good sense to assume Philemon, Apphia, and Archippus were, in effect, co-leaders of their church

---

[36]The same language (fellow soldier) is also attributed to the Philippian leader Epaphroditus, who risked his health and safety to aid Paul (Phil 2:25).

community, which met in Philemon's house. If Apphia was Philemon's wife, one can imagine a scenario similar to that of the ministry couple Prisca and Aquila (1 Cor 16:19). This is the only place Apphia is mentioned in the whole New Testament (and Philemon for that matter), so we don't really know anything else about her. Her name is Phrygian, as attested by inscriptions and documentary evidence from the Lycus Valley. One thing worthy of note is how unusual it is for Paul to mention a woman's name at the *beginning* of a letter (i.e., as an addressee).[37] This affords her some level of importance as a part of this believing community. Furthermore, if Apphia was Philemon's wife, as materfamilias (sharer in household leadership) she would have a key role to play in welcoming Onesimus home—the household matron often executed the practicalities of household slave management.[38] She would need to be persuaded by Paul's letter as well.

What about Paul's title "sister" for Apphia? When used with a named individual, "brother" or "sister" appears to be his way of talking about a ministry colleague. So, for example, Timothy is often referred to as "brother Timothy" (2 Cor 1:1; Col 1:1; 1 Thess 3:2; Philem 1). So too Titus (2 Cor 2:13) and Epaphroditus (Phil 2:25). Phoebe, a *diakonos*, is called "sister Phoebe." This was Paul's way of acknowledging a ministry co-worker and faithful leader.[39] It was a title of honor and respect. This makes sense since each addressee in the letter to Philemon is given an honorific title: friend and coworker Philemon, sister Apphia, fellow soldier Archippus. Whatever the exact relationship between these three people, we can confidently say that if there was a Christian leadership meeting in Colossae, these three people would be there.

Nympha (Colossians 4:15). Nympha just might be "the most important early Christian leader you've never heard of." That is because

---

[37]See Batanayi I. Manyika and Cornelia van Deventer, "The Curious Case of Apphia, Our Sister," *Conspectus* 29 (2020): 134-50.

[38]See Richard P. Saller, "Women, Slaves, and the Economy of the Roman Household," in *Early Christian Families in Context: An Interdisciplinary Dialogue*, ed. David L. Balch and Carolyn Osiek (Grand Rapids, MI: Eerdmans, 2003), 185-206.

[39]See Manyika and van Deventer, "Curious Case," 145; also Nicholas R. Quient, "Was Apphia an Early Christian Leader?," *Priscilla Papers* 31, no. 2 (2017): 10-13.

she is (1) the only known and named Christian from first-century Laodicea and (2) a female Christian householder that was, perhaps,
that community's main leader. Here is what Paul writes about her to
the Colossians:

> Give my greetings to the brothers and sisters at Laodicea, and to Nympha
> and the church in her house.
>
> After this letter [Colossians] has been read to you, see that it is also
> read in the church[40] of the Laodiceans and that you in turn read the
> letter from Laodicea. (Col 4:15-16)[41]

From this tidbit of information at the end of Paul's letter to the Colossians, we gather that Paul also sent a letter to Nympha's church and that
these two communities (Colossians and Laodiceans) were meant to read
their own letters and then exchange them with each other. This is something to ponder for a moment. If Paul had sent a letter to Laodicea,
Nympha would have been a key recipient and may have been responsible
for circulating the letter (if there were multiple house churches), and
perhaps she even read it out loud to her community.

The fact that Paul mentions Nympha without association with a man
is an indicator of a few possible situations. Perhaps she was a Christian
but her husband was not.[42] Or she was a widow who functioned as the
manager of her household (similar to Lydia).[43] And it could be that she
was unmarried, though that is uncommon and unlikely. Paul's comment
about *her* house reinforces the possibility that she was householder and

---

[40]Obviously this word "church" (*ekklēsia*) here does not refer to a church building but to a Christian community, presumably assembled in Nympha's house.

[41]There is a question about whether this figure is female or male. Some ancient manuscripts have
the name of a male (Nymphas). But the earliest and most reliable manuscripts have the female
name (Nympha). Our best guess as to how the male version of the name got into manuscripts
of Colossians is well expressed by R. McL. Wilson: "Scribes might not have believed that a
woman could hold so prominent a position" (*Colossians and Philemon*, International Critical
Commentary [London: T&T Clark, 2014], 304). For a key discussion of the evidence favoring
the female name, see Amanda C. Miller, "Paul's Social Network in Colossians," *Review and Ex-
positor* 116, no. 4 (2019): 436-45, at 442.

[42]See Wilson, *Colossians and Philemon*, 304; Florence M. Gillman, "Nympha," in *Anchor Bible
Dictionary* (New York: Doubleday, 1992), 4:1162.

[43]See Margaret Y. MacDonald, *Colossians and Ephesians*, Sacra Pagina (Collegeville, MN: Liturgical Press, 2000), 183; Wayne A. Meeks, *The First Urban Christians: The Social World of the Apostle
Paul* (New Haven, CT: Yale University Press, 2003), 143.

host. This would have naturally thrust her into a position of central leadership in the Laodicean church. As Margaret MacDonald explains, "Perhaps the most important service that a first-century believer could provide for a church group was to offer a house for meetings. Thus Nympha no doubt played a key leadership role in the churches of the Lycus Valley."[44] *If* Nympha was a (widow) householder in Laodicea and hosted a church in her house, and if she hosted the majority of believers there—a well-to-do person could fit a few dozen people in their atrium—then she naturally functioned as the *episkopos* of that community. Yes, that's speculative, but we know that household hosts (like Priscilla and Aquila, Stephanas, and Philemon) *were* key church leaders giving oversight to their congregations.

Again, it should reshape how we think about first-century Christianity when we consider that the only named person we know from the Laodicean community is a woman, Nympha. This offers yet another reminder that ministry leadership in the apostolic period was *not* a man's job. People, both women and men, of skill and gifting, with resources and experience at their disposal, were called on to care for the people of God in Jesus Christ—people like Apphia and Nympha.

THINKING ABOUT CO-LABORERS FOR TODAY

One of the things that becomes clear as we look closely at the many women involved in ministry leadership in the first century is that they were recognized by Paul because of their commitment, competency, and perseverance in the *work* of the gospel. Some leaders were probably wealthy; others were not—that didn't factor into Paul's praise. Some were high status; others were freedpersons, perhaps even slaves. Paul did not distinguish one from the other in terms of commendation. Some were Jews, others Greeks, Romans, and Phrygians. Paul lumped them all together as "coworkers" in ministry. And, of course, some were men and some were women. Paul did *not* see fit to honor men separately from

---

[44]MacDonald, *Colossians*, 188; cf. Margaret Y. MacDonald, "Can Nympha Rule This House? The Rhetoric of Domesticity in Colossians," in *Rhetoric and Reality in Early Christianities*, ed. Willi Braun (Waterloo, ON: Wilfrid Laurier University Press, 2005), 99-120, at 104.

women. Names are all jumbled together as a *corpus mixtum*. To him, they were brothers and sisters working side by side with him, and each had equal importance according to God's gifting of members to support the one body. In Paul's time, it would have been natural, expected even, for him to list the most important people first, especially those with the highest social status. If Paul were playing that game, lower-class women would be included last (or not at all). But because of the gospel of Jesus Christ, we don't see *those* kinds of lists in the New Testament. What we see is a diverse network of leaders throughout the Roman Empire serving as missionaries, local house-church leaders, and interchurch liaisons.

What Paul saw in this group was not the virtues of a particular trait, like sex or skin color, but grit and ambition, the will to labor and suffer for the sake of the gospel. For those in ministry today, we have much to learn from these early leaders. They were willing to endure social rejection for their faith, and in the face of that they still rolled up their sleeves to serve the church with love and loyalty.

7

Phoebe, Paul's Trusted Proxy

In the Roman world there was no postal service for private correspondence. If you wanted to mail a letter to a friend or relative, you needed to send someone you knew (like a personal slave or a relative) or hire someone. Of course, in many cases you didn't want the private information in the letter compromised, so you were careful to select a trustworthy courier. On the other end of the communication, the recipient might worry about a forged document and a potential stranger showing up at their doorstep. So a personal recommendation letter or letter section from the sender was appropriate. This is an example of a typical commendation of a personal letter carrier:

> Theon to his esteemed Tyrannus, many greetings.
>
> Heraclides, the bearer of this letter is my brother. I therefore entreat you with all my power to treat him as your protege. I have also written to your brother Hermias asking him to communicate with you about him. You will confer upon me a very great favour if Heraclides gains your notice. Before all else you have my good wishes for unbroken health and prosperity. Good-bye.[1]

Paul's letters, we know, sometimes contained information about the letter carrier. In the case of Philippians, we gather that Epaphroditus was sent by the Philippians to deliver a gift to support Paul in prison (Phil 4:18). Paul sent Epaphroditus back to them with his letter in hand,

---

[1]P.Oxy. 292, cited in Peter M. Head, "Named Letter-Carriers Among the Oxyrhynchus Papyri," *Journal for the Study of the New Testament* 31, no. 3 (2009): 279-99, at 285.

commending Epaphroditus for his faithful ministry to Paul (Phil 2:25-30). A certain Tychicus was sent by Paul to the Colossians with his letter. Paul commends him to them as "a dear brother, a faithful minister and fellow servant in the Lord" (Col 4:7). He was commissioned not only to deliver the letter but also to update them on Paul's situation in prison, and eventually bring back good news from them to Paul (Col 4:8).

Romans 16:1-2 offers another commendation: "I commend to you our sister Phoebe, a deacon [*diakonos*] of the church in Cenchreae. I ask you to receive her in the Lord in a way worthy of his people and to give her any help she may need from you, for she has been the benefactor of many people, including me." It is clear from this statement that Phoebe was Paul's letter carrier to the Roman churches (more on that below). His words fit the general pattern of courier commendation, but also we know that he chose trusted ministry colleagues to bear his letters and prepared them to minister to the churches as well. Because Phoebe is here recognized for her ministry position in her own hometown (as a *diakonos*), no doubt she also had a ministry role to play in Rome too. Despite the fact that most Christians throughout history and today haven't spent much time thinking about this Cenchreaean Christian woman, we can easily recognize that she played a crucial role in Paul's apostolic ministry.[2] He entrusted her with this massively important, sixteen-chapter letter. He trusted her and relied on her in ways similar to other traveling ministry colleagues like Timothy and Titus.

WHO WAS PHOEBE?

The name Phoebe is Phrygian and means "bright, radiant as the moon."[3] Because we have record of some slaves and freedwomen bearing this name, it is possible that she, too, was a freed slave who went on to obtain

---

[2]See Amy B. Peeler and Jennifer Powell McNutt, "Paul's Most Beloved Letter Was Entrusted to a Woman," *Christianity Today*, October 20, 2020, https://www.christianitytoday.com/ct/2020/november/phoebe-paul-women-new-testament-first-interpreter.html. Also check out the fascinating work of historical fiction that imagines the life and ministry of Phoebe by Paula Gooder, *Phoebe: A Story* (Downers Grove, IL: IVP Academic, 2018).
[3]Robin Gallaher Branch, "Female Leadership as Demonstrated by Phoebe: An Interpretation of Paul's Words Introducing Phoebe to the Saints in Rome," *In Luce Verbi* 53, no. 2 (2019): 1-10, at 2.

an impressive level of status and perhaps also wealth.[4] Paul mentions her hometown as Cenchreae, the eastern seaport of Corinth (Acts 18:18), some thousand kilometers southeast of Rome. That she could travel freely, apparently without a husband, supports the notion that she was a woman of means. In fact, some scholars surmise that the scribe of Paul's letter, Tertius (Rom 16:22), was Phoebe's slave—an unprovable notion, but a thought worth pondering.[5] In her own town she was a ministry leader, and we know she had some personal connection to Paul, since he mentions her as a benefactor. We will look at each of these details about Phoebe more carefully.

"Ministry provider" Phoebe. Paul commends Phoebe as a respected Macedonian church leader, a *diakonos* (Rom 16:1). We have already talked about this terminology in chapter five; suffice it to say here that some translations have missed the mark by calling Phoebe a "servant" (NASB) or "deaconess" (RSV) here. As for "servant," it is true that that is the basic definition of this word, but it seems to be used in a more technical sense here in Romans 16. While *diakonos* was generally used as a simple term for someone who serves, in a commendation text like this, *diakonos* represented a title of respect and honor. That *diakonos* did become some kind of leadership title is evident in Philippians 1:1 (see also 1 Tim 3:8-13). It would seem that the *diakonoi* ("ministry providers," as I have called them) were under the leadership of managers, *episkopoi*, but note that the Corinthian leader Stephanas (1 Cor 16:15), whom one might expect to fit the description of "overseer," is said to have a diaconate (*diakonia*) ministry.[6]

The translation "deaconess" is also problematic. The Greek word *diakonos* is technically a masculine word (grammatically) and is a generic term for "ministry provider." Paul never employed the grammatically

[4]Joseph Fitzmyer, *Romans*, Anchor Yale Bible (New Haven, CT: Yale University Press, 2008), 729; Robert Jewett, *Romans: A Commentary*, Hermeneia (Minneapolis: Fortress, 2006), 943.
[5]See Richard N. Longenecker, *Introducing Romans: Critical Issues in Paul's Most Famous Letter* (Grand Rapids, MI: Eerdmans, 2011), 12.
[6]Craig Keener notes that even though Paul differentiates between managers and ministry providers in 1 Timothy, both groups had to adhere to sound teaching and both were required to demonstrate administrative skills (1 Tim 3:12; cf. 3:4-5); see *Paul, Women & Wives: Marriage and Women's Ministry in the Letters of Paul* (Peabody, MA: Hendrickson, 1992), 239.

feminine form *diakonissa*, though it did develop into more common use later on in Christian history.[7] Just as today we refer to women in film and theater as "actors" (and the term *actress* as a genderized label is falling out of favor), so too *diakonos* as a (grammatically masculine) term was not restricted to just men. The bottom line is this: for Paul, there was just one term that covered both men and women, *diakonos*, so it is misleading to call her a "deaconess."

We cannot say specifically what it meant that Phoebe was a Cenchreaen *diakonos*, except that Paul found it worthy of mention.[8] My preference is to use the title "ministry provider" rather than "deacon," because "deacon" has developed into a very specific role in some church traditions.[9] Perhaps the most straightforward way to explain this title is in reference to "an agent with a sacred commission."[10] The church father Origen used Paul's commendation of Phoebe to affirm that "women were appointed to the ministry of the church" and that they served as "ministers" in that context.[11] Theodoret observed that Phoebe is evidence of Paul's preaching of the gospel not only in big cities like Corinth but in smaller villages like Cenchreae, such that a church there could produce a woman leader like Phoebe, "who was highly regarded and famous."[12]

Before moving on from our discussion of *diakonos*, it is helpful to look at how Paul used this language elsewhere in the same letter, Romans.

---

[7]Fitzmyer, *Romans*, 730.

[8]Barbara Reid imagines that a *diakonos* like Phoebe would have carried out a ministry of the Word in preaching and teaching, presiding over the Lord's table, and caring for God's people in more general ways socially and financially; see *Wisdom's Feast: An Invitation to Feminist Interpretation to the Scriptures* (Grand Rapids, MI: Eerdmans, 2016), 83; see also Efrain Agosto, *Servant Leadership: Jesus and Paul* (St. Louis: Chalice, 2012), 148; Carolyn Osiek, "The Politics of Patronage and the Politics of Kinship: The Meeting of the Ways," *Biblical Theology Bulletin* 39, no. 3 (2009): 143-52, esp. 149.

[9]See Reid, *Wisdom's Feast*, 80; Susan Mathew, *Women in the Greetings of Romans 16.1-16: A Study of Mutuality and Women's Ministry in the Letter to the Romans* (London: T&T Clark, 2013), 74; Philip Barton Payne, *Man and Woman: One in Christ* (Grand Rapids: Zondervan, 2015), 61.

[10]For this quote and an extended discussion, see Marg Mowczko, "What Did Phoebe's Position and Ministry as *Diakonos* of the Church at Cenchrea Involve?," in *Deacons and Diakonia in Early Christianity*, ed. Bart J. Koet, Edwina Murphy, and Esko Ryökäs (Tübingen: Mohr Siebeck, 2018), 91-102, at 97.

[11]J. Patout Burns Jr., *Romans: Interpreted by Early Christian Commentators* (Grand Rapids, MI: Eerdmans, 2012), 381-82.

[12]Burns, *Romans*, 382.

This provides the best framing and shaping for how we are meant to understand the venerable "service" of Phoebe.

> I [Paul] am talking to you Gentiles. Inasmuch as I am the apostle to the Gentiles, I take pride in my ministry [*diakonia*] in the hope that I may somehow arouse my own people to envy and save some of them. (Rom 11:13-14)

> Now . . . I am on my way to Jerusalem in the service [*diakoneō*] of the Lord's people there. For Macedonia and Achaia were pleased to make a contribution for the poor among the Lord's people in Jerusalem. (Rom 15:25-26)

> I appeal to you, brothers and sisters, by our Lord Jesus Christ and by the love of the Spirit, to join me in earnest prayer to God on my behalf, that I may be rescued from the unbelievers in Judea, and that my ministry [*diakonia*] to Jerusalem may be acceptable to the saints. (Rom 15:30-31 NRSV)

In Rom 11:13-14, Paul refers to his own apostleship as "ministry" (*diakonia*), the verbal noun form of the same term he uses for Phoebe as "minister" (*diakonos*). He also mentions a specific project, the collection and gift for the poor saints in Jerusalem, as a "ministering" (*diakoneō*) activity (Rom 15:25-26), an important part of his apostolic service (Rom 15:30-31).

> We have different gifts according to the grace given to each of us. If your gift is prophesying, then prophesy in accordance with your faith; if it is ministry [*diakonia*], then minister [*diakonia*]; if teaching, then teach. (Rom 12:6-7, my translation)

This is one of Paul's most generalized references to ministry as a gift and grace given by God for the building up of the community, a member's individual contribution to the whole body.

> For [governing] rulers hold no terror for those who do right, but for those who do wrong. Do you want to be free from fear of the one in authority? Then do what is right and you will be commended. For the one in authority is God's servant [*diakonos*] for your good. But if you do wrong, be afraid, for rulers do not bear the sword for no reason. They are God's

servants [*diakonos*], agents of wrath to bring punishment on the wrongdoer. (Rom 13:3-4)

Here Paul refers to city authorities (like magistrates, judges, perhaps military officers) as "servants" of God who carry out civic good by God's grace. These leaders possess *authority*, and Christians must seek to participate respectfully in civic life (including paying taxes). In what way are magistrates "servants of God"? Paul was not talking about *Christian* magistrates; hardly any Christians would have been in such powerful positions in the middle of the first century. In some way, Paul saw non-Christian rulers and judges as "common grace" leaders who serve the wider orderliness of creation. They contribute to harmony-making in God's world. They carry out a service under God's supreme authority. Especially in this context, *diakonos* is not a lowly term marking a lower-echelon function of leadership—quite the opposite, these are *the* ruling authorities. This little section of Romans demonstrates that *diakonos* was able to reflect *any* kind of service, from that of what we think of as hourly-wage-earning table servants up to the highest leaders in society, like judges and governors.

> Accept one another, then, just as Christ accepted you, in order to bring praise to God. For I tell you that Christ has become a servant [*diakonos*] of the Jews on behalf of God's truth, so that the promises made to the patriarchs might be confirmed and, moreover, that the Gentiles might glorify God for his mercy. (Rom 15:7-9)

Christ himself is called here a *diakonos*, a servant of God ministering to the circumcised as part of God's grand plan. When we put all of these occurrences of this language together, it is obvious that Paul was paying honor and respect to Phoebe, but not as a "deacon" (if by that we mean a title with specific tasks that are menial or hold little or no authority). He was treating her as someone like himself, dedicated to the hard work of *ministry*, not least in her tireless efforts to support Paul's mission in Rome.

"Benefactor" Phoebe. In Paul's commendation of Phoebe in Romans 16:2, he makes much of her benefaction and support of him and many others. He uses the Greek term *prostatis*. This was language

used about a patron supporting others in need. "Helper" (NASB) misses the social dynamics involved in this terminology. In this first-century Roman context, this was terminology used for someone of power and status serving as a guardian and protector of a person or a group.[13] A *prostatis* was someone who stepped in with resources and influence to aid someone in need. Phoebe was the benefactor; Paul and many others were recipients.

To imagine what this benefaction ministry might have looked like, scholars sometimes turn to a fascinating case study involving a woman named Junia Theodora. She was a wealthy citizen of Roman Corinth in the first century AD. No less than five inscriptions testify to her benefaction.[14] In particular, she was committed to supporting Lycians[15] visiting or staying in Corinth.[16] She provided hospitality in her home and extended to them other supports. In some cases, she took in people who were exiled from Lycia. Here is a sampling of some of the inscriptions honoring her:

> Since Junia Theodora, a Roman, a benefactress of the greatest loyalty to the Lycian federation and our city has accomplished numerous ... benefits for the federation and our city, and dwelling in the city of the Corinthians welcomes in her own house Lycian travellers and citizens ... supplying them with everything ... ; displaying her patronage [*prostasia*] of those who are present.[17]

The people of Myra (in Lycia) sent a letter to the magistrates of Corinth commending Junia Theodora.

> Many of our (citizens) who travelled to your territory testified concerning a citizen of yours, Junia Theodora, daughter of Lucius, and the devotion and zeal which she used on their behalf, occupying herself continually for

[13]See Erlend D. MacGillivray, "Romans 16:2, *Prostatis/Prostates*, and the Application of Reciprocal Relationships in New Testament Texts," *Novum Testamentum* 53 (2011): 183-99, esp. 194.
[14]See Konstantinos Mantas, "Independent Women in the Roman East: Widows, Benefactresses, Patronesses, Office-Holders," *Eirene* 33 (1997): 81-85.
[15]Ancient Lycia was in Anatolia, modern-day Turkey.
[16]See R. A. Kearsley, "Women in Public Life in the Roman East: Iunia Theodora, Claudia Metrodora and Phoebe, Benefactress of Paul," *Tyndale Bulletin* 50, no. 2 (1999): 189-211, at 194.
[17]Jerome Murphy-O'Connor, *St. Paul's Corinth: Texts and Archaeology* (Collegeville, MN: Liturgical Press, 2002), 83.

our people particularly at the time of their arrival in your city; that is why, according her our approval for her loyalty to the city, we hold her in the greatest esteem, and have decided at the same time to write to you as well in order that you may know of the gratitude of the city.[18]

Another city of Lycia, Patara, sent a similar notice to Corinth honoring Junia Theodora.

> Since Junia Theodora, a Roman, living in Corinth, a woman of the greatest honour, living modestly, who is a friend of the Lycians and had dedicated her life to earning the gratitude of all the Lycians, has bestowed numerous benefits also on many of our citizens; and, revealing the generosity of her nature, she does not cease, because of her goodwill, from offering hospitality to all the Lycians and receiving them in her own house and she continues particularly to act on behalf of our citizens in regard to any favour asked—so that the majority of our citizens have come before the Assembly to give testimony about her.[19]

Jerome Murphy-O'Connor notes that Junia Theodora did more than just offer space for Lycians to reside in her (what we can assume to be large) house. She used her connections to put Lycians in good stead with Corinthian authorities, and she also may have introduced Lycian merchants to her business contacts. Robert Kearsley underscores that benefaction of this kind was common in the ancient world; what was *unusual* was this coming from a woman, especially one who was not associated with a husband (a widow?). This must point to her high social status that afforded her such independent power and influence.[20] It appears that Junia Theodora was acting independently, "living a very public life circulating freely within the high-ranking, predominantly male world of government and commerce in Corinth."[21] One can easily imagine Phoebe fitting a similar social profile. Perhaps she opened up her house to traveling Christian leaders, like Paul, but above and beyond that she

---

[18]Murphy-O'Connor, *St. Paul's Corinth*, 83.
[19]Murphy-O'Connor, *St. Paul's Corinth*, 83.
[20]Kearsley makes note of another socially powerful woman, this time in the city of Histiaea, who held offices normally occupied by men, demonstrating that "the boundary between male and female in public life was not entirely inflexible" ("Women in Public Life," 194).
[21]Kearsley, "Women in Public Life," 197.

had "access" to power and social influence to protect and support ministry work.[22] Bradley Blue reasons that the skills that enabled Phoebe to aid and protect people like Paul were also the kind of gifts that would make her a natural administrative leader in her church.[23]

"Sister" Phoebe. Let's turn back to Phoebe's role as letter carrier. I regularly hear from students that they had never heard before that Phoebe was entrusted with bringing Paul's important epistle to Rome. But this is not a modern observation or insight. Going back to some of the ancient Greek manuscripts of Romans, we find subscriptions (end of document "tags," if you will) that say things like this:

> Written to the Romans through Phoebe from Corinth[24]

> Written to the Romans from Corinth through Phoebe the minister [or "ministry provider," *diakonos*][25]

> Epistle written to the Romans through Tertius; and sent through Phoebe from Corinth[26]

Peter Abelard (1079–1142) mentions in his commentary on Romans that Paul sent his letter through Phoebe, and he quotes approvingly from Jerome that Paul did not favor men over women when it came to carrying out such important tasks.[27] John Calvin (1509–1564) also mentions as a matter of fact that Phoebe was given this letter by Paul to carry to Rome.[28]

Now, it is crucial to understand that in the ancient world, letter carriers played a more important role than just "delivering mail." One would not make such a long journey, especially with such a vital message as Romans, and simply drop it off. Peter Head has done important research

[22]Carolyn Osiek and Margaret Y. MacDonald, with Janet H. Tulloch, *A Woman's Place: House Churches in Earliest Christianity* (Minneapolis: Fortress, 2006), 194-243, esp. 227-28

[23]Bradley Blue, "Acts and the House Church," in *The Book of Acts in Its Graeco-Roman Setting*, ed. David W. J. Gill and Conrad Gempf (Grand Rapids, MI: Eerdmans, 1994), 119-222, at 184.

[24]Ms 35, similarly 201.

[25]Mss 42, 90, 216, 339 462, 566*, 642.

[26]Ms 337. Her home city of Cenchreae was very close to the larger city of Corinth, so you could think of it as part of "Corinth metro."

[27]See Peter Abelard, *Commentary on the Epistle to the Romans*, trans. Steven R. Cartwright (Washington, DC: Catholic University of America Press, 2011), 90

[28]Joseph Haroutunian, ed., *Calvin: Commentaries* (Philadelphia: Westminster, 1958), 468.

on the responsibilities of letter carriers and their mediatorial relationship with the sender and their communicative authority. After analyzing hundreds of letters from the Roman world, many dozens of which mention letter carriers, Head concluded that these couriers played a crucial role in "extending the communication initiated by the letter."[29] As an agent of the sender, the letter carrier acted as a kind of proxy, operating on behalf of the sender. On occasion the named letter carrier did function in some way or another to "represent" the sender, to expand on details with the letter, and even to expound and reinforce the primary message of the letter in oral communication.[30]

When it comes to Phoebe in particular, Head and others recognize that she would possess a kind of apostolic agency, operating on Paul's behalf in Rome, especially since she was going to stay in town and could ensure a clear understanding of his messages and potentially bring back a response or report on how the churches were assimilating his teachings.[31] Along the same lines as Head's conclusions, Lincoln Blumell argues that letter carriers like Phoebe would have been given instructions regarding the intended impact of the communication.

> The letter carrier served to extend and clarify the message so that it was properly contextualized and interpreted in the intended manner by the recipient. . . .
>
> [The letter carrier] was thought to be a trusted friend or an associate/agent who could accurately and faithfully relay the oral component of the message. In such cases it even seems that at times the letter carrier acted not just as an intermediary between the sender and recipient but that he was invested with authority to carry on and extend the dialogue and in a way vicariously stood in for the sender who could not be physically present.[32]

---

[29]Head, "Named Letter-Carriers," 297.

[30]Head, "Named Letter-Carriers," 297.

[31]Head, "Named Letter-Carriers," 298. See also Allan Chapple, "Getting *Romans* to the Right Romans: Phoebe and the Delivery of Paul's Letter," *Tyndale Bulletin* 62, no. 2 (2011): 195-214, at 213-14.

[32]Lincoln Blumell, "The Message and the Medium: Some Observations on Epistolary Communication in Late Antiquity," *Journal of Greco-Roman Christianity and Judaism* 10 (2014): 24-67, at 57 and 64.

It is very important that we draw out the implications of Paul's choice of the church leader Phoebe for this particular task. Paul *knew* that this letter to the Romans was instrumental to his mission for several reasons. First, as the great imperial city, this would be a hub for Christian communities. As people traveled for business to Rome, these churches would be representative of the Christian faith for many observers. Second, these Roman believers did not know Paul personally, so this letter was their introduction to Paul, his gospel message, and his apostolic ministry to Gentiles. Paul would have placed this letter only into the care of someone he trusted with "apostolic" wisdom and shrewdness. In a way, Paul was sending Phoebe as an ad hoc apostle, a Cenchreaen ministry delegate to operate on his behalf.

This is reinforced by his labeling of Phoebe as "sister," a detail often overlooked in the discussion of this minister. True, Paul could refer to any fellow Christian as "brother" or "sister."[33] But this language takes on more of a technical meaning in commendation passages, where he would be recognizing their peer status—*this person is just like me.* Paul does this regularly with his coworker Timothy ("brother Timothy"; 2 Cor 1:1; Col 1:1; 1 Thess 3:2), Titus (2 Cor 2:13), and the letter carriers Tychicus (Col 4:7; Eph 6:21) and Epaphroditus (Phil 2:25). For example, Paul had to flee Thessalonica suddenly but worried about the believers there and sent Timothy to check up on them and bring back a report. He commends Timothy to them as a worthy substitute for his own presence, "our brother and co-worker" (1 Thess 3:2). As Charles Wanamaker explains, "Timothy's credentials . . . entitle him to act as Paul's representative. In context they may be intended to reassure the Thessalonians that Timothy had Paul's complete confidence when he visited them by himself."[34] Similarly, calling her "sister Phoebe" would offer a status indicator: she was a leader like Paul.[35] The Romans ought

---

[33]See Paul Trebilco, *Self-Designations and Group Identity in the New Testament* (Cambridge: Cambridge University Press, 2014), 16-67.

[34]Charles A. Wanamaker, *The Epistles to the Thessalonians*, New International Greek Text Commentary (Grand Rapids, MI: Eerdmans, 2015), 127.

[35]See Trebilco, *Self-Designations*, 23; E. Earle Ellis, "Paul and His Co-workers," *New Testament Studies* 17, no. 4 (1971): 13-22; Branch, "Female Leadership"; Jeremy Punt, "(Con)figuring Gender in Bible Translation," *HTS* 70.1 (2014): 1-8, at 6.

to treat her accordingly, a sentiment reinforced by Paul's request that they should afford her warm hospitality.[36]

DID PHOEBE READ THE LETTER?

A matter that relates closely to the duties of a letter carrier is whether Phoebe was given the responsibility from Paul to read the letter aloud. Beverly Gaventa argues that Phoebe would have been the most natural choice for lector (letter reader), as someone Paul knew well; he could easily have trained her to vocally perform his letter in the presence of the Roman Christians.[37] This makes good sense, though it is hard to be sure.[38] While we cannot have certainty about who read the letter out loud, we *can* have confidence that Phoebe took responsibility for engaging with the letter's contents in communication with Roman leaders. Philip Esler imagines Phoebe going from one house church to another, discussing the contents of the letter after it was read. In that sense, she was indeed the first interpreter of Romans.[39] And if that is the case, Paul would have ensured that she truly understood his main ideas and could reinforce them among the Roman house churches. Furthermore, presumably she would eventually return to Cenchreae and make contact with Paul about the letter's reception (or perhaps she would send him a letter, discussing the responses from the Romans). She would, again, play the role of agent or proxy, delivering back to Paul any key decisions or questions coming from the Roman Christian leadership.

---

[36]For a more extensive discussion of Paul's use of "sister," see Nijay K. Gupta, "Sister Phoebe: *Adelphē* as An Honorific Descriptor in Rom 16:1-2," in *Rhetoric, History, and Theology: Interpreting the New Testament*, ed. Todd D. Still and Jason A. Myers (Minneapolis: Fortress, 2022), 133-56.

[37]Beverly R. Gaventa, *When in Romans: An Invitation to Linger with the Gospel According to Paul* (Grand Rapids, MI: Baker Academic, 2018), 29-31. Elsa Tamez takes for granted that Phoebe read the letter aloud and devises an imaginative depiction of her introducing the letter and reinforcing some of its contents; Elsa Tamez, "Phoebe, Bearer of the Letter to the Church in Rome, Explains Romans 12:1-2," *Reformed World* 67, no. 2 (2017): 4-12.

[38]Some scholars wonder whether Phoebe was literate. This is hard to know, but if she was somewhat wealthy and held a more elite status, she would be the *kind* of person that had such an education. See Gaventa, *When in Romans*, 18.

[39]See Philip F. Esler, *Conflict and Identity in Romans* (Grand Rapids, MI: Eerdmans, 2003), 117-19.

WHAT WAS PHOEBE'S BUSINESS IN ROME?

One thing we learn from Paul's short commendation of Phoebe is that she was traveling to Rome from Cenchreae not just to hand deliver Paul's letter to those churches but also to conduct some other business. Those receiving the letter, especially the Roman church leaders, I presume, were meant to show her proper hospitality and to "give her any help she may need" (Rom 16:2). So, just to make it clear, she was staying put in Rome and Paul was encouraging them to aid her as needed.

What exactly was she doing there? One possibility is that she had personal business, unrelated to Paul's letter and mission. Joseph Fitzmyer, for example, wonders whether the "affair" (*pragma*) Paul refers to is perhaps supporting someone embroiled in a lawsuit.[40] The Greek term *pragma*, though, is a generic word and really divulges nothing at all about the situation. Furthermore, if Phoebe was in Rome for personal matters, perhaps Paul might have asked Christian colleagues to support her, but this could have been done in a separate message or letter. Why "publicize" this to all the churches who would hear this letter read aloud? Besides, Phoebe appears to have been a woman of means, so what aid could they have provided that she needed?

More likely, she was staying in Rome at Paul's behest and helping to secure and promote his ministry there. Arland Hultgren imagines Phoebe going from one house church to another to "fill them in on Paul's plans, secure arrangements for his arrival, alleviate any concerns they might have about his coming and being with them, and, above all, interpret the Letter to the Romans among its recipients, prior to Paul's arrival."[41] This would make sense of Paul's overall commendation of Phoebe, not just as the letter's carrier, but as a representative of Paul, an apostolic agent acting on his behalf.

Robert Jewett takes Phoebe's ministry role one step further and proposes that Paul sent her as a kind of "advance team" representative to

---

[40]Fitzmyer, *Romans*, 731; James D. G. Dunn, *Romans 9–16*, Word Biblical Commentary 38B (Dallas: Word Books, 1988), 888.

[41]Arland J. Hultgren, *Paul's Letter to the Romans: A Commentary* (Grand Rapids, MI: Eerdmans, 2011), 570.

establish Rome as a strategic base of operations for taking the gospel westward to Spain: "Her patronage would involve gaining the cooperation of the Roman house churches in creating the logistical base and arranging for the translators that would be required for the Spanish mission."[42] If this is true, one could imagine that the many people Paul greets in the remainder of Romans 16 would be important colleagues who would serve as "advisers and supporters" of this gospel mission.[43]

PHOEBE FOR TODAY

Beverly Gaventa has inspired readers to imagine how Phoebe was engaged with Paul *before* bringing the apostle's letter to the Romans.[44] Here Paul was entrusting into her care this massively important message and theological instruction and exhortation to the churches in the empire's capital city. You can imagine the care with which he discussed his mission and intentions with Phoebe. Was she excited? Was she nervous? What did she ask for clarity about? Did she encourage him to make any changes?

We can also imagine that Phoebe was probably not sent to Rome alone, and yet no one else is specifically mentioned as accompanying Phoebe on this auspicious journey of many hundreds of miles. Paul would have had many colleagues to choose from who could have gone with or instead of Phoebe. He mentions the Corinthian leaders Gaius, Erastus, and his brother Quartus—the fact that they sent their salutations to the Romans probably meant they were known leaders (Rom 16:23). We could also mention Stephanas, Fortunatus, Achaicus, and Crispus (1 Cor 1:14; 16:15). But Paul chose Phoebe to safeguard his ministry in Rome, to serve as an apostolic proxy.

From what Paul said about Phoebe, we know that she was a self-giving, generous leader, using her gifts and everything at her disposal to help others. Just like Junia Theodora, Phoebe was known to be a person that

---

[42]Jewett, *Romans*, 947.
[43]Jewett, *Romans*, 947.
[44]See her important lecture, now on YouTube: "Listening to Phoebe Read Romans," United Theological Seminary of the Twin Cities, March 17, 2012, https://www.youtube.com/watch?v=89TeH0HbelI&t=312s.

went out of her way to support people that needed her, people like Paul. I wonder too if she was sent to Rome as a *model* of the self-giving Christian that Paul wanted to see flourish in the Roman churches as well.

Phoebe serves for us today as a model of the generous leader—one who, though blessed with many gifts, pours them out for the greater good, benefiting needy people and advancing the greater gospel mission.

8

Prisca, Strategic Church Leader and Expert Teacher

The most prominent couple involved in the first-century expansion of Christianity.

Jerome Murphy-O'Connor

Prisca . . . was the most important early Christian who is not a household name.

Michael Peppard

While you may not have been familiar with the names Damaris, Syntyche, or Tryphaena before reading this book, perhaps you have heard of Prisc(ill)a and her husband, Aquila. They are "persons of interest" in Paul's lengthy list of greetings in Romans 16 (16:3), but their names also appear elsewhere in Paul's letters (1 Cor 16:19; 2 Tim 4:19) and in Luke's account of the apostolic spread of the gospel in his book of Acts (18:1-4, 18-27). They were highly active, not only in their shared labor as craftworkers, but also in ministry throughout the empire.[1] And not just

---

[1]See Christoph Stenchke, "Married Women and the Spread of Early Christianity," *Neotestamentica* 43, no. 1 (2009): 145-94; Carolyn Osiek and Margaret Y. MacDonald, with Janet H. Tulloch, *A Woman's Place: House Churches in Earliest Christianity* (Minneapolis: Fortress, 2006), 34; Lynn

anywhere in the empire, but in major cities like Corinth, Ephesus, and Rome. Paul knew them well and commended them for their shared ministry work, including bailing out Paul on at least one occasion. To this couple *all* the Gentile churches owe a special debt of gratitude.

WHO ARE PRISCA AND AQUILA?

Prisca was her official name; the other form of her name, Priscilla, is called a diminutive, a kind of affectionate nickname ("little Prisca"). Her name means "ancient" (as in venerable), and Aquila's name means "eagle."[2] We know they were tentmakers like Paul; they were probably not dependent laborers but "independent craftspersons."[3] This is evident in their ability to move from city to city for ministry, while still able to ply their craft. What kind of tents did Prisca and Aquila make and for whom? Peter Lampe guesses that they fabricated "sun awnings of linen for private customers seeking protection from the hot Roman sun."[4] But this independent business work did not necessarily mean they were wealthy.[5] Craftspeople like Prisca, Aquila, and even Paul could have periods of success and profit, and also times of struggle and lack. That is consistent with how Paul describes his own experience; Aquila and Prisca appear to have been savvy businesspeople, such that they could afford living space that could accommodate a church group.[6]

One interesting consideration in terms of this couple is the ordering of their names in Acts and Paul's letters.[7] When their names appear in

---

H. Cohick, *Women in the World of the Earliest Christians: Illuminating Ancient Ways of Life* (Grand Rapids, MI: Baker Academic, 2009), 129-32.

[2]Marie Noel Keller, *Priscilla and Aquila* (Collegeville, MN: Liturgical Press, 2010), xiii.

[3]Peter Lampe, *Christians at Rome in the First Two Centuries: From Paul to Valentinus* (London: Continuum, 2006), 187.

[4]Lampe, *Christians at Rome*, 188-89; see Pliny, *Natural History* 19.24; see similarly Keller, *Priscilla and Aquila*, 25.

[5]For scholars who argue for a relatively high status and wealth, see Robert Jewett, *Romans: A Commentary*, Hermeneia (Minneapolis: Fortress, 2006), 956; Wayne A. Meeks, *The First Urban Christians: The Social World of the Apostle Paul* (New Haven, CT: Yale University Press, 2003), 59.

[6]Susan Mathew, *Women in the Greetings of Romans 16.1-16: A Study of Mutuality and Women's Ministry in the Letter to the Romans* (London: T&T Clark, 2013), 87-88.

[7]In the Greco-Roman world, it was standard practice to list the husband's name before that of his wife, probably to recognize the head of household. However, a study of thousands of Roman epitaphs shows a small percentage of exceptions where the wife was named first. In many such cases, the wife held citizenship while her husband was a slave. There does not appear to be a

close proximity, on four occasions Prisca's name appears before Aquila's (Acts 18:18, 26; Rom 16:3; 2 Tim 4:19). On only one occasion, 1 Corinthians 16:19, Aquila is mentioned first. Given the male-centered nature of society and the tendency to give honor through rhetorical features *like* name order, this is noteworthy, though it is not exactly clear what it means.[8] Some have proposed that this indicates that Prisca had a higher social status than her husband.[9] But there are a couple of problems with this theory. First, why the switch in name order in 1 Corinthians 16:19 (with Aquila's name first)? Second, Paul does not seem to be the kind of person who focused on worldly status, so to speak.[10] He utilized the social privileges of colleagues and friends for the sake of the gospel, but he didn't treat it as something to acknowledge all by itself.

A more likely theory is that Prisca was the more active (and therefore more widely known) ministry leader.[11] This aligns with comments made by the early theologian John Chrysostom. He claimed that in Romans 16:3 Paul names Prisca before her husband "in recognition of the fact that her piety was superior to her husband's."[12] It is unclear what Chrysostom meant here by "piety," but it seems reasonable that this prior mention

---

particular set of rules around name order, but this research does acknowledge that name order is an indicator of status or prominence in some way; see Marleen Boudreau Flory, "Where Women Precede Men: Factors Influencing the Order of Names in Roman Epitaphs," *The Classical Journal* 79, no. 3 (1984): 216-24.

[8] In at least one early Greek manuscript (D), the scribe seemingly switched the order of the names in Acts 18:26, putting Aquila's name first; see Ann Graham Brock, "Scribal Blunder or Textual Plunder? Codex Bezae, Textual-Rhetorical Analysis, and the Diminished Role of Women," in *Her Master's Tools? Feminist and Postcolonial Engagements of Historical-Critical Discourse*, ed. Caroline Vander Stichele and Todd Penner (Atlanta: SBL Press, 2005), 253-64, at 260. This same manuscript famously eliminates the story of the conversion of the Athenian woman Damaris (Acts 17:34) and changes "not a few of the honorable Greek women and men" (Acts 17:12) to "of the Greeks and the honorable, many men and women"; see Dominka Kurek-Chomycz, "Is There an 'Anti-Priscan' Tendency in the Manuscripts? Some Textual Problems with Prisca and Aquila," *Journal of Biblical Literature* 125, no. 1 (2006): 107-28.

[9] Meeks, *First Urban Christians*, 59; Jewett, *Romans*, 955.

[10] See Michael Peppard, "Household Names: Junia, Phoebe, and Prisca in Early Christian Rome," *Commonweal*, June 1, 2018, 11-14, at 14.

[11] See Peter Lampe, "Prisca," in *Anchor Bible Dictionary* (New York: Doubleday, 1992), 5:468; Christine Schenk, *Crispina and Her Sisters: Women and Authority in Early Christianity* (Minneapolis: Fortress, 2017), 37.

[12] Margaret M. Mitchell, *John Chrysostom on Paul: Praises and Problem Passages* (Atlanta: SBL Press, forthcoming); see also Mikeal C. Parsons, *Acts*, Paideia (Grand Rapids, MI: Baker Academic, 2008), 250-51.

identified her as more prominent in gospel activity.[13] Jerome Murphy-O'Connor is explicit about what the intentional name ordering means for gender and social status in the early church: "The public acknowledgement of Prisca's prominent role in the Church, implicit in the reversal of the secular form of naming the husband before his wife, underlines how radically egalitarian the Pauline communities were."[14] Before getting into what Christian ministry and mission looked like for this important couple, let's go back and get a basic rundown of their history and locations.

FROM CITY TO CITY

Scholars have reconstructed a plausible travel chronology of this ministry couple. Acts 18 makes clear that the first location we can place them is Rome. They were already married at this point and perhaps came to Christian faith in the capital city. Luke mentions too that an edict by Roman emperor Claudius forced Jews to leave Rome (Acts 18:2).[15] Murphy-O'Connor argues that controversies of Jesus Christ whipped up turmoil in the Roman synagogues, leading to a crackdown by the emperor.[16] Perhaps Prisca and Aquila were partly to blame for this, as they proclaimed Jesus to their Jewish kinspeople. Where they went from Rome we cannot know for sure, but we do know they settled down for a year and a half in Corinth where they met Paul (Acts 18:2-3). They offered Paul hospitality, and he stayed with them for a long while. Their relationship was enriched not only by their shared faith in Christ but also by their common profession. Then Prisca and Aquila left Corinth with Paul and landed in Ephesus. They stayed, but Paul left again after a short while to continue his itinerant ministry (Acts 18:18-21). While Paul was with Prisca and Aquila in Ephesus, he wrote the letter we know as 1 Corinthians. He wrote to the Corinthians, "The churches in the province of Asia send you greetings. Aquila and

---

[13]Jerome Murphy-O'Connor, "Prisca and Aquila: Travelling Tentmakers and Church Builders," *Bible Review* 8, no. 6 (1992): 40-51, 62, at 41.

[14]Murphy-O'Connor, "Prisca and Aquila," 42.

[15]This event is also mentioned by Suetonius, *Claudius* 25.4.

[16]Murphy-O'Connor, "Prisca and Aquila," 45.

Priscilla greet you warmly in the Lord, and so does the church that meets at their house" (1 Cor 16:19).

It was also during Prisca and Aquila's time in Ephesus that they encountered Apollos, the traveling evangelist from Alexandria. We will go into more detail about this Acts episode later on, but suffice it to say here that Prisca and Aquila seem to have been the central leaders in the Ephesian Christian community, such that they took it upon themselves to give Apollos a more thorough understanding of "the way of God" (Acts 18:24-28).

When the Claudian edict ended and Jews could return to Rome, Prisca and Aquila availed themselves of this opportunity. Perhaps this is what they planned all along, or maybe Paul encouraged them to go back "as Paul's vanguard to Rome, where he wanted to establish a firm footing for his gospel before continuing to Spain."[17] In his letter to the Romans, Paul commends them for their ministry work, even risking their lives to help Paul. In Rome, Prisca and Aquila hosted a Christian assembly in their house (Rom 16:5). But eventually they left Rome again and went back to Ephesus, according to 2 Timothy 4:19. Osiek and MacDonald make a thoughtful observation about this couple's unique ministry:

> One of the most fascinating features of the description of Prisc(ill)a and Aquila's activities in Acts and presentation of their contribution by Paul in his letters is that they combined aspects of an itinerant existence with the more settled existence of hosting a house church; their lives may, therefore, offer very important insight into how the Jesus movement managed to establish itself in the Greco-Roman city. Their missionary pattern was literally one of moving and setting up house.[18]

HOUSE-CHURCH LEADERS

We have already talked about householders as church leaders, but it is worthwhile here to contemplate again the important roles that such women and men played as "hosts" (this term doesn't do justice to their

---

[17]Lampe, "Prisca," 5:468.
[18]Osiek and MacDonald, Woman's Place, 33.

impact as community leaders providing more than space and a meal). House-based Christian communities were the norm in the earliest stages of Christianity, and in all likelihood it was a strategic choice for Paul to call on people like Prisca and Aquila to go from place to place, establishing house-based assemblies—and, indeed, to preach the gospel to influential people like Lydia (Acts 16:11-15) who would then bring the gospel to their own households (which included not only family and relatives but also slaves and dependent laborers socially connected to the "house").[19] No doubt, then, the head of household (the norm being a male) would naturally serve as a central leader in the church community. But, as Vincent Branick is quick to point out, the household mother (materfamilias) often carried a household administrator role (1 Tim 5:14). "The mother in many ways was the manager of the household. The widow often stood in the place of her deceased spouse for business activities. Most probably, the mother would not have been reduced to a passive spectator in the church that met in her house."[20] Branick goes on to mention several women who seem to share leadership in some of the house churches mentioned in the New Testament: Nympha (Col 4:15), Apphia (Philem 1), possibly Chloe (1 Cor 1:11), Lydia (Acts 16:11-15), and, of course, Prisca.

So what exactly did house-church leaders like Prisca and Aquila do? We can expect that in addition to providing space and organizing a communal meal, they helped preside over the assembly worship. Many members of the household would have seen the householders as wise leaders and capable managers. Did they teach as well? This is unclear. But given Paul's connections to people like Stephanas (one of a few people whom Paul baptized [1 Cor 1:16; 16:15]), it would seem that he did train

---

[19] Again, see Roger Gehring's important book, *House Church and Mission: The Importance of Household Structures in Early Christianity* (Peabody, MA: Hendrickson, 2004); also Vincent Branick, *The House Church in the Writings of Paul* (Eugene, OR: Wipf & Stock, 2012): "Most probably the conversion of a household and the consequent formation of a house church formed the key element in Paul's strategic plan to spread the Gospel to the world. . . . It is not surprising then to see frequent mention of baptisms, not just of individuals, but of whole households. . . . Acts makes such a household conversion almost a theme in itself (Acts 10:2; 16:15; 16:33; 18:8; cf. also Jn 4:53)" (18; on Prisca and Aquila, see 60-61).

[20] Branick, *House Church*, 21.

and commission such householders to form their assemblies, especially reinforcing the apostolic tradition. In the case of Prisca and Aquila, we must remember *how close* Paul was to this couple, having spent months, perhaps even years, in ministry with them, for some of this time living with them. How many other Christian leaders in the world at that time had such intimate and close interaction with Paul, absorbing his knowledge and benefiting from his spiritual insights?[21] There were probably only a handful of people Paul would put in this close circle of associates who could be fully confident of their understanding of the apostolic tradition he sought to pass down, people like Timothy, Titus, and Silas.

RISKY MINISTRY?

I am intrigued by the reference in Romans 16:4 to Prisca and Aquila risking their lives for Paul, which implies putting themselves in some kind of danger. Paul claims that not only he but also all the Gentile churches were in their debt. That's a major commendation. They deserve a place in the Christian hall of heroes, as it were, for their intrepid intervention. But what was Paul referring to? What kind of jeopardy could this have been? In this matter we can only guess. Susan Mathew considers the possibility that this aid took place in Ephesus, as Paul mentions to the Corinthians how the apostles and their colleagues were "putting [themselves] in danger every hour" (1 Cor 15:30 NRSV).[22] Paul refers to fighting "wild beasts" there, not literally contending with animals, but more likely a symbol-laden reference to the wild and fanatical worshipers of Ephesian Artemis.[23] Perhaps when Paul's life was in danger, they came to his rescue, maybe hiding him in their home. Or perhaps they were advocating for him in some way using what Robert Jewett calls their "patronal capacity."[24] This

---

[21]This is a point repeatedly reinforced by Chrysostom.

[22]Mathew, *Women in the Greetings*, 90.

[23]Artemis was widely associated with the forest and wild animals; see Daniel Frayer-Griggs, "The Beasts at Ephesus and the Cult of Artemis," *Harvard Theological Review* 106, no. 4 (2013): 459-477; Morna D. Hooker, "Artemis of Ephesus," *Journal of Theological Studies* 64, no. 1 (2013): 37-46.

[24]That is, using their social capital to get him out of hot water; Jewett, *Romans*, 957.

could include using connections to get Paul released from incarceration in Ephesus (or elsewhere).[25]

Chrysostom, taking note of the many women Paul praises in Romans 16, comments, "Here [Paul] hints at their hospitality, and pecuniary assistance, holding them in admiration because they had poured forth their blood, and had made their whole property open to all. You see these were noble women, hindered [in] no way by their sex in the course of virtue."[26] Taking note of how Paul consistently mentions and honors Prisca alongside her husband, Chrysostom adds,

> For what is greater or so great, as to have been a succorer [savior] of Paul? At her own peril to have saved the teacher of the world? And consider: how many empresses there are that no one speaks of. But the wife of the tent-maker is everywhere reported of with the tent-maker [Paul]; and the width that the sun sees over, is no more of the world than what the glory of this woman runneth unto. Persians, and Scythians, and Thracians, and they who dwell in the uttermost parts of the earth, sing of the Christian spirit of this woman, and bless it. . . . [Paul] does not feel ashamed to call a woman his helper [i.e., savior] but even finds an honor in doing so. For it is not the sex that he minds, but the will is what he honors. . . . Look at their labor for the preaching, the crown in martyrdom, the munificence in money, the love of Paul, the charm they found in Christ. . . . Vie with this woman . . . and learn whence Priscilla became such as she was.[27]

One reason Chrysostom is so complimentary of Prisca is that she was an advanced teacher for the evangelist Apollos. It is now time to look more closely at that fascinating story in Acts.

INSTRUCTING APOLLOS

This is the episode as told by Luke:

> Meanwhile a Jew named Apollos, a native of Alexandria, came to Ephesus. He was a learned man, with a thorough knowledge of the Scriptures. He

---

[25]Joseph Fitzmyer, *Romans*, Anchor Yale Bible (New Haven, CT: Yale University Press, 2008), 735.
[26]See Mitchell, *John Chrysostom on Paul*.
[27]John Chrysostom, *Homilies on the Acts of the Apostles and the Epistle to the Romans*, in *Nicene and Post-Nicene Fathers*, series 1, vol. 11, ed. Philip Schaff, trans. J. B. Morris, W. H. Simcox, and George B. Stevens (New York: Christian Literature, 1889), 551.

had been instructed in the way of the Lord, and he spoke with great fervor and taught about Jesus accurately, though he knew only the baptism of John. He began to speak boldly in the synagogue. When Priscilla and Aquila[a] heard him, they invited him to their home and explained to him the way of God more adequately.

When Apollos wanted to go to Achaia, the brothers and sisters encouraged him and wrote to the disciples there to welcome him. When he arrived, he was a great help to those who by grace had believed. For he vigorously refuted his Jewish opponents in public debate, proving from the Scriptures that Jesus was the Messiah. (Acts 18:24-28)

Alexandria (Egypt) was known at the time for producing passionate and learned philosophers (like Philo of Alexandria). Apollos is described here as both highly intelligent and richly eloquent. Put simply, he was a gifted and persuasive evangelist, a fact reinforced by Paul's references to Apollos in 1 Corinthians (1 Cor 1:12; 3:4-5; 4:6). In fact, Paul had to cool the Corinthians' passions for Apollos, noting that such gifted leaders are merely servants, while God alone deserves praise (1 Cor 3:5). But the situation in Ephesus (Acts 18) seems to be that Prisca and Aquila detected in Apollos's gospel message some gaps. Before we get to those gaps, it is worth pondering, What were Prisca and Aquila doing in the synagogues? And what gave them the "right" to pull Apollos aside for instruction? Presumably, as Jews, Prisca and Aquila tried to establish warm connections with local Jewish communities as a positive witness to Jesus. And within the Ephesian Christian community, we know that Prisca and Aquila had significant standing, not least because of their close association with Paul. That they took it upon themselves to give Apollos further instruction makes good sense; they were the most qualified to fill out his understanding of the apostolic tradition after Christ's resurrection.[28]

Priscilla and Aquila approached Apollos and offered to supplement his knowledge with a more complete understanding of the Christian faith. So they took him to their home. Much is made by scholars of the fact that Priscilla is mentioned first in this episode. As we discussed above, name order was meaningful, and here it seems to suggest that *she*

---

[28]Parsons, *Acts*, 263.

took the lead role in teaching Apollos (Acts 18:26). Chrysostom makes it seem as if she was primarily responsible for taking Apollos aside and instructing him, and she "perfected him as a teacher."[29] Similarly, the church father Ammonius (175–242) claims on the basis of this episode that "women passed on the faith": "He [Apollos] did not become conceited as if he were receiving a rebuke from a woman. . . . [Priscilla] explained to him in her teachings the things of faith, and Apollos listened and received them, for . . . his knowledge was imperfect."[30] That, over time, Priscilla became the more famous (and presumed to be the more active in ministry leadership) is supported by Chrysostom and Ammonius and also Ambrosiaster's brief remark, "Aquila is Priscilla's husband."[31] One would expect, in a patriarchal world, for the woman to be described in terms of the man ("Priscilla is Aquila's wife").[32]

The language used by Luke for their instruction of Apollos is *ektithēmi*, "to convey information by careful elaboration, explain, expound."[33] Now, one might try to make the case that this is not the same as professional instruction, but the same Greek verb is used by Luke for Peter's telling Jewish Christians about his encounter with the Gentile Cornelius (Acts 11:4). At the very end of the book of Acts, the same verb is used again for Paul's response to Jews in Rome who wished for him to explain his religious sect, which was developing a bad reputation. "They arranged to meet Paul on a certain day, and came in even larger numbers to the place where he was staying. He witnessed to them from morning till evening, *explaining* about the kingdom of God, and from the Law of Moses and from the Prophets he tried to persuade them about Jesus"

---

[29]Mitchell, *John Chrysostom on Paul.*

[30]Francis Martin, ed., *Acts,* Ancient Christian Commentary on Scripture (Downers Grove, IL: InterVarsity Press, 2006), 231.

[31]J. Patout Burns Jr., *Romans: Interpreted by Early Christian Commentators* (Grand Rapids, MI: Eerdmans, 2012), 384.

[32]It is important to point out, though, that not all early Christian writers focused on Priscilla. Eusebius does not give attention or prominence to one over the other (*Church History* 18.9); Irenaeus only mentions Aquila (*Church History* 21.1).

[33]Walter Bauer, Frederick W. Daker, William F. Arndt, and F. Wilbur Gingrich, eds., *A Greek-English Lexicon of the New Testament and Other Early Christian Literature,* 3rd ed. (Chicago: University of Chicago Press, 2000). The Latin equivalent, used in the Vulgate translation, is *exponō,* where we get the word "exposit."

(Acts 28:23). What these texts have in common is careful argumentation, a point-by-point explanation in order to convince. Prisca and Aquila are thus presented as well-educated teachers of the faith, willing and able to sharpen even such an intelligent evangelist as Apollos.

Some have tried to minimize the teaching ministry of Prisca by pointing to the house context: "Perhaps most important is the fact that the instruction of Apollos took place in a private setting."[34] This comment demonstrates poor understanding of the first-century Roman world *and* the first several decades of the early Christian mission. The idea that Prisca and Aquila *could* have chosen a "public" space but *then* chose a "private" one raises the question *Where would they go instead?* Let's say, for argument's sake, that Prisca and Aquila (or just Aquila) are the overseers of the Ephesian Christian community. Where might they take Apollos for official and public discussion? They wouldn't go to the synagogues, where they had no authority. To their workshop? Perhaps, but they likely rented living space that doubled as their workspace (so they would still be "at home"). To their "church office"? There were no professional church buildings! In fact, leaders' houses *were* the church's meeting space, so it makes perfect sense for that to be where Apollos was taken.

But I personally don't think they took Apollos to their home *because* it was their "church." That is an anachronistic way of thinking about it. They probably took Apollos home because *that* is the place where you offer hospitality; in addition, it would afford their conversation privacy. Emily Hemelrijk is one of the leading world scholars on the lives of women in the Greco-Roman world. She observes that we would be mistaken to think of the Roman home as a "private" space. Some parts of a house were indeed for family use only (like a bedroom). But the *atrium* (central courtyard), the *tablinum* (another open room, often decorated with art and statues), and the *triclinium* (dining room) served as "reception halls" for clients and visitors.[35] Even the Roman *cubiculum*, a

---

[34]Andreas J. Köstenberger and Margaret Elizabeth Köstenberger, *God's Design for Man and Woman: A Biblical-Theological Survey* (Wheaton, IL: Crossway, 2014), 140.

[35]Emily Hemelrijk, *Hidden Lives, Public Personae: Women and Civic Life in the Roman West* (Oxford: Oxford University Press, 2015), 10.

small leisure room, was a place where more intimate gatherings could be held with friends and guests. So, Hemelrijk explains, "there was a sliding scale between public and more private areas within the houses of the elite, indicating gradations of publicity or intimacy. This was emphasized by architectural and decorative elements, such as columns and wall paintings."[36] Hemelrijk rightly cautions against retrojecting modern assumptions about women and "the house" onto the Roman world: "The ideal of female domesticity did not imply privacy or a life of seclusion. On the contrary, the reception of numerous clients and visitors put her in the public eye even within her own house."[37]

Now, Prisca and Aquila were not wealthy elites, and we can assume they did not have a sprawling mansion in Ephesus or Corinth or Rome. But even in a smaller house, the household sociology would be similar on scale. Houses were simply *the* place for Christians to gather comfortably, as in the case of Paul naturally going to the house of Lydia in Philippi, or Peter going to the house of the mother of Mark.[38] One thing we might consider: personal homes sometimes have a personal library, and it very well could be that Prisca and Aquila immediately took Apollos "home" so that they could verify what they were teaching him by pulling out records of apostolic texts or traditions. In that sense, they weren't just taking Apollos *home*; they were taking him for further instruction to their *school*!

PRISCA FOR TODAY

There are many ways in which Prisca is an inspiration for Christian faith and leadership today. One could point to her dedication to properly educating Christian leaders (like Apollos)—a case for the work of seminary professors! And Prisca is also a model of the "tentmaker" minister who is able to earn money plying a trade while dedicating time to serving the church. But I am especially impressed with Prisca's active faith and nimble spirit. I have moved from city to city almost ten times in my

---

[36]Hemelrijk, *Hidden Lives,* 10.
[37]Hemelrijk, *Hidden Lives,* 11.
[38]See the helpful discussion by Kevin Giles, "House Churches," *Priscila Papers* 42, no. 1 (2010): 6-8.

lifetime, and it is always hard. New surroundings. New home. New people. New shops. New culture. Prisca and Aquila moved several times, sometimes (we can assume) for missionary work. It is a choice to let go of some of the comforts and conveniences of being "settled," and perhaps most significantly it is a decision to leave behind a social network of one's family and friends. There was no FaceTime, email, or texting. No telephones. No bullet train to pop "home" for the weekend. Prisca and Aquila were called to a life of novelty—which can be exciting, but also difficult and wearisome. They did not heed this calling for the prospect of riches, fame, or pleasure. They did it for the sake of the gospel mission, to bring the good news of Jesus to places far and wide.

9

Junia, Venerated Apostle and Imprisoned Hero

Among the women leaders mentioned in the New Testament, Junia is perhaps the most well known today, thanks to the attention of scholars like Scot McKnight, Lynn Cohick, Richard Bauckham, Eldon Epp, Lucy Peppiatt, and Cindy Westfall.[1] But, as you might know, it hasn't always been that way. About a half century ago, most academic commentaries were undecided or unclear on whether the person mentioned in Romans 16:7 was a man or a woman; virtually all translations had the name Junias, presumed to be a male name. But now, well into the twenty-first century, there is widespread consensus that the name should be read "Junia," a woman's name, and that *she* was a key leader in early Christianity. Paul also refers to Junia (and her husband Andronicus)[2] as *apostoloi*, the Greek word that is often translated "apostle." In fact, Paul says this ministry couple was *prominent*—noteworthy, distinguished, special—among the *apostoloi*. Andronicus and Junia were not "apostles" in the

---

[1]Scot McKnight, *Junia Is Not Alone* (Englewood, CO: Patheos, 2011); McKnight, *The Blue Parakeet: Rethinking How You Read the Bible*, 2nd ed. (Grand Rapids, MI: Zondervan Academic, 2018), 227-36; Lynn H. Cohick, *Women in the World of the Earliest Christians: Illuminating Ancient Ways of Life* (Grand Rapids, MI: Baker Academic, 2009); Richard Bauckham, *Gospel Women: Studies of the Named Women in the Gospels* (Grand Rapids, MI: Eerdmans, 2002); Eldon Jay Epp, *Junia: The First Woman Apostle* (Minneapolis: Fortress, 2005); Lucy Peppiatt, *Rediscovering Scripture's Vision for Women: Fresh Perspectives on Disputed Texts* (Downers Grove, IL: IVP Academic, 2019); Cynthia Long Westfall, *Paul and Gender: Reclaiming the Apostle's Vision for Men and Women in Christ* (Grand Rapids, MI: Baker Academic, 2016), 243-78.

[2]Technically, Rom 16:7 does not state that this pair, Andronicus and Junia, were married, but the naming of a man and a woman together would naturally imply they were a couple, and we know that ministry couples were in leadership because of people like Prisca and Aquila.

way Paul was. There was a small group of gospel-mission leaders that were especially commissioned by the Lord Jesus to spread the good news; these were the "official" apostles. But Paul sometimes uses the term *apostolos* for a larger group of men and women who served the same mission but didn't carry the same level of authority. Nevertheless, these "non-official" apostles, like Andronicus and Junia, were a key part of carrying the gospel to the world.

Junia Was a Woman: Rediscovering Her Sex

For more than half a millennium—from the thirteenth century to the 1980s—"Andronicus and Junias" (notice the *s*) were taken to be biological brothers or male ministry colleagues. The presumed male name Junias was assumed to be a short form of the name Junianus. The 1995 version of the New American Standard Bible, for example, has this reading: "Greet Andronicus and Junias, my kinsmen." But here's the problem: in the Greek text of Romans 16:7, the form of the name (*Iunian*) technically *could* be masculine or feminine, so it is unclear whether this is a man's name or a woman's name. So how would you know? It's kind of like seeing the name Chris—you might wonder if it is short for Christopher or Christina. But the example of Chris is not exactly like what we have with this situation with the Greek word *Iunian*. You see, Junia is a widely attested woman's name from Greco-Roman antiquity. On the other hand, the theoretical name Junias (hypothetically a male name) is not attested at all.[3] As far as we can tell from collecting information about ancient Roman names, Junianus *was* a male name, and although men and women sometimes went by short name forms, Junias does not appear in any extant record as a short form.[4] Put simply, the odds are *strongly* in favor

---

[3]Bernadette Brooten sums up the matter well: "To date not a single Latin or Greek inscription, not a single reference in ancient literature has been cited by any of the proponents of the *Junias* hypothesis. My own search for an attestation has also proved fruitless. This means that we do not have a single shred of evidence that the name *Junias* ever existed." Brooten, "Junia . . . Outstanding Among the Apostles (Romans 16:7)," in *Women Priests: A Catholic Commentary on the Vatican Declarations*, ed. Leonard Swidler and Arlene Swidler (New York: Paulist Press, 1977), 141-44, at 142; see also Bauckham, *Gospel Women*, 168.

[4]At least 250 occurrences of the female name Junia have been discovered from the Roman world; for the theoretical male name Junias, we have no evidence whatsoever; see Peter Lampe, "The

of *Iunian* being a woman's name, not a man's. So why is there a debate over the sex of this person? The questioning of the sex of Junia appears to be related to the identification of her as an apostle (that's a complicated issue as well; see below). While the early church of the first millennium seemed to take for granted that the Christian woman Junia was an *apostolos*, sometime in the medieval period this became more problematic, and scholars (and also translators) came to the conclusion that Paul *could not* have been talking about a woman.[5] So how did the interpretation swing back to recognizing Junia as a woman?[6] A major factor involves New Testament scholars taking more seriously early commentaries and comments on Paul's letter to the Romans found especially in patristic writings of the fourth and fifth centuries.

On matters of interpretation where a textual reading is unclear, an important methodological technique used by New Testament scholars involves looking at how the earliest interpreters read and understood the matter. So, when it comes to Junia, we benefit from having numerous patristic writings that mention her. That does not automatically mean those early theologians were always right. But we must take into account that (1) they stood closer in time to the New Testament writers, (2) they had more in common with them culturally, and (3) some of them were hellenophones—that is, Greek was their native language. Thus, if enough of the patristic writers identified Junia as a woman's name, then it would take some serious evidence to the contrary to argue against their assumptions.

The most explicit attestation of Junia's sex comes from John Chrysostom (347–407). About Junia he wrote,

---

Roman Christians of Romans 16," in *The Romans Debate*, ed. Karl Donfried (Peabody, MA: Hendrickson, 1991), 216-30, at 226.

[5]Joseph Fitzmyer remarks that Giles of Rome (1247–1316) may have been the first person (we know) who departed from the patristic tradition and presented Andronicus's ministry partner as the man "Junias"; see Fitzmyer, *Romans*, Anchor Yale Bible (New Haven, CT: Yale University Press, 2008), 737. See Beth Allison Barr, *The Making of Biblical Womanhood: How the Subjugation of Women Became Gospel Truth* (Grand Rapids, MI: Brazos, 2021), 290; her discussion of Junia is brief, but I encourage everyone to read Barr's book.

[6]Anthony Thiselton remarked in 2016 that the scholarly view that Junia is a woman is now "unanimous"; that is a bit of an exaggeration, but we can say that anyone arguing otherwise has to overcome a mountain of evidence; see Thiselton, *Discovering Romans* (Grand Rapids, MI: Eerdmans, 2016), 257.

> It was the greatest of honors to be counted a fellow prisoner of Paul's.
> . . . Think what great praise it was to be considered of note among the
> apostles. These two were of note because of their works and achievements.
> Think how great the devotion of this woman Junia must have been, that
> she should be worthy to be called an apostle! But even here Paul does not
> stop his praise, for they were Christians before he was.[7]

Chrysostom takes for granted that Junia is a woman *and* an "apostle." We
will address the apostle matter later, but it is worth noticing here that
Chrysostom doesn't entertain the possibility that Junia was a man, even
though the whole matter is a bit shocking to him! Similarly, the feminine
name Junia is attested by ancient Christian writers Origen, Ambrosiaster,
Jerome, Theodoret, John Damascene, Peter Abelard, and Peter Lom-
bard.[8] A tenth-century church calendar observes May 17 as the feast of
Saints Andronicus and Junia, mentioning the latter as the former's traveling partner in godly preaching, "who, dead to the world and the flesh,
but alive to God alone, carried out her task."[9]

With evidence like this, widespread and voluminous, scholars today
have "rediscovered" the true sex of Junia—Andronicus's wife, but also a
coworker in ministry and mission for the sake of the gospel, not unlike
Prisca and Aquila. But unlike Prisca and Aquila, Andronicus and Junia
were called *apostoloi*—or were they?

Junia Was an *Apostolos*: Recognizing Her Ministry

Alongside the sex debate regarding Junia (which is now all but settled),
there has also been extensive discussion of the phrase *hoitines eisen
episēmoi en tois apostolois*, which has been variously translated, representing basically two divergent interpretations:

> They are well known *to* the apostles. (NET)

> They are outstanding *among* the apostles. (NIV)

---

[7] As translated and cited in Gerald Bray, ed., *Romans*, Ancient Christian Commentary on Scripture
(Downers Grove, IL: InterVarsity Press, 1998), 372.

[8] See Epp, *Junia*, 32-33.

[9] *Acts Sanctorum, Maii* 4, cited in Fitzmyer, *Romans*, 737.

Theoretically, the Greek text in question could be understood either way. The first interpretation (NET) treats Andronicus and Junia as *outside* the circles of apostles: Andronicus and Junia were well known *to* the apostles, but they themselves were not apostles. The second option (NIV) includes them as apostles: Andronicus and Junia were outstanding or prominent *among* the apostles.[10] Numerous articles and essays—most of them highly technical and hard to follow unless your Greek knowledge is advanced—have addressed this matter.[11] But crossing swords over the minutiae of Greek syntax is not going to settle this matter definitively. Again, there are other resources and tools at our disposal to seek more clarity on this—namely, early testimony. (And, again, it's not foolproof, but it shines a bit of extra light on this seemingly irresolvable debate.) No early Christian writer as far as I have read has given credence to the reading that Junia and Andronicus were *not* apostles. Alternatively, there are several patristic writers who take for granted that Junia was an *apostolos*, as we have seen with Chrysostom. Chrysostom considered this a high office, a status of work and ministry that belongs to only the most venerated of Christian leaders (see the quote above). Ambrosiaster (fourth century) also attested that Junia was an *apostolos*; he took this to mean some sort of second generation of apostolic ministry.[12] Theodoret of Cyrus (423–457) referred to *apostoloi* as "men and women of note, not among the pupils but among the teachers, and not among the ordinary teachers but among the apostles."[13] This is fascinating to me, because Theodoret seems to have automatically presumed that *apostoloi* were teachers of the highest authority in

---

[10]See Linda Belleville, "Women Leaders in the Bible," in *Discovering Biblical Equality: Biblical, Theological, Cultural & Practical Perspectives,* ed. Ronald W. Pierce, Cynthia Long Westfall, and Christa L. McKirland, 3rd ed. (Downers Grove, IL: IVP Academic, 2021), 69-90.

[11]Michael H. Burer and Daniel B. Wallace, "Was Junia Really an Apostle? A Re-examination of Rom 16.7," *New Testament Studies* 47, no. 1 (2001): 76-91; Linda Belleville, "*Iounian . . . episēmoi en tois apostolois:* A Re-examination of Romans 16.7 in Light of Primary Source Materials," *New Testament Studies* 51, no. 2 (2005): 231-49; Epp, *Junia,* 72-79; Michael H. Burer, "*Episēmoi en tois Apostolois* in Rom 16:7 as 'Well Known to the Apostles': Further Defense and New Evidence," *Journal of the Evangelical Theological Society* 58, no. 4 (2015): 731-55.

[12]Theodore S. de Bruyn, *Ambrosiaster's Commentary on the Pauline Epistles: Romans* (Atlanta: SBL Press, 2017), 267.

[13]Translation from Bray, *Romans,* 372.

the church. If we read between the lines of this statement, he could barely imagine anyone ranking higher in the church worldwide than people like Junia and her husband, Andronicus.

One of the earliest patristic writers, Origen (184–253), likewise acknowledged that Junia and Andronicus were *apostoloi*, and he went one step further, theorizing what this meant in light of Paul's reference to their preceding him in the faith: "He might have called them prominent among the apostles and among the apostles who preceded him because they were among the seventy-two who were also called apostles (Luke 10:1)."[14] Let's briefly look at Luke's account. We tend to think of twelve disciples following Jesus, but as we have already seen (in chapter four of this book), there was a much larger group that followed Jesus, learned from him, and did ministry. In Luke's tenth chapter, Jesus appointed seventy disciples to go out in pairs from town to town. He said, "The harvest is plentiful, but the workers are few. Ask the Lord of the harvest, therefore, to send out workers into his harvest field. Go! I am sending you out like lambs among wolves" (Lk 10:2-3). They were meant to go out and cure the afflicted, proclaiming and embodying the coming kingdom (Lk 10:9). Jesus blesses them to serve as his own agents: "Whoever listens to you listens to me; whoever rejects you rejects me; but whoever rejects me rejects him who sent me" (Lk 10:16). Luke does not narrate exactly what happened in their dispersed ministry, just that they returned with joy that the demons submitted to their power (Lk 10:17).

Whenever I had read Luke 10 in my early studies of the Bible, I simply *assumed* Luke's "pairs" were all men. But it makes good sense that Jesus sent them out as married couples to minister well to both men and women. This would naturally follow Luke's own interest in the lives (and conversion) of women.[15] And, again, following Origen's logic, how else

---

[14]Translated and cited in J. Patout Burns, *Romans: Interpreted by Early Christian Commentators* (Grand Rapids, MI: Eerdmans, 2012), 385.

[15]William Klassen argues that the couple that Jesus talks to on the road to Emmaus (Lk 24) is Cleopas and his wife. This coheres with places in the Gospels where women are directly commissioned, such as Jn 4 (the Samaritan woman) and the resurrection accounts; see Klassen, "Musonius Rufus, Jesus, and Paul: Three First-Century Feminists," in *From Jesus to Paul: Studies in Honour of Francis Wright Beare*, ed. Peter Richardson and John C. Hurd (Waterloo: Wilfrid Laurier University Press, 1984), 185-206, at 198-200.

can we account for this senior couple (Andronicus and Junia) fitting the label of "apostles," except as part of this larger group? It may be that Origen also put together the fact that when Jesus "sent out" the seventy, Luke uses the word *apostellō* (Lk 10:1), which is the verbal form of the noun *apostolos*, "apostle"—that is, one who is sent out.

Think about it this way: while Paul called himself "least" and last of the apostles, the last one that Jesus appeared to after his resurrection (1 Cor 15:8-9), Paul was still considered an official apostle, the "thirteenth" apostle, as it were (1 Cor 9:1-2). Now, note that in Romans 16 Paul mentions Andronicus and Junia's *prior* conversion as a part of his commendation. In some way, he looked up to them. They held some form of seniority to him, as if *they* were part of an even *earlier* generation than him. It's hard for me to imagine that this did *not* imply that they walked with Jesus in his earthly ministry. Can you imagine that?

So I hope by now it seems clear that, with the support of patristic evidence, we can comfortably conclude that Paul was commending Andronicus and Junia *as* apostles, respected ministry leaders who were distinguished and remarkable among the *apostoloi*. But rarely have I seen a discussion reflecting on what exactly this couple *did* in ministry. Yes, they were "sent out," but sent out to do what? Above, we noted Theodoret's presumption that they were teachers, probably assuming that they were responsible for passing on the apostolic tradition as they shared the gospel (see 1 Cor 11:2). But the word *apostolos* itself (in the context of early Christianity) tends to imply taking the good news of Jesus Christ out into the world, as Paul and Peter did.[16] The closest concept we have to this today, I suppose, would be church planting (see 1 Cor 3:6). But the *apostoloi* would be a more organized and centrally dispatched group of church-planting leaders sent to share the gospel and establish flourishing communities of believers. Now, what would distinguish Andronicus and Junia among the *apostoloi*? Perhaps it was their "success," though I doubt Paul measured faithfulness by numbers. More likely, what brought Junia and Andronicus repute was their courage and resilience in the face of

---

[16]See Elisabeth Schüssler Fiorenza, "Missionaries, Apostles, Coworkers: Romans 16 and the Reconstructions of Women's Early Christian History," *Word & World* 6, no. 4 (1986): 420-33.

persecution and resistance. Paul tells us they got themselves in trouble, such that they landed in prison because of their ministry (we will go into more detail on that below). Almost certainly it was this intrepid, "do-or-die" faith that impressed Paul and his ministry colleagues. Combine this and the fact that this couple walked with the earthly Jesus, and we can see that, of anyone we meet in the New Testament, these two were probably Paul's heroes, models of the faith for him. And as fellow Jews, as Paul points out, they were like his spiritual "auntie and uncle."

JUNIA IN CHAINS: PRISONER OF JESUS CHRIST

The final piece I want to discuss in this last section on Junia is the often neglected and underappreciated comment by Paul that she and Andronicus were fellow prisoners with Paul. There are so many questions raised by this comment that are not answered in Romans: Why were they in prison? Where? Were they together with Paul? How did they get released? Though we are given very little information, it is worth slowing down to consider the kinds of situations and circumstances that stand behind this short comment.[17]

War captives. The first thing that would strike the reader of Paul's letter to the Romans is the Greek word he uses for "prisoner." Here he does not use the more basic term *desmios*, which refers to the chains of incarceration (see Philem 1, 9; cf. Acts 27:1, 42). Rather, he uses the word *synaichmalōtos*, which is often translated in academic scholarship as "prisoner of war." In modern usage, "prisoner of war" often implies that the incarcerated is captured military personnel, but *synaichmalōtos* simply refers to a war captive, military or civilian. So, to avoid confusion, I prefer the translation "war captive." In any case, it is a term that is used for people conquered and taken captive by a foreign enemy.[18] What is interesting about Paul's use of this word (Rom 16:7; Phil 1:23; Col 4:10) is that it is metaphorical. The apostles were not fighting in an actual war

---

[17]For a more advanced and detailed discussion, see Nijay K. Gupta, "Reconstructing Junia's Imprisonment: Examining a Neglected Pauline Comment in Romans 16:7," *Perspectives in Religious Studies* 47, no. 4 (2020): 385-97.

[18]See Aristeas 23; *Psalms of Solomon* 2.6; Lk 21:24.

against Romans and Greeks. Nor were they technically captured as plunder. Paul probably chose this language to represent frontline ministry as a kind of spiritual battleground that was full of danger. But given the number of occasions when Paul *did* end up in a real prison, we can assume that he and Andronicus and Junia were in fact taken into Roman custody and that Paul was *interpreting* these events spiritually.

Junia's crimes. Very few scholars have engaged with an important question: For what sort of crime would someone like Junia end up in prison? Roman prisons weren't the sort of place where one was sent for petty crimes, especially in the case of women. Our best understanding is that for minor infractions in the Roman world, women would be handed over to their husbands or fathers to be punished and shamed.[19] For that reason, we have precious little information about the presence and treatment of women in ancient prisons. But before getting into that, let's imagine what kinds of crimes might land someone like Andronicus or Junia in prison.

When we look at "higher crimes" in Roman law, we can rule out things that Paul would never commend and these leaders would never do: robbery, theft, murder, and so on. When we eliminate, as well, other crimes that would result in execution (like treason), we are left with a couple of legitimate possibilities—namely, civil disturbance and inciting a riot.[20] I am reminded of the "disturbance" in Ephesus that Luke narrates in Acts 19:23-41. Local businessmen who sold local religious goods were upset by Paul's ministry that saw many turn to the Lord and the Way and then repudiate their local gods and their trappings. At the battle cry of "Great is the Artemis of the Ephesians!" these enraged locals whipped up a mob and hunted down Paul and his companions. The frenzied crowd would not listen to reason, and a local man named Alexander warned them that there would be trouble if the authorities arrived to

---

[19]See Jane F. Gardner, *Women in Roman Law and Society* (London: Routledge, 2015), 5-30; Craig S. Wansink, *Chained in Christ: The Experience and Rhetoric of Paul's Imprisonments* (Sheffield: Sheffield Academic Press, 1996), 55.

[20]For a look at Roman crimes and imprisonment, see Brian Rapske, *The Book of Acts and Paul in Roman Custody*, The Book of Acts in First Century Setting 3 (Grand Rapids, MI: Eerdmans, 1994), 41-42; cf. T. J. Cadoux, "The Roman Carcer and Its Adjuncts," *Greece and Rome* 55, no. 2 (2008): 202-21.

disperse the mob and settle the din: "If there is anything further you want to bring up, it must be settled in a legal assembly. As it is, we are in danger of being charged with rioting because of what happened today. In that case we would not be able to account for this commotion, since there is no reason for it" (Acts 19:39-41). In that particular situation the uproar died down (Acts 20:1), but certainly on other occasions Paul and his companions were rounded up and questioned, perhaps even incarcerated. Indeed, later in Acts, Paul is found in Jerusalem, accused of defying Jewish law and desecrating the holy place (Acts 21:27-28). Again, a mob was whipped up, but this time Paul was arrested and put in chains. Now, Paul was eventually released, but he was questioned and beaten first. These scenarios help us imagine how someone like Paul or Andronicus or Junia could wind up in prison for their ministry work.

Conditions of Roman prisons. Now, the first thing to know about Roman prisons is that incarceration was not itself a sentence or form of punishment. That is, no judge or magistrate gave the convicted a certain prison sentence like "thirty years" or "life." Prisons, or places of confinement and custody, were designed to hold the accused in one location until sentencing and punishment.[21] Having said that, though, Roman prisons were often described (in histories, personal accounts, and novels) as dark, dank, disgusting, and dangerous. The Roman statesman Cicero famously described prison this way: "There is the darkness—the chains—the prison—the tortures of being shut up, of being shut off from the sight of parent and child, nay, from drawing free breath and looking upon the common light of day; from such evils escape may well be bought with life itself."[22]

Prisoners were thrown into overcrowded rooms where disease and suffocation were common threats. Some prisoners died during their confinement on account of beatings and torture, but others met an early fate on account of the grotesque conditions. Libanius grimly confesses, "No one comes out [of prison]—or precious few, at least—though many go in. They are doubly afflicted, by the actual imprisonment and by the

---

[21]See Robert Jewett, *Romans: A Commentary*, Hermeneia (Minneapolis: Fortress, 2006), 962-63.
[22]Cicero, *Against Verres* 2.5.9.

manner of it."[23] One more factor to consider is the famous metal shackles worn by the prisoners. It was widely known that the prison chains were large and heavy, such that they would cut into the skin and cause infections and scars.[24] The Roman satirist Juvenal joked that iron workers found themselves so busy manufacturing prison chains that they were constantly running a shortage on farming equipment.[25]

As hard as it is to read about these horrible conditions for the incarcerated, it is helpful to paint a vivid picture of what the apostles were constantly facing. Of course there were occasions where they were in prison briefly or merely under "house arrest." But at least on some occasions they did face more serious criminal accusations and thus did "hard time." And I would imagine when Paul used the term (*syn*)*aichmalōtos* (war captive), this reflected just such situations.

Women prisoners. As mentioned, we have scant information about the experiences of women in prison. As far as we can tell, few women populated Roman prisons. The rare bit of information we have tells us that their lives were in grave danger and their bodies vulnerable. Unlike in modern Western prisons, in the ancient world women were not confined separately from the men. They were all together. Women were fearful of sexual violence and abuse, victimized by both other prisoners and guards.[26] In *The Passion of Perpetua and Felicity*, an ancient Christian text (ca. 200), we read about the martyrdom of well-to-do Perpetua and a slave named Felicitas. Part of the story is a kind of diary entry from Perpetua, who describes the darkness of the prison, stocks, the heat and overcrowded conditions, and mistreatment by the guards. Under these kinds of circumstances, one would imagine that women in the Roman world would avoid prison at all costs. If prison conditions were difficult for men, all the more for women thrown into that population.

Prisoner Junia. So, as we turn our thoughts again to Junia, it is indeed a significant thing for Paul to mention that she spent time in prison for

---

[23]Libanius, *Orations* 45.8.

[24]Plutarch, *Moralia* 165E.

[25]Juvenal, *Satires* 3.309-11.

[26]Roman historian Suetonius talks about the poor treatment of young girls (virgins) who were sometimes raped in prison before execution (*Life of Tiberius* 61.5).

the sake of the gospel. Obviously, she survived her prison time and was let go at some point, but who knows what she went through in prison. The *fact* of her surviving prison time is amazing in itself. Add to that the fact that she apparently returned to apostolic ministry (such that she was commended by Paul and sent greetings). If Andronicus and Junia left prison and engaged in the same (dangerous) ministry as before, they were opening themselves up to the possibility of incarceration again—an even riskier endeavor for a woman.

JUNIA FOR TODAY

In the past few decades, numerous academic studies, as well as some more popular works, have given attention to Junia as a key figure in early Christianity. There has been a general recovery of her female sex and her apostolic ministry. In this chapter I have also tried to reckon with her sacrifices for the gospel mission, which include enduring imprisonment. As Junia was almost certainly part of Jesus' earthly ministry and sent out by Jesus himself in mission, I have confidence that Paul regarded Junia as one of his heroes, a "senior" mentor in the faith along with Andronicus. And what in particular did Paul admire about Junia? I believe it would be her courage and faith to work on the frontline of God's worldwide mission of spreading the good news, work that can easily get you in trouble. Where we might stay in our comfortable homes and neighborhoods, Junia ventured out into the world because people needed to hear about Jesus.

In order for Junia to have been rounded up for questioning and confinement, she had to have been out and about in public. Had she been operating only privately among women, I doubt this would have gotten the attention of the Roman authorities. If she was imprisoned alongside Andronicus (and perhaps with Paul as well), she must have been regarded as a threat to the public order. She must have known the risks. She must have heard stories from others (or witnessed for herself) how believers who incited disturbances could get themselves into serious trouble. But she did this dangerous ministry work anyway. And even when she faced the consequences, she dusted herself off and got right back out there. That is an inspiring testimony of God's indescribable grace and of Junia's amazing faith.

Conclusion

Putting It All Together

It is time now to wrap up and take stock of our study of women in the history of God's redemptive work, especially in the ministry of the early churches in the Roman world. We will reflect on five key ideas and themes developed in this book.

God's People Have Needed Wise, Faithful, and Brave Women from the Beginning

We started with the Israelite judge and prophet Deborah—rather than with the traditional approach of talking about Genesis and the creation stories—because we can talk theory and theology all day, but I find it incredibly clarifying to look at specific *people* in God's good news story, and how the biblical writers actually reflect on those people. And when people say, "Women can't" or "Women shouldn't," I say, "But Deborah did!" She judged wisely. She held steadfastly to God's prophetic direction and promptings. She modeled courage in Israel's clash with its enemies. And she was not alone, as if some kind of exception to the "rule" of patriarchy and the superiority of male wisdom and leadership. We could easily pivot to another highlighted woman in Scripture: Mary, the mother of Jesus. Luke 1 finds the action in a setting quite the opposite of Deborah's, away from Israel's high court, away from the battlefield and the war room. Luke shines the spotlight on a humble teenage girl visiting her cousin in the Judean hill country. Despite these opposing circumstances and settings, Mary and Deborah have a lot in common. Both are favored by God. Both are found living, pondering, and acting without much mention of their husbands. Both sing richly theological songs of divine triumph. Deborah had a hard job, no doubt about that. But Mary might just have the biggest burden on her shoulders of any Israelite in the whole Bible. What faith and courage, hope and perseverance, patience and resilience must have been required for her to bear, raise, and follow this special child?

For too many years, I neglected the stories of such women in the Bible. I am willing to take responsibility for that. I treated the Bible as a man's world, where women were just supporting characters. I hid them. I hid them from myself, and eventually I hid them from others. But now I realize that God inspired, gifted, and held women responsible for fortifying the life of his people. Whether in the home with the children, in the hill country in song and verse, in the high court of the land giving judgment, or at the tomb memorizing angelic instructions, women populate Scripture as examples of faith and obedience.

WOMEN OF ALL KINDS ENCOUNTERED JESUS AND HIS PEOPLE

Another thing to notice in the Bible is how Jesus interacted with women. He did not treat it as a scandal to converse with women in close contact, even in spite of what others might think or say. He accepted invitations of hospitality from women. He sometimes listened patiently to their pain. He had theological discussions with women. He received care from them. He talked about their everyday lives in some of his parables. He healed them of diseases and cast out demons to free them from bondage. He encouraged those women who wanted to follow him.

Put simply, women were an important part of Jesus' earthly life and ministry. And this did not change after he ascended. We see Paul share the gospel with a group of women he encountered in Philippi. Lydia came to faith in Jesus and became a Christian leader and patron. For one reason or another, women found this Jesus faith attractive, perhaps even empowering, so much so that Christianity eventually developed a reputation for recruiting devotees from the ranks of slaves, women, and children, groups that Roman elites considered thoughtless and gullible.[1] Of course, that is not why the apostles and early Christian missionaries preached to women and slaves. They did so because the gospel is beautifully blind to privileging people on the basis of sex and status. The church could not be a gentlemen's club or for citizens only. And I believe they subscribed to a "blind demographic" form of leadership, meaning that qualifications for leadership were not limited to Jewish ethnic heritage, a specific age standard, or males only (like the Jewish priesthood). This did not eradicate sex, but those differences had no bearing on legitimacy for serving God's people and God's gospel mission as leaders and teachers.

PAUL PREACHED HARMONY BETWEEN MEN AND WOMEN IN THE HOME AND THE CHURCH

It is easy to walk away from "prohibition" passages in the New Testament with the (mistaken) impression that the apostles were constantly trying to put women in their place below men in the pecking order of leadership in the home and the church (see my discussion in the section "What About . . . ?" at the end of this book). The fact that no two prohibition texts are exactly the same—and some of them have very odd and cryptic (to us now) language (1 Cor 11; 1 Tim 2)—indicates that these appear to be situation-specific teachings. Also, they have more to do with harmony and unity in the church, and less to do with "gender roles." If Paul believed in separate spheres (women in the home, men at work and leading the church) and genderized roles, he was a living contradiction. He sent Phoebe *away from home* to do apostolic work on his behalf. He instructed Nympha to take responsibility for having the Colossian letter read (and presumably also obeyed) by her church. He partnered with Prisca and Aquila in city-to-city missionary work, treating them as equals in leadership. In fact, there is good reason to believe *she* was the more active partner in ministry.

---

[1] This is famously expressed by an early opponent of Christianity named Celsus; the theologian Origen summarizes and refutes the arguments of Celsus in his work *Against Celsus* (see 3.44).

I think when we are reading situation-specific advice from Paul related to conflict between men and women, we are not always thinking about *why* these matters arise and therefore must be addressed. It seems like more than one community in the early Christian world wrestled with a "battle of the sexes" for one reason or another. Paul's primary goal was not submission of one group, or supremacy of another. At the end of the day, he wanted mutual care and respect and harmony. When we remove these controversial passages from their respective contexts, it is all too easy to create a gender-roles handbook, but we do so at too great a price. We must ask, *What was going on? How does Paul respond? And what aspects of his instruction can legitimately be universalized for all God's people in all places at all times?* That is not to say there can be no "timeless takeaways" from Paul's letters. There very much can be. But these questions must be asked, properly discussed and answered, and then applied with fear and trembling.

PAUL RELIED ON NUMEROUS WOMEN LEADERS AS COWORKERS IN THE GOSPEL MISSION

We began this book by talking about the figures mentioned in Romans 16, and it is an appropriate occasion to reflect on them again at the close. I'd barely have known who Phoebe was twenty years ago, let alone Tryphaena and Tryphosa. But reading and studying the catalog of people Paul commends in that chapter, especially the several women, has completely reshaped my mental image of early Christian communities and their leadership and ministry dynamics. Paul talks about these women in a way that suggests he actually knows them. This is not just a roster; it's an honor roll. These women were *ministers*. They labored in ministry, they traveled, they networked, they taught, they used strategic resources at their disposal, and they risked their necks for the gospel cause. If we counted heads at early church "leadership summits," yes, men would outnumber women. That is without question. But my point is this: women were there, when we so often imagine that they weren't. And they weren't there as some sort of initiative on diversity, or to get a "woman's perspective." Paul doesn't use gender-specific stereotypes for how women exercise influence and leadership in contrast to men. They all work and labor for the same cause. It would have made sense that women were in a strategic position to minister to other women, and men to men. But it doesn't seem like there were walls built to separate men and women from engaging each other. In fact, Paul seems to have especially relied on widows as independent leaders with much to bring to ministry and mission—which brings us to our next point.

INDEPENDENTLY POWERFUL WOMEN EXISTED IN THE ROMAN WORLD—AND IN THE EARLY CHURCHES TOO

An important part of our conversation in this book involves making sense of how some women could wield great influence and occupy positions of prominence in a patriarchal society. One factor is social status and class, hence *class* patriarchy. While the dynamics of patriarchy could and did suppress the opportunities for women to experience rights, privileges, and benefits available to men, there is another sociocultural "layer" on the grid of Roman society that allowed women to navigate through the cracks, so to speak, toward more power and influence. Women could even operate independently, or with a large amount of freedom, in certain circumstances. It's not enough to say, then, that the "biblical world" was a man's world, and our job today as Christians is to turn the clock back to the good ol' days. Women did not experience equality in every way, shape, or form, and sexism, misogyny, and violence against women were pervasive. We should be clear and honest about that. But independently powerful women did exist, women like Plancia Magna of Perge, Junia Theodora of Corinth, and Eumachia of Pompeii.

One could easily say, "That was the pagan world, but God's people are called to a separate gender ethic." Now, there is a point to be made there. I am *not* saying about the early churches that the apostles and ministry leaders simply assimilated to whatever trends and conventions were fashionable in society. We know Christians were radically countercultural when it came to repudiating privileges based on ethnicity, elite social status, or wealth. Christians rejected prostitution and the common practice of infant abandonment. So, in theory, the earliest Christians could have said no to Rome's allowance of women holding positions of influence and power. But what we *actually* see in the Pauline churches is the respect and promotion of women that is similar to wider Roman trends. The commendation of the Cenchreaen Phoebe, for example, is remarkably similar to honorific inscriptions praising (nearby) Corinthian Junia Theodora.

I am not sure how much of this, for the apostles, was very directly and intentionally decided from the beginning in respect to women and power. What might be more likely is that Paul and other leaders were encountering gifted women and then recognizing the work of God in them—and then they had to search the Scriptures, pray, and discuss what God was up to. No official encyclical or pronouncement was made about exactly what women could and couldn't do, but what we see is that women were recognized for their gifts and then supported in their ministries.

PAUL SAW NO DEFICIENCY OF INTELLECT, SKILL, OR MORALITY IN WOMEN

A crucial implication of the presence and affirmation of women in ministry is that Paul clearly saw no deficiency of intellect, skill, or morality in women *as* women. Correspondingly, Paul did not see men as inherently better leaders. This is important to point out, because if a church today decides to bar women from eldership, preaching, teaching, or pastoral leadership, I think the burden falls on them to explain why. It is not enough to say, "Go read 1 Timothy 2:11-15." Behind all the moral commands in Scripture are reasons and rationale. God doesn't give instructions and prohibitions without reason. The Ten Commandments forbid stealing because it is economically unfair. There is to be no adultery, because it destroys the marriage. If women ought not to preach, there has to be a reason. We can't just say, "It's a divine mystery." I do believe there are theological mysteries we will never fully understand. (How exactly does the trinitarian three-person-oneness of God work? What is the nature of Jesus' resurrection body?) But when it comes to social ethics and real life in the church together, we need to answer the *why* question. If someone tried to answer the question by saying, "Women are not very good at . . ." (or "not as good as men at . . ."), I would want to say, "Is that provable? Who decides? Is it true for all women? Most women? Some women? Is that deficiency ever present in men? A few? Some? Many?"

Let's look again at Phoebe: she was a strategic and important partner in Paul's ministry to Rome. Here is a situation where Paul was in or near Corinth, and he writes this massively long letter to the Roman churches. It is clearly an important communication. He expresses his gospel to a set of communities he has never met in person. He is concerned about how it will be received. He wants to get every jot and tittle right. He is not able to deliver it himself, so he has to entrust it to one of his co-workers. We have already talked about how Phoebe was almost certainly the letter carrier and the interpreter of the letter. In that role, any concerns and questions about Paul's letter from the listeners in Rome would naturally be directed at Phoebe. That's quite a responsibility. Paul had to put his trust in someone, and Phoebe is the person he chose. Corinth was a city that Paul was very familiar with, and there were probably numerous options for letter carriers (Stephanas, Gaius, Crispus, male leaders mentioned in 1 Corinthians). Phoebe may have *already* been going to Rome for other reasons, but even if that were the case, Paul's decision to use her as his apostolic proxy is significant. He could have sent a trustworthy man *with* her and her entourage, but as far as we can tell, he didn't.

What I have tried to do in this book is paint a more detailed and realistic picture of life in the first-century Roman world, including social dynamics in Pauline churches. Before I went to seminary, I had a particular image in my head of Christian homes and churches neatly divided into genderized roles, where men did the serious "theological" and executive work of leadership and ministry, and women assisted quietly in supportive roles. I would have assumed this paralleled the patriarchy of the wider ancient world. But things are not quite that simple. That mental image doesn't reflect a more complex reality of women's lives as recorded in inscriptions, personal letters, and other nonliterary documents—and as recorded in the Bible. Scientist Alfred Korzybski famously said, "The map is not the territory." His point was that we use and study maps, we become dependent on them for thinking about the world, but sometimes we lose sight of the fact that the map is not reality. The map is an overly simplified depiction to use as a tool. When you step foot on the land itself, the differences between map and territory become palpable. I hope this book has offered you a chance to step on territory where women lived, worked, laughed, cried, hoped, dreamed, gave, learned, taught, received ministry, wisely led, felt the shame and shackles of imprisonment for the sake of Jesus Christ, and reflected and shared Christ's gospel in the world. It is precisely these kinds of experiences that can help us become better theological cartographers.

What About . . . ?

This book is about the many women leaders of the early church who are talked about in the New Testament but who have not been remembered well by the church throughout time up to today. The focus has been on telling the stories of these women who "worked hard" (as Paul writes) in ministry and labored in the gospel mission. Where men have sometimes said, "Women can't," the Old and New Testaments testify: *they did.* That is the main message that I have tried to communicate. But I know that some readers will still wonder about the so-called prohibition texts that appear to prevent women from serving in ministry or seem to locate them under the authority of men. I never intended to ignore these important texts, but I didn't want to make them the foundation or center either. Here I add a "bonus section" to this book to explain how I understand some of these hotly debated and discussed passages and how they relate to the lives of the many women leaders talked about in the Bible and in this book. We will address two "what about" issues: What about Paul prohibiting women from teaching in the church in 1 Timothy 2? And what about the submission texts in the New Testament household codes?

What About Paul Prohibiting Women from Teaching in the Church?

We have seen how women were active in ministry in the early church, the apostolic era, and participated in every area of leadership. There was nothing that was "off limits." Women were not in the majority in leadership positions, of course, but neither were they entirely absent or excluded on theological grounds. This perspective, though, raises questions about how this can be squared with the so-called prohibition texts. In this chapter I will focus on the most important and (seemingly) most relevant one: 1 Timothy 2:11-15.[1]

1 TIMOTHY 2:11-15 IN CONTEXT

I desire, then, that in every place the men should pray, lifting up holy hands without anger or argument; also that the women should dress themselves modestly and decently in suitable clothing, not with their hair braided, or with gold, pearls, or expensive clothes, but with good works, as is proper for women who profess reverence for God. Let a woman learn in silence with full submission. I permit no woman to teach or to have authority over a man; she is to keep silent. For Adam was formed first, then Eve; and Adam was not deceived, but the woman was deceived and

---

[1]For an extensive discussion from the viewpoint of the Council of Biblical Manhood and Womanhood, see Andreas J. Köstenberger and Thomas R. Schreiner, ed., *Women in the Church: An Interpretation and Application of 1 Timothy 2:9-15*, 2nd ed. (Wheaton, IL: Crossway, 2016).

became a transgressor. Yet she will be saved through childbearing, provided they continue in faith and love and holiness, with modesty. (1 Tim 2:8-15 NRSV)

Here Paul[2] directs his protege Timothy regarding how he should handle serious problems in the Ephesian Christian community. The second chapter of Paul's first letter to Timothy concentrates on how the people in the church can put themselves in a godly posture to seek the welfare of all and work toward a common good. In 2:8-15 Paul first gives counsel for men to make peace and not be hostile to one another. Out of respect to God, they should worship as one (1 Tim 2:8). Next, Paul appeals to women in the church with a more extensive teaching (1 Tim 2:9-15). First, Paul addresses the need for humble and modest attire. Then he comments on their behavior in the church community. They should be calm, quiet, and respectful, especially toward the men who are present. Paul adds an argument from Scripture, namely that Eve fell into sin. But there is a path to redemption for women, "through childbearing" (1 Tim 2:15). The upshot of this passage, from one perspective (which I will refute), is that women ought to play no executive function in the church because they are gullible and hasty by nature, and their proper place is caring for family in the home.

But I will argue that a careful reading of this passage raises some important questions that challenge that common misreading. Why must women be silent? If women are especially prone to deception or gullible, why allow them to teach women, or even children for that matter (who cannot use more advanced discernment faculties in their tender age)? As

---

[2]The authorship of 1 Timothy is contested in Pauline studies. Suffice it to say, I take this to be a "genuine" letter from Paul in the sense that these are his own ideas and teachings to a real Timothy. Now, some of the writing style and vocabulary in 1 Timothy do not match up with letters like Galatians and 1 Corinthians, so I consider it possible that an associate of Paul (with his permission or in collaboration) helped craft the wording and influenced the style; see Luke Timothy Johnson, *The First and Second Letters to Timothy*, Anchor Yale Bible (New Haven, CT: Yale University Press, 2008); also Johnson's newer work, *Constructing Paul*, vol. 1 of *The Canonical Paul* (Grand Rapids, MI: Eerdmans, 2020), 19-92; cf. Gordon Fee, *1 and 2 Timothy, Titus*, New International Bible Commentary (Peabody, MA: Hendrickson, 1995), 23-26; Stanley E. Porter, "Pauline Authorship and the Pastoral Epistles: Implications for Canon," *Bulletin for Biblical Research* 5 (1995): 105-23.

for the creation story, wasn't Adam also a liability, letting sin come into the world through his transgressions (Rom 5:12-20)?

There is an even bigger problem that prevents this text from serving as a linchpin in the discussion about prohibiting women from authoritative leadership in the church: the Greek word translated as "have authority (over)" (*authenteō*) is an *extremely* rare word from antiquity, and it is genuinely unclear (and passionately debated) how one ought to understand and translate it. We will discuss this further below, but for now we can mention that scholars disagree about whether it has a neutral meaning of "have authority" or more of a negative meaning of "domineer" or "control (in an abusive way)." That makes a big difference in the interpretation and application of this text. Did Paul prohibit women from having any ecclesial authority over men in general, or more specifically from trying to domineer over men, to stick it to them or put them in their place, as it were?

To lay out all my cards on the table, I will offer my own understanding of this text and what Paul was trying to communicate to Timothy. Then I will talk through the key interpretive issues for this much-debated text.

Here is my reading of this text in short form. Paul instructed Timothy to shut down destructive patterns that were forming in the Ephesian community, fueled by outside false teaching that was making inroads in the church. Some Christian women were convinced that they held some superior wisdom and directly challenged the church's leaders (most or all of whom were men). Paul wanted to put a stop to "the battle of the sexes" in this community. Women who had fallen prey to false teaching should not disrupt the church gathering. Whoever carried that attitude that women have some leg up over men religiously ought to be reminded that Eve shares the blame in letting sin into the world. God is not honored when one group dominates another; rather, new creation is evident in men and women coming together in faith and love, showing humility, holiness, and self-restraint.

We need to stop treating this text as if it is something Paul taught to everyone everywhere. There are enough peculiarities in this passage to say that Paul needed to communicate this to *this* Ephesian community at *this*

time, and universalizing it should *not* be an unquestioned assumption.[3]
We will begin our discussion with a broader matter relating to Paul's letters
to Timothy (and Titus) as a whole: What kind of texts are these?

"PASTORAL EPISTLES"?

We know that in the ancient church the three epistles 1 Timothy,
2 Timothy, and Titus were circulated together to churches and appeared
together in canon lists, and that they have similarities in topics, style, and
argumentation. In that sense, they are a trio that belong together. But
they are often talked about today under the label "Pastoral Epistles,"
which was not specific terminology used by the early churches. The language of "Pastoral Epistles" dates back to the eighteenth century.[4] Now,
precursors for this can be found in Thomas Aquinas (thirteenth century),
who viewed these letters together as a kind of "pastoral rule." But before
that it is not clear these three letters were given some special status as
general guidance for church leadership. On the contrary, it would be
misleading and unwise to treat them as comprehensive instructions for
clergy or a universal guide for all churches. First Timothy and Titus do
give direction on virtues of Christian leaders, but much less so 2 Timothy.[5] Philip Towner calls for an end to the title "Pastoral Epistles," precisely because it is inaccurate and prevents each letter from being ap-
preciated for its individual context and argumentation.[6]

How does this relate to our discussion of 1 Timothy 2:11-15? If we take
the "Pastoral Epistles" as a kind of pastoral rule for all churches for all
times, we are bound to see this passage as universally relevant, as if this
was what Paul taught to all churches. Knowing that the early church did
not label these letters in that way helps us raise the question of whether
this was more of a generalized teaching or more of a situation-limited one.

---

[3]Craig S. Keener, *Paul, Women & Wives: Marriage and Women's Ministry in the Letters of Paul* (Peabody, MA: Hendrickson, 1992), 101.
[4]Attributed to P. Anton, *Exegetische Abhandlung der Pastoral-briefe Pauli an Timotheus und Titum*, ed. J. A. Maier (Halle: Waysenhaus, 1753-1755).
[5]See P. N. Harrison, *The Problem of the Pastoral Epistles* (Oxford: Oxford University Press, 1921), 15-16.
[6]Philip Towner, *Letters to Timothy and Titus*, New International Commentary on the New Testament (Grand Rapids, MI: Eerdmans, 2006), 88.

One important point to make along these lines is that 1 Timothy, far from being a one-size-fits-all ministry manual, is addressing a church dealing with rampant and destructive false teaching.[7] From the very start of the letter, Paul warns Timothy to be on his guard against heretical doctrines (1 Tim 1:3).[8] Paul mentions different features of the false teaching throughout the entire letter (1 Tim 1:3-7, 18-20; 4:1-3; 6:3-10, 20-21). We also know that women were a specific target of the false teachers (1 Tim 5:15), and that gender and marriage issues were a factor (1 Tim 4:3).

This, then, has bearing on whether 1 Timothy 2:8-15 is a universal leadership rule or a specific set of instructions targeted at a particular situation in Ephesus. First, we can say that if women not teaching men is a universal apostolic mandate, then why does Paul present it to his close friend and longtime ministry associate Timothy *as if* it is new information?[9] Paul would merely need to say, "Timothy, you know what we teach about women; enforce that here as well." But he offers such formal instruction, with particular supportive information, that it appears to be something he needs to explain to Timothy. The additional details about Adam and Eve would seem entirely unnecessary *if* Paul were simply repeating here doctrine he held always and everywhere. Second, the message to men is responsive to some issue in *this* particular Ephesian church, so it would make sense if the matter with women had the same circumstantial urgency.[10] Third, if we (today) are so apt to universalize 1 Timothy 2:12, then why do we not do so for Paul's commands in the same letter that young widows must remarry (1 Tim 5:14)?[11]

What I have said so far does not yet make a full case that 2:8-15 is a context-specific matter not to be universalized toward prohibiting women from having leadership roles over men. What I have tried to put

---

[7]See I. Howard Marshall, *New Testament Theology: Many Witnesses, One Gospel* (Downers Grove, IL: IVP Academic, 2004), 404.

[8]Gordon D. Fee, "The Great Watershed, Intentionality and Particularity/Eternality: 1 Timothy 2:8-15 as a Test Case," *Crux* 26 (1990): 31-37, at 32; Klyne Snodgrass, "A Case for the Unrestricted Ministry of Women," *The Covenant Quarterly* (2009): 26-44, at 37-39.

[9]Keener, *Paul, Women & Wives*, 112.

[10]Fee, *1 and 2 Timothy, Titus*, 70.

[11]Fee, *1 and 2 Timothy, Titus*, 77.

into question is the tendency to appeal to this text as a trump text for disallowing women from preaching and serving as teachers, pastors, or elders. Now I want to address the issues of "teaching" and what Paul meant in bringing this up.

THE NATURE OF "TEACHING" (*DIDASKŌ*) IN THE CHURCH

When Paul mentions "teaching" in this text, we need to be clear about what he is talking about and what he is not talking about. He is not talking about any and every kind of teaching (like reading, 'riting, and 'rithmetic). And he is probably not talking generically about teaching spiritual truths or even what we think of as Bible study. The language of *didaskō* within a church setting tends to focus on passing on foundational apostolic tradition related to the core truths of the gospel and the faith (1 Cor 4:17; Gal 1:12; Col 2:7; 2 Thess 2:15).[12] In the context of what was happening in Ephesus, the prohibition of women "teaching" appears to be a concern with someone stepping in to pass on a *new* kind of apostolic teaching, or one that deviates from what is part of the tradition.[13] Timothy was qualified to teach this tradition (1 Tim 4:11; 6:1). Others were as well, as long as they had been properly trained (2 Tim 2:2).

We get a hint from the letter to Titus about what might have prompted Paul to issue a warning of silence: "For there are many rebellious people, full of meaningless talk and deception, especially those of the circumcision group. They must be silenced, because they are disrupting whole households by teaching things they ought not to teach—and that for the sake of dishonest gain" (Titus 1:10-11). In *that* situation, some were spreading false teaching and had to be stopped. In the situation of 1 Timothy, it was *women* who were perpetuating false teaching, so that was who Paul was concerned about. Paul wasn't saying women shouldn't exercise their ministry gifts to form the church in wisdom and edification. He took for granted that women would prophesy in church

---

[12]Note that in Col 3:16 Paul talks about Christians "teaching" one another, which probably involves sharing spiritual insights and learning from one another, as we do today in a Bible study setting.

[13]See Towner, *Letters to Timothy and Titus*, 320.

(1 Cor 11:4-5), one of the most powerful spiritual gifts (1 Cor 13:2; 14:1-5). James D. G. Dunn argues that, since teaching is listed as a spiritual gift as well (Rom 12:7), prophecy and teaching bear some didactic similarities. Both depend on the Spirit for insight oriented toward their own context and assembly, for example. "Consequently the line between teaching and prophecy becomes very thin—the latter characterized more as new insight into God's will, the former more as new insight into old revelation."[14] Therefore, if Paul had no problem with women prophesying among the people (including men and women), why would he give a blanket prohibition against women teaching in the church?

Those who promote a patriarchal interpretation of 1 Timothy 2:11-15 sometimes make the argument that women cannot teach over men because they are prone to being deceived (Eve's original sin). There are two brief points to make about this (more on Eve below). First, if women struggle with discerning faithful teaching from false teaching, why let them teach other women? Were this the case, men should do *all* the teaching. Second, to go back to the Israelite judge Deborah, she arbitrated Israel's judicial cases, presumably requiring keen intellect and meticulous and wise interpretation of God's Word. Would Paul have allowed a woman like Deborah to teach with authority in a mixed setting in the church, in the way Deborah led the people of God in one of its darkest eras? It makes more sense, in this light, that Paul's teaching prohibition was local and limited, not generic and universal.

I want to make one more point here about women as teachers, this time drawing from one of the church fathers, Theodore of Mopsuestia (350–428). In his commentary on 1 Timothy, Theodore felt it necessary to explain this text *because* he thought it was awkward. In his explanation, he first affirms that female prophets were led by God to speak to the church, so he does not want to deny that women had much to offer to the people of God. Furthermore, he makes the important point that Paul desired and expected Christian women to teach the gospel to their

---

[14]James D. G. Dunn, *Romans 9–16*, Word Biblical Commentary 38B (Dallas: Word Books, 1988), 729. This seems to be corroborated by the close pairing of prophecy and teaching in 1 Cor 14:6: "revelation or knowledge or prophecy or teaching" (NRSV).

"godless husbands" (1 Cor 7:16). Paul issues the prohibition in 1 Timothy, Theodore reasons, because of teachings that might cause trouble and "disturbance" in the church community, not because women were deficient *in themselves* as teachers of the church.[15] Now, that does not make Theodore equivalent to a modern-day egalitarian when it comes to affirming women in ministry of the Word, but it does reinforce what we have said here that Paul was not placing a blanket judgment on women as teachers, as if there was some deficiency in their capabilities.

THE VERB *AUTHENTEŌ*—WHAT DOES IT MEAN?

One of the most discussed and debated elements of this passage pertains to what Paul meant when he referred to not allowing a woman to "have authority over a man" (1 Tim 2:12 NRSV). On face value, it would seem that this means women should not bear God-given leadership over men. But it is not quite as simple as that. The Greek word Paul uses here, *authenteō*, is an extremely rare word in this time period, so much so that it is not clear *why* Paul used this word, and it very well could carry a more negative connotation—note how Eugene Peterson paraphrases it: "I don't let women take over and tell men what to do" (MSG). From that perspective, Paul wasn't forbidding women from having *any* authority over men; he was preventing women from trying to domineer over men, as it would appear was happening in the Ephesian church in this particular situation.

This might seem like a slippery argument, to say that we should take the word *authenteō* in a negative sense and read it within the limits of a particular contextual problem in ancient Ephesus. But consider this: the King James Bible (in the early seventeenth century) translated *authenteō* as "usurp authority over the man," taking this verb with a negative meaning. In fact, that has been a more historical approach to the meaning of this verb until the late twentieth century. For example, Linda Belleville has traced a unified reading of this verb through the centuries:

---

[15]See Theodore of Mopsuestia, *The Commentaries on the Minor Epistles of Paul*, trans. Rowan A. Greer, Writings from the Greco-Roman World (Atlanta: SBL Press, 2010), 559.

Erasmus (1519): "usurp authority"

Geneva (1560): "Usurpe authority"

Webster (1833): "usurp authority"

Fenton (1917): "dominate"

Goodspeed (1923): "domineer"

Williams (1937): "domineering"

Spanish UBS (1966): *dominar*[16]

So, what changed? In the 1980s, a few scholars produced articles questioning conventional translations of *authenteō*.[17] The argument was made that, while *authenteō* may have had a negative connotation at one point in history, over time it came to be used in a more neutral way.[18] This is actually true, but that progression is not reflected in the New Testament period, but rather centuries later. Comparative examples of word usage should ideally come from the same time period. If you can't find the exact same word form in the same century or close time period, it is helpful to look at cognates, word forms built on the same word root (i.e., part of the same word family). It is hard to find occurrences of the verb *authenteō* from the time of Paul, but we *do* have a few occurrences of other forms. So, for example, the noun form (*auntenēs*) appears in the Jewish text Wisdom of Solomon 12:6: "and *murderous parents* who kill innocent lives, you willed to destroy by the hands of our fathers" (my translation). Similarly, the Jewish philosopher Philo of Alexandria (contemporary with the apostles) used the same noun with the meaning "murderer."[19] This reinforces the negative connotation of the verb *authenteō* used in 1 Timothy.

---

[16]See Linda Belleville, "Lexical Fallacies in Rendering *authentein* in 1 Timothy 2:12: BDAG in Light of Greek Literary and Non-Literary Usage," *Bulletin for Biblical Research* 29, no. 3 (2019): 317-41, 318.

[17]See esp. George Knight, "*AYΘENTEΩ* in Reference to Women in 1 Timothy 2:12," *New Testament Studies* 30 (1984): 143-57; Leland E. Wilshire, "The TLG Computer and Further Reference to *Authenteō* in 1 Tim 2:12," *New Testament Studies* 34 (1988): 120-34.

[18]See Wilshire, "*Authenteō* in 1 Tim 2:12," 131.

[19]Philo, *That the Worse Attacks the Better* 78.

So, what exactly does *authenteō* mean? Cynthia Long Westfall has conducted the most thorough and up-to-date study of this verb and has come to this insightful conclusion:

> In the Greek corpus, the verb [*authenteō*] refers to a range of actions that are not restricted to murder or violence. However, the people who are the targets of these actions are harmed, forced against their will (compelled), or at least their self-interest is overridden, because the actions involve the imposition of the subject's will over against the recipient's will, ranging from dishonor to lethal force.[20]

It is a mistake, she goes on to say, to pretend that this is a positive verb regarding the exercise of authority, such that it might refer to servant leadership or pastoral care. It is about *overpowering* someone or something else for one's own advantage or gain. Westfall further supports her case by noting that Paul does not go on to say, "Rather, men should *authenteō* over women."[21] This verb expresses abuse of power, not neutral or positive use of power.

Think about it this way: Paul had over a dozen words to choose from in Greek that carry the meaning "govern" or "have authority" with a positive or neutral value.[22] Why would he choose *authenteō*, which is exceptionally rare, when he could have chosen a more common word for positive authority? Let's illustrate this with an example. There are about five uses of *authenteō* (other than 1 Tim 2:12) from around the time of the New Testament.[23] Unless you are engaged in translation work, it's hard to understand just how rare that is. Imagine you are testing a new product out, and you have just five people you can test it on—surely that is not enough of a sample. The more, the better, and you would prefer

[20]Cynthia Long Westfall, *Paul and Gender: Reclaiming the Apostle's Vision for Men and Women in Christ* (Grand Rapids, MI: Baker Academic, 2016), 242; see also her important (and very technical) article "The Meaning of *authenteō* in 1 Timothy 2.12," *Journal for the Study of Greco-Roman Christianity and Judaism* 10 (2014): 138-73.

[21]Westfall, *Paul and Gender*, 294.

[22]Some of the most commonly used words relating to authority and power are *exousia, dynamis, epitagē, epitropē, kyrieuō, archē, poimainō, ēgemonia/ēgemoneuō*.

[23]Philodemus, *Rhetorica* 2.133; BGU 1208.38 (Letter from Tryphon); Aristonicus Alexandrinus, *De signis Iliadis* 9.694; Ptolemy, *Tetrabiblos* 3.13.10; Moeris Atticista, *Lexicon Atticum*; see Jamin Hübner, "Translating *authenteō* in 1 Timothy 2:12a," *Priscilla Papers* 29, no. 2 (2015): 16-26.

hundreds, if not thousands. Translators feel the same; they want hundreds of occurrences of a word to really get a grasp on its meaning in a particular time period. So, with only a handful of occurrences of *authenteō*, there just isn't much to work with.

One of the most common words in Greek is *kai*, which means "and." It occurs approximately 500,000 times in all existing ancient Greek texts (from Homer to Herodotus and beyond). Let's take a somewhat common word, *anthrōpos*, which means "person." We find about 15,000 occurrences. The most common word for authority in the ancient world is *exousia*, which appears about 1,500 times in Greek literature. What about *authenteō*? If we tried to include the maximum number from antiquity, we would come up with about five to twelve (there is some debate on which occurrences are considered legitimate). That is pretty much the definition of a rare word. We need to ask, Why would Paul opt for an exceptionally rare verb (*authenteō*) for such an important statement, if there were other similar terms that were far more familiar and commonplace? He would have no reason to do that— *unless* it had a special nuance or connotation that necessitated its usage. Rare circumstances lead to more specialized terminology.

When people say, "First Timothy 2:12 offers 'clear teaching' that women can't preach or teach men in the church," I like to use this illustration: Imagine you use a word today—let's call it *frundify* (I just made that up). Now imagine that you have never said it before, you've never seen it written, you've never heard anyone else say it. Now imagine you will never see it, hear it, or say it again for the rest of your life. That is the kind of rarity we are dealing with when it comes to *authenteō*. It simply *can't* mean "have authority" in a neutral or positive sense. It stretches logic too far and doesn't fit how interpreters from the ancient world and most of the modern world have read the word. It is much more likely that Paul was appealing to a relatively rare word that carries a sense of abuse of power to prohibit women (who had succumbed to false teaching) from taking over the church and seeking to put men "in their place." It would make sense that Paul put his foot down on this matter, encouraged Timothy to put a stop to this, and imposed strict standards on a church going through major turmoil.

WHAT WAS GOING ON IN EPHESUS?

Our task now is to consider the situation on the ground in Ephesus that
may have led to Paul's prohibition of women trying to overpower male
teachers in the church. This is an important consideration, because
some might think it outlandish that "way back then" in a "patriarchal"
world women might attempt such a coup. But a couple of theories have
been put forward that are plausible and grounded in legitimate historical and cultural information from the ancient Roman world.

"New women"—a women's liberation movement? Several scholars
have made a case for the rise of a new social movement in the first-
century Roman Empire, a kind of women's sexual liberation.[24] According to the theory of classical scholars Elaine Fantham, Helene
Peet Foley, Natalie Boymel Kampen, Sarah B. Pomeroy, and H. Alan
Shapiro, in the late Roman Republic women of wealth and status were
emboldened to freely attend social gatherings where it was not socially appropriate for them to appear previously. These women
wanted to express their sexuality more freely, especially at parties.
Fantham and her colleagues propose that this came about as husbands went away for war, leaving wives free from their watchful gaze.
Furthermore, at this time women were able to experience more financial independence from their husbands. And perhaps there was a
motivation of "payback": "Unless women had learned chastity as a
moral imperative they might claim for themselves the self-indulgence
practiced by their husbands."[25]

Roman historian and politician Sallust (86–35 BC) pointed to a
high-class married woman, Sempronia, as a model of the Republic's
"crumbling morals."[26] Sallust claims that Sempronia was

[24]See Bruce W. Winter, *Roman Wives, Roman Widows: The Appearance of New Women and the
Pauline Communities* (Grand Rapids, MI: Eerdmans, 2003); Carolyn Osiek and Margaret Y. Mac-
Donald, with Janet H. Tulloch, *A Woman's Place: House Churches in Earliest Christianity*
(Minneapolis: Fortress, 2006), 23; Elaine Fantham et al., *Women in the Classical World* (Oxford:
Oxford University Press, 1995), 280-93; R. A. Bauman, *Women and Politics in Ancient Rome*
(London: Routledge, 1992).
[25]Fantham et al., *Women in the Classical World*, 289.
[26]Victoria E. Pagan, *A Sallust Reader* (Mundelein, IL: Bolchazy-Carducci, 2009), 43.

able to play the lyre and dance more skillfully than an honest woman should, and having many other accomplishments which minister to voluptuousness. But there was nothing which she held so cheaply as modesty and chastity. Her desires were so ardent that she sought men more often than she was sought by them. . . . She was a woman of no mean endowment; she could write verse, bandy jests and use language which was modest or tender or wanton.[27]

A similar cultural concern was expressed by other ancient writers in the Roman world like Cicero and Plutarch.[28] This seems to correspond with new legislation imposed by Augustus regarding marriage. Laws cracked down on adulterous behavior of married women. Caesar Augustus punished his own daughter for adultery, and he exiled the poet Ovid for supporting this moral decay with his love poetry.

Philip Towner, who has written one of the leading 1 Timothy commentaries, considers it plausible that this "new women" movement became a problem for the early churches precisely in places like Ephesus. This could account for Paul's concern with immodest apparel and the flouting of traditional Roman family values.

This text [1 Tim 2:9-10] addresses a group of wealthy women (probably wives for the most part) for whom respectability and regard for an approved dress code (apparel, hairstyles, jewelry, respectable demeanor) were apparently not high on the agenda. . . . Paul was faced with cultural development influencing the behavior of well-to-do Christian women in worship that posed a risk to the church's public image.[29]

The advantage of this approach to the situation behind 1 Timothy 2:8-15 is that it accounts for the apostolic teachings about dress, modesty, and piety. What is less clear is how it relates to the false teaching, except perhaps that false teachers preyed on wealthy women in particular.

Ephesian Artemis—patron goddess of female empowerment? Another approach to the situation in Ephesus relates to the patron deity of

---

[27]Sallust, *Catiline* 25; translation from Bruce W. Winter, "The 'New' Roman Wife and 1 Timothy 2:9-15," *Tyndale Bulletin* 51, no. 2 (2000): 285-94, at 288.
[28]Cicero, *Letters to Atticus* 6.1.24-25; Plutarch, "Advice to Bride and Groom," *Moralia* 139-40.
[29]Towner, *Letters to Timothy and Titus*, 196.

the city, Artemis (also known as Ephesian Artemis). The people of
Ephesus worshiped many gods, including the high Olympians, but Artemis had a special connection to the city, as Jerome Murphy-O'Connor
explains: "Artemis permeated the consciousness of the Ephesians to the
point that it was a rock-bottom element in their collective and individual
identities."[30] According to legend, she was born nearby and watched over
the city.[31] Ephesians hailed her as greatest of all deities, hence Acts 19:28:
"Great is Artemis of the Ephesians!"[32] The ancient writer Himerios reported, "When the leader of the Muses divided all the earth beneath the
sun with his sister, although he himself dwells among the Greeks, he
appointed that the inheritance of Artemis would be Ephesus."[33] Ephesian
Artemis was associated with many things in antiquity. She was hailed a
virgin goddess.[34] Classically, she was conceived of as a master hunter who
kept company with wild animals. On coins she was often depicted as
riding on a chariot with four horses, and she was associated with other
creatures, such as a bee, a lion, and a stag.

Morna Hooker explains that in Asia Minor the worship of Artemis
fused with the worship of a god called Cybele (who was also associated
with wild animals).[35] The cult of Artemis in Ephesus was known for its
violent tendencies, like ritual killing.[36] And it promoted a message of
female empowerment, fixated as it was on this wild, warrior-like goddess.
This was influenced by the legend that Ephesus was founded by Amazonian women.[37] Ancient Greek geographer Strabo writes, "Who could

[30]Jerome Murphy-O'Connor, *St. Paul's Ephesus: Texts and Archaeology* (Collegeville, MN: Liturgical Press, 2008), 16.
[31]Strabo, *Geography* 14.1.20.
[32]Pausanias, *Description* 4.31.8. See Murphy-O'Connor, *St. Paul's Ephesus*, 16. Paul Trebilco notes that the Ephesian temple dedicated to Artemis was massive, four times the size of the Parthenon; see his discussion of Artemis in *The Early Christians in Ephesus from Paul to Ignatius* (Grand Rapids, MI: Eerdmans, 2007), 19-30.
[33]Murphy-O'Connor, *St. Paul's Ephesus*, 17.
[34]Xenophon, *Ephesian Tale* 1.2; Achilles Tatius 6.21.2.
[35]Morna D. Hooker, "Artemis of Ephesus," *Journal of Theological Studies* 64, no. 1 (2013): 37-46; see also Rick Strelan, *Paul, Artemis, and the Jews in Ephesus* (New York: de Gruyter, 1996), 91.
[36]See Aída Besançon Spencer, *1 Timothy*, New Covenant Commentary (Eugene, OR: Cascade Books, 2014), 16.
[37]See Strabo, *Geography* 11.5-34; cf. 12.3.21; Pausanius, *Guide* 7.2.6-9; 7.4.2-3; Pliny, *Natural History* 5.31.115.

believe that an army of women, or a city, or a tribe, could ever be organized without men, and not only organized, but even make inroads upon the territory of other people. . . . For this is the same as saying that the men of those times were women and that the women were men."[38] Murphy-O'Connor articulates the cultural deviation of this Amazonian origin tale: it is "all the more remarkable that a male-dominated world should have ascribed the founding of seven important cities to women who were not goddesses."[39] The fact that the Amazonian women were associated with both Artemis and Ephesus is demonstrated by the fact that statues of them were placed in Artemis's temple in the city.[40] This central focus on Artemis along with the origin legend of the Amazons gave the city a unique quality of female empowerment. Ancient Roman architect Vitruvius mentioned how the Artemis temple had a "feminine" look, various features made to look like the hair, body shape, or clothing of a woman.[41]

This could explain why Paul wrote to Timothy that he must intervene in a situation where Ephesian Christian women were trying to be domineering—not because they were striving for equality with the male leaders, but because they were trying to overpower them, influenced by a spirit of female strength. Aída Besançon Spencer summarizes this perspective well: "*Authenteō* [domineer, 1 Tim 2:12] might very well allude to the traditional destructive pagan feminine principle at Ephesus. . . . [Paul] was using *authenteō* . . . to describe destructive attitudes of the women toward the men, modeling themselves on Artemis, the 'slaughterer.'"[42]

It should be said that neither of these situational theories (new women, Ephesian Artemis) explains all the confusing bits of 1 Timothy 2:8-15. But each can offer a reasonable sense as to why Paul would issue such a strongly worded prohibition of women teaching (with a heavy hand) over men.

---

[38]Strabo, *Geography* 11.5-34.
[39]Murphy-O'Connor, *St. Paul's Ephesus*, 8.
[40]Pliny, *Natural History* 34.19.53.
[41]Vitruvius, *On Architecture* 4.1.5-8.
[42]Spencer, *1 Timothy*, 65; see a similar reading in I. Howard Marshall, *The Pastoral Epistles*, International Critical Commentary (London: T&T Clark, 2007), 441-42.

ADAM AND EVE

In 1 Timothy 2:13-14, Paul reinforces his teaching prohibition with an appeal to the story of Adam and Eve: "For Adam was formed first, then Eve; and Adam was not deceived, but the woman was deceived and became a transgressor" (NRSV). Sometimes, these verses are discussed as if Paul's mention of the creation stories is meant to demonstrate the universal application of his teaching about women and men. But this is only partly true. Yes, Paul's argument "from creation" is meant to carry weight and authority based on the actions that happened at the beginning of human history. But Paul may have been using the creation story to make a more limited point.

On the face of it, it might seem that Paul was saying this: *Adam was made first and therefore has superior authority. Eve was deceived, Adam was not, so she shouldn't have "taught" him.* But it is difficult to connect these pieces back to the situation in Ephesus that Paul was addressing. What does Adam's prior creation have to do with women teaching? And what does Eve's being deceived and her sin have to do with teaching? Are we to conclude that her sinful choice completely disqualifies all women from teaching men? Paul does not connect the dots by saying women can't be teachers because they were not created first. What *is* made explicit in these verses is that Eve fell prey to the serpent's snare and passed on its lie to Adam. Eve was not immune from accepting and propagating false teaching. This is directly relevant to the situation behind 1 Timothy, where women were the targets of false teaching. Paul wasn't offering a universal ban on women teachers because Eve was created second. He was humbling arrogant women teachers in Ephesus by reminding them that their foremother Eve was duped.

There is a danger in working too hard to universalize Paul's message about Adam and Eve. After all, Paul casts blame on Adam in other texts (Rom 5:12-21; 1 Cor 15:22). The point of calling out Eve's transgression was that she passed on information without adequate education and discernment, which is what Paul was concerned with in Ephesus as well.[43]

---

[43]Keener, *Paul, Women & Wives,* 116; cf. Towner, *Letters to Timothy and Titus,* 227.

As Klyne Snodgrass observes, the only other time Paul mentions the deception of Eve in his letters is also in the context of false teachers devastating the church (2 Cor 11:3).[44]

Linda Belleville makes an interesting suggestion that Paul's mention of the biblical creation story may have been a part of his strategy to counteract the Ephesian origin story where Artemis was born before her twin brother Apollos: "While some may have believed that Artemis appeared first and then her male consort, the biblical story states just the opposite. Adam was formed first, then Eve (v. 13). And Eve was deceived to boot (v. 14), hardly a basis on which to claim superiority."[45]

SAVED THROUGH CHILDBEARING?

The last piece of the puzzle that we should discuss here is Paul's note that "she will be saved through childbearing, provided they continue in faith and love and holiness, with modesty" (1 Tim 2:15 NRSV). There are some oddities to note here. Observe the shift from singular "she" (Eve?) to the plural "they" (Ephesian women?). More importantly, in what sense does Paul conceive of salvation "through childbearing"? Numerous theories have been proposed, without any clear consensus. Does this point forward from Eve to the birth of the Messiah (Gen 3:15)? Or does it mean women in general will be spared (i.e., not die) in labor (though obviously some Christian women still died in labor then and now)? Or is this about commitment to family life and rearing children? Paul's wording,

---

[44]Snodgrass, "Unrestricted Ministry," 38. It should also be pointed out that the reference to Eve here is in analogy to the whole church (men and women) succumbing to false teaching, not just the women. (Thank you to the anonymous reviewers of this book for reminding me of this contextual detail!)

[45]Belleville, "Lexical Fallacies," 339. Similarly, Sandra L. Glahn argues, "For Gentiles—the focus of Paul's ministry—the Genesis narrative was new. . . . In these Gentiles' [Artemesian] creation narrative, the woman came first, and that gave her preeminence as the first twin. Competition persisted between cities that worshiped one or the other of the twins, with Artemis's followers insisting she was superior because she was born first" ("The First-Century Ephesian Artemis: Ramifications of Her Identity," *Bibliotheca Sacra* 172 [2015]: 450-69, at 463). Glahn sums up Paul's Genesis counterargument in this way: "The female is not superior; Genesis proves it" (464). What we see in Paul's appeal to Genesis is not a generic appeal to gender roles based on creation principles but a "clash" of origins and how they shape social identity. Genesis was brought into the discussion not to prevent women from teaching anywhere and everywhere but to refute any justifications for women trying to overpower men.

unfortunately, is too concise and even a bit too cryptic for us to understand his meaning and how it relates to the flow of his argumentation and our knowledge of the situation in Ephesus. Given the emphasis on love, piety, and modesty in this passage, Gordon Fee is probably correct that Paul wanted Ephesian Christian wives to turn toward their husbands in affection and unity rather than to undermine or overpower them. Every Ephesian Christian woman was called on to be a "model, godly woman, known for her good works . . . includ[ing] marriage, bearing children, and keeping a good home."[46] Now, Paul wouldn't be calling for this in order to domesticate all women, encouraging them to cook, sew, and nurse rather than carry out leadership in the church. On the contrary, Paul worked with and supported many women leaders as colleagues. But here he was exhorting rebellious Christian women to care about their marriages and families, counteracting the destructive anti-marriage messages of the false teachers.[47]

Conclusion

What I see happening in 1 Timothy is that Paul was telling his colleague and apprentice Timothy to impose a kind of lockdown on the Ephesian church because of the infectious spread of a false teaching that especially preyed on women and made aberrant teachings about marriage. Women who had taken it upon themselves to overpower male leaders were told to step back and take the posture of learners rather than teachers. This was not because of some genderized deficiency in their mental, didactic, or leadership capacities. Teaching was a gift that could and should be nurtured. But because of a local "battle of the sexes" in Ephesus, bold restrictions were necessary to extinguish the false teaching and to help restore healthy relationships.

The bottom line for our purposes here is that Paul was not denying women the rights and roles of church leadership, and he wasn't even forbidding teaching. He was putting a stop to women promoting unsound doctrine and upsetting male and female relationships. Today, we

---

[46]Fee, *1 and 2 Timothy, Titus*, 75.
[47]Towner, *Letters to Timothy and Titus*, 234-35.

still have a lot of unanswered questions about 1 Timothy 2:11-15: What exactly does *authenteō* mean? Why appeal to Adam's prior creation? What does Paul mean by "childbearing"? The complexities and nuances of this dense passage should give us pause before stating that "the Bible clearly says." Some things in this passage are clear; others are not. And what we read here we should try to fit into a wider picture of Paul's ministry and teaching in which he was constantly engaging and working with women leaders who were exercising leadership, teaching, serving in evangelism, partnering in Paul's missionary strategy, and working on the frontiers of the gospel mission.

What About the Submission Texts in the New Testament Household Codes?

Whenever I teach on the subject of women leadership in the New Testament, inevitably there are questions about the New Testament "household codes" where submission language appears (Col 3:18–4:1; Eph 5:22–6:9; 1 Tim 2:8-15; 6:1-2; Titus 2:1–3:8; 1 Pet 2:18–3:7). How could Paul support and promote women leaders, specifically women teachers, when he told them to be submissive? How could women have any kind of executive power in the church if they could not hold such power in the home?

I have to admit that in my early years of Christian faith I could not reconcile these submission texts with any perspective that allowed women to exercise authority in the church. But I changed my mind about the seemingly prohibitory nature of these passages when I studied them in their historical context and paid more careful attention to what they say—and don't say—about women as members of households. While there are several passages of similar style and content related to this in the New Testament, we will use Colossians as our representative case study throughout this chapter.

COLOSSIANS 3:18–4:1

> Wives, submit yourselves to your husbands, as is fitting in the Lord.
> Husbands, love your wives and do not be harsh with them.
> Children, obey your parents in everything, for this pleases the Lord.

Fathers, do not embitter your children, or they will become discouraged.

Slaves, obey your earthly masters in everything; and do it, not only when their eye is on you and to curry their favor, but with sincerity of heart and reverence for the Lord. Whatever you do, work at it with all your heart, as working for the Lord, not for human masters, since you know that you will receive an inheritance from the Lord as a reward. It is the Lord Christ you are serving. Anyone who does wrong will be repaid for their wrongs, and there is no favoritism.

Masters, provide your slaves with what is right and fair, because you know that you also have a Master in heaven. (Col 3:18–4:1)

There is no getting around the fact that the terse commands and directives in these texts are very off-putting to read. It's not just about wives being submissive; Paul also tells slaves to obey their masters *in everything*. How could Paul, the great apostle of Christian liberty, write such conformist nonsense?[1] Well, before we succumb to the temptation to rip these passages out of our Bibles, we need to recognize that Paul was drawing from widely recognized social language from the Greco-Roman world about proper household management. Several ancient moral philosophers (like Aristotle and Seneca) addressed the proper way of running the household for the greater civic good.[2] The common pattern among these discourses is the threefold dynamic of husband/wife, parent/child, master/slave. These household statements are about power and control—who has the power, and how to maintain order in the house. This specific social construction does not trace back to the Old Testament or Hebrew tradition, it should be noted. Rather, it is grounded in ancient Greek philosophy regarding ideal human life and politics, the individual and the city.

---

[1]With a bit of cheek, Andrew Lincoln encourages those who find the household codes irritating to preach from the common lectionary. (The lectionary excludes these passages from their weekly readings!) Lincoln, "Colossians," in *New Interpreter's Bible*, vol. 11 (Nashville: Abingdon, 2000), 551-669.

[2]Aristotle, *Politics* 1.253-54; Dio Chrysostom, *Orations* 5.348-51; Seneca, *Epistles* 94.1; Dionysius of Halicarnassus, *Roman Antiquities* 2.25.4–26.4; see also Jewish writers Philo, *On the Special Laws* 2.224-41; Josephus, *Against Apion* 2.199-208.

THE GRECO-ROMAN HOUSEHOLD ECONOMY

In his highly influential *Politics*, Aristotle explains how social order should reflect human nature.

> Of household management we have seen that there are three parts: one is the rule of a master over slaves, . . . another of a father, and the third of a husband. A husband and father rules over wife and children, both free, but the rule differs, the rule over children being a royal, over his wife a constitutional rule. For although there may be exceptions to the order of nature, the male is by nature fitter for command than the female, just as the older and full-grown is superior to the younger and more immature.[3]

Aristotle concludes this section by commenting that "the courage of a man is shown in commanding, of a woman in obeying."[4] He saw women as incompetent, gullible, mischievous, and weak-willed.[5] Over time, Greek and Roman philosophers became more and more convinced that society would rise or fall on the basis of well-ordered and obedient households. Dio Chrysostom writes this:

> The safety [of our households] depends not only on the likemindedness of master and mistress, but also on the obedience of the servants, yet both the bickering of master and mistress and the wickedness of the servants have wrecked many households. . . . And the good marriage, what else is it save concord between man and wife? And the bad marriage, what is it save their discord? Moreover, what benefit are children to parents when through folly they begin to rebel against them?[6]

Women had their place, and men had theirs. These roles must be respected for the good of the city and country. According to Roman historian Livy, tribune Lucius Valerius argued that women absolutely must not be allowed in leadership in government, religion, or war. Rather, their honor comes from "elegance of appearance, adornment, and apparel."[7]

---

[3] Aristotle, *Politics* 1258a37-b17; translation from Mary R. Lefkowitz and Maureen B. Fant, *Women's Life in Greece and Rome: A Sourcebook in Translation* (London: Bloomsbury, 2016), 64-65.
[4] Aristotle, *Politics* 1260a24.
[5] Aristotle, *Politics* 1269b12-1270a31.
[6] Dio Chrysostom, *Discourses 37–60*, trans. H. Lamar Crosby, Loeb Classical Library (Cambridge, MA: Harvard University Press, 1940), 38.15-16. See also Plutarch, *Moralia* 139-40.
[7] Livy, *History of Rome* 34.7.8-9.

Similar kinds of household expectations are described in Hellenistic Jewish texts. For example, Philo of Alexandria writes this:

> The women are best suited to the indoor life which never strays from the house. . . . Organized communities are of two sorts, the greater which we call cities and the smaller which we call households. Both of these have their governors; the government of the greater is assigned to men under the name of statesmanship, that of the lesser, known as household management, to women. A woman, then, should not be a busybody, meddling with matters outside her household concerns, but should seek a life of seclusion.[8]

Similarly, ancient Jewish sage Ben Sira urges fathers to keep their sons in line, protect the purity of their daughters, rebuke a wife's bad attitude, and honor one's parents (Sir 7:23-27). Again, the point was to protect the household as a major building block of society. The patriarchal ideas behind the household codes are not distinctive to the Greeks and Romans, but the format became more concretely and identifiably Greco-Roman. If the household code system comes from Aristotle and company and not Moses and the prophets, why did some of the New Testament writers include such codes?

APPROACHES TO THE NEW TESTAMENT HOUSEHOLD CODES

There is a lively discussion in the scholarship of 1 Peter that I believe is insightful for thinking through the household codes in the New Testament more generally. When it comes to why 1 Peter includes a household code, and what the expectations for the first readers were, two divergent views have been proposed respectively by David Balch and John Elliott.[9] Balch has argued that 1 Peter's household code was given to urge the readers to conform to social norms in order to fit into

---

[8]Philo, *On the Special Laws* 3.169-71, cited in Eric G. Lovik, "A Look at the Ancient Household Codes and Their Contributions to Understanding 1 Peter 3:1-7," *Calvary Baptist Theological Journal* 11 (1995): 49-63, at 55.

[9]See David L. Balch, *Let Wives Be Submissive: The Domestic Code in 1 Peter* (Chico, CA: Scholars Press, 1981); John H. Elliott, *A Home for the Homeless: A Social-Scientific Criticism of 1 Peter, Its Situation and Strategy* (Minneapolis: Fortress, 1990); Elliott, *1 Peter*, Anchor Bible (New York: Doubleday, 2000).

society and demonstrate "good behavior" on the part of Christians before their neighbors. Put another way, the code reflects an "outward-looking" perspective, attempting to show respectable behavior in society. We might call this an "apologetic" function, whereby accommodation to culture offered opportunities to build bridges where the Christian faith could be shared.[10]

John Elliott offers a different view. The author of 1 Peter does not appear to be primarily interested in helping believers "fit in" within society, assimilating to the world's norms and values. The letter as a whole is concentrated not on pleasing outsiders but on developing a robust Christian identity that *resists* conformity. When it comes to 1 Peter's household code, Elliott admits that the form and basic relational dynamics are borrowed from broader Greco-Roman society, but he argues that the author of this Christian letter presents a distinctive adaptation that focuses on the unique lordship of Christ and deep respect and dignity for all parties, whether those with more power or those with less.[11]

I think elements of both perspectives (Balch's and Elliott's) can be brought together. The fact that the New Testament contains Greco-Roman-style household codes *at all* means that the writers were borrowing from culture, and that the early Christians reinforced, to at least some degree, household relationships according to wider cultural expectations.[12] They wanted to maintain the respect of their neighbors as best they could (Rom 12:18; Gal 6:10; 1 Pet 2:12).[13] But there is a key point to be made here by Elliott: the *differences* or *divergences* from Aristotle and

---

[10]A helpful summary of the views of both Balch and Elliott can be found in David G. Horrell, *1 Peter*, New Testament Guides (London: T&T Clark, 2008), 79-81.

[11]See John Elliott, "1 Peter, Its Situation and Strategy: A Discussion with David Balch," in *Perspectives on 1 Peter*, ed. Charles H. Talbert (Macon, GA: Mercer University Press, 1986), 61-78; see also Balch's essay in the same volume, "Hellenization/Acculturation in 1 Peter," 79-102.

[12]James D. G. Dunn explains that some conformities to wider household practices by Christians "attest clearly to any suspicious outsiders, or even government spies, that Christian discipleship was not disruptive but rather supportive of society's basic structure." Dunn, "The Household Rules in the New Testament," in *The Family in Theological Perspective*, ed. Stephen C. Barton (Edinburgh: T&T Clark, 1996), 43-63, at 57.

[13]Tacitus recounts how Jews had a reputation of despising the (Roman) gods, disowning their country, and having little care for the integrity of the family (*Histories* 5.5); Tacitus describes Christians as hating the whole human race (*Annals* 15.44).

others are deeply meaningful. The New Testament writers did not simply "cut and paste" from standard domestic codes; the codes are "Christianized." With a view toward Paul's household codes, Loveday Alexander sums up well a both/and perspective.

> Paul seems to be caught between the values and ethos of the surrounding culture and the radical challenge offered to those values by the new thing that was happening "in Christ." It looks very much as if Paul was concerned not to rock the boat: he retains the traditional dress code for women, while treating men and women as equal partners in marriage and allowing women freedom to exercise their God-given ministry within the church. Given the entrenched strength of the cultural ethos, it is in many ways remarkable that Paul was able to move as far as he did in accepting women as friends, colleagues, and fellow-workers "in the Lord."[14]

Let's look at Colossians 3:18–4:1 again. Note that, first of all, several of the commands and expectations are set in the context of regard toward "the Lord." The paterfamilias is not the "ultimate authority"; there is a Sovereign who watches over the behavior of all, including the head of household. Second, generous virtues are promoted, including love and gentleness. While Greco-Roman codes tend to focus on *obedience*, the New Testament codes also reinforce care and compassion.[15] There is genuine concern for the well-being of the parties with less, little, or no power; Paul was concerned with protecting not only their bodies but also their hearts (Col 3:21). Furthermore, what Paul calls for here is offered in hope. Slaves, while still "stuck" in their servile positions, are promised a beautiful and lavish inheritance by God; those who have no family or inheritance are given more than they could ask for or imagine (Col 3:24).

One reason why the early Christians may have supported the *potestas* (authoritative power) of the paterfamilias is that he carried *legal* power over the household, generally speaking. This naturally gave the "man of the house" more legal leverage. We need to think of the more well-to-do

---

[14]Loveday Alexander, "Women as Leaders in the New Testament," *Modern Believing* 54, no. 1 (2013): 14-22, at 20.

[15]See Ben Witherington III, "Was Paul a Pro-Slavery Chauvinist?," *Bible Review* 20, no. 2 (2004): 8, 44.

paterfamilias as the manager of a small business. Historian Richard Saller makes this point nicely: "Whereas today *pater familias* conjures up the image of a severe, patriarchal male head of household, for classical Romans it brought to mind, first and foremost, an estate owner."[16] The New Testament writers may have supported the household codes for the sake of some form of expediency; they give us no reason to believe it was because they believed that women were incapable of leadership or inferior to men in this capacity. On the contrary, if we take an example from 1 Timothy, there is a clear expectation that young widows should remarry, have children, and *oikodespoteō*—govern their household well (1 Tim 5:14). First Timothy treats women not as subordinates and followers but as managers and leaders in their own right.

SUBMISSION?

Let's take a closer look at the husband-wife relationship in the household code, and especially the *s* word: submission. The Greek verb *hypotassō* is regularly used in these contexts (Eph 5:24; Col 3:18; 1 Pet 3:5). It refers to organizing oneself under the power, authority, or leadership of someone else. For example, Christians ought to "be subject/submissive" (*hypotassō*) to rulers and civil authorities (Rom 13:1, 5; Titus 3:1). There is a sense of respect that comes with this verb, and also compliance, but it is not exactly the same thing as "obedience." Wives, as Christians, must act according to conscience, not simply blind obedience like a robot or pet. Put another way, the New Testament writers would *not* have expected wives to "submit" to any directives from their husbands that would be considered sinful or harmful to themselves or others. That might seem obvious, but it is worth stating because "submission" was not absolute. If a Christian wife were asked to lie, cheat, or steal, this ought not to be done, that much is clear.

Paul makes some statements in 1 Corinthians that shed light on this dynamic. Husbands, Paul writes, don't have absolute authority over their wives. When Paul states that a husband has authority over his wife's body

---

[16]Richard P. Saller, "*Pater Familias, Mater Familias*, and the Gendered Semantics of the Roman Household," *Classical Philology* 94, no. 2 (1999): 182-97, at 192.

(1 Cor 7:4a), this would have been a natural assumption in the Greco-Roman world. But Paul immediately adds the inverse: "likewise the husband does not have authority over his own body, but the wife does" (1 Cor 7:4b NRSV). That would have been a pretty radical and even dangerous notion in the ancient world! This reciprocity and partnership, Paul urges, should not result in a tug of war over who should have more power. Rather, husbands and wives should come together in mutual care and unity (1 Cor 7:5).

We have mentioned in an earlier chapter that women sometimes were not under the direct power of their husbands; that is, their marriage arrangement was *sine manu* (without the hand of authority of the husband). In that case, the wife remained under the authority of her father (who may have lived elsewhere). By the time of the Roman Empire, *sine manu* marriage became the norm. Women *could* operate with some independence from their husbands. Saller explains that women sometimes had their own money and their own slaves, and perhaps even generated their own (private) income.[17] Perhaps part of the message of the New Testament household codes was that neither the husband nor the wife should try to subvert the other. You see, in some *sine manu* situations, there could be bad blood between the family of the wife and that of the husband over money issues. The household codes promote unity and harmony in the household.

Let's address a couple of myths and questions about the Greco-Roman household codes and the submission commands. First, did wifely submission imply women couldn't "work"? No. Roman women could and sometimes did work, often inside and through the home, but sometimes also outside. Priscilla and Aquila provide a clear example of this, and the wife of Tobit worked in business independently of her husband (Tob 2:11-14). Second, did submission relegate women to domestic duties in the house, like cooking and cleaning? In the Roman world, women were expected to manage the household, and this included tidiness and efficiency. But keep in mind, many households had slaves and low-wage

---

[17]Saller, "*Pater Familias*," 197.

workers that did what we think of as "domestic" work.[18] Elite women spent their time doing all sorts of non-domestic activities, including networking and euergetism.[19] Submission was more about cooperation in general than the carrying out of specific gendered duties.

One final word about submission before moving on. Ephesians 5:21 offers an important insight into how Paul thought about the use of position and power as a Christian: "Submit to one another out of reverence for Christ." This verse, in a way, introduces the Ephesian household code, where we read in Ephesians 5:22, "Wives, submit yourselves to your own husbands as you do to the Lord." Initially, this might seem like a contradiction. How can you have wives submitting to husbands when all are subject to one another? The household codes lay out structure and leadership in a more formal way, but Paul's statement in 5:21 sets the tone and environment for *all* relationships. Mutual submission is not about each one blindly obeying the other and vice versa—that would lead to confusion and chaos. It is more about mutual respect, care, concern, and a spirit of graciousness. No one, no matter how high in the pecking order, should consider themselves "the boss," because only Christ occupies that spot. And Christ's own humility should inspire a spirit of meekness for even the most powerful.

The Ruling Materfamilias

The fact of the Greco-Roman household codes might appear to lead to the assumption that a man's rule of the household was absolute, that it was a right based on sex. Given the misogynistic statements made about women by all manner of ancient writers and in popular culture, this may

---

[18]In the famous parable of the prodigal son, when the son finally returns, the overjoyed father calls for a celebratory meal. He directs his commands not to his wife (she does not appear in the story at all) but to his slaves: "Quickly, bring out a robe—the best one—and put it on him; put a ring on his finger and sandals on his feet. And get the fatted calf and kill it, and let us eat and celebrate" (Lk 15:22-23 NRSV). If there was a wife (in the imaginative world of this made-up parable), she might help supervise the party and manage the slaves, but there would be no cultural assumption that she would do any of the work herself of cooking, decorating, and so forth.

[19]*Euergetism* refers to activities that support the civic good, like sponsoring and donating to public services and local programs. See Sophia Aneziri, "Aspects of Female Euergetism in the Ancient Greek World: Endowments Offered by Women," *Dossier: Des femmes qui comptent: Genre et participation sociale en Grèce et à Rome, Mètis* 18 (2020): 103-22.

reflect the origins of patriarchal household rule. But from a legal and practical standpoint, there appear to be circumstances in the Roman world where a woman became the ruling authority of the household as materfamilias.[20] I have mentioned before that women could and did serve as heads of household in the Roman Empire (see chapter five). We have already talked about Christian women in this situation, like Lydia and Nympha.[21] But as we process the household codes, it is helpful to ponder how a householder like Nympha would have read or reacted to the Colossian code.[22] Gordon Fee argues that in the absence of a husband (she was probably a widow), she would have put *herself* in the position of the paterfamilias: "There would have been no husband to submit to, and she would have assumed the man's role in the other relationships."[23] Fee points out that, in the case of slave couples, Roman law and the household codes did not put authority in the hands of the male slave but in the hands of the householder: "The word to wives has to do with the *householder's* wife, not the wife in a slave couple, who herself would be required to obey the householder, because she was owned by the former."[24] In that case, the household codes are not so much about male

---

[20]The details of Roman law get a bit complicated and are sometimes unclear, but what I gather is that if the paterfamilias died and there was no adult male heir in the household, the materfamilias would wield household authority (*patria potestas*), but she could not possess or bequeath the patrimony (passing down by herself full inheritance of the family name). See Mary Harlow, "In the Name of the Father: Procreation, Paternity, and Patriarchy," in *Thinking Men: Masculinity and Its Self-Representation in the Classical Tradition*, ed. Lin Foxhall and John Salmon (London: Routledge, 1998), 155-69.

[21]See chapter six above; also see Linda Belleville, "Women Leaders in the Bible," in *Discovering Biblical Equality: Biblical, Theological, Cultural & Practical Perspectives*, ed. Ronald W. Pierce, Cynthia Long Westfall, and Christa L. McKirland, 3rd ed. (Downers Grove, IL: IVP Academic, 2021), 70-89, at 86-87.

[22]As you might recall, Nympha is probably a householder and house-church leader in Laodicea; Paul sent a letter to the Laodicean church through her, and she was asked to swap letters with the Colossian church (Col 4:15). So we are imagining here how she received and read the household code in Colossians (3:18–4:1). For some helpful observations along these lines, see Margaret MacDonald, "Can Nympha Rule This House? The Rhetoric of Domesticity in Colossians," in *Rhetoric and Reality in Early Christianities*, ed. Willi Braun (Waterloo, ON: Wilfrid Laurier University Press, 2005), 99-120.

[23]Gordon D. Fee, "Hermeneutics and the Gender Debate," in *Discovering Biblical Equality: Complementarity Without Hierarchy*, ed. Ronald W. Pierce and Rebecca Merrill Groothuis, 2nd ed. (Downers Grove, IL: IVP Academic, 2004), 364-81, at 375. Note that this essay by Fee appears in the second edition of this book and not in the third.

[24]Fee, "Hermeneutics," 375.

power as about household order. Yes, men were the default for *patria potestas* ("fatherly power" over the household), and, yes, men would have comprised the majority of householders in society, but the system did not per se fall apart without a man of the house. Women stepped into this role with some regularity and exercised leadership over children, slaves, and other members of the household estate (like hired workers).

Now, it appears that Nympha is an exception to the norm of male leadership in the house church. She is something of a rarity, probably the only named solo female house-church leader in the New Testament.[25] But she was not alone if we look ahead a bit in time. If we widen our perspective to include second-century Christian texts, we find some interesting information about women house-church leaders. In the postscript of his letter to Polycarp, Ignatius of Antioch first greets "the widow of Epitropus together with the whole household belonging to her and the children."[26] In another letter, Ignatius greets "the household of Tavia," offering his prayer that she may be firm in faith and love.[27] Again, as we consider the New Testament household codes, we must take into account that it was not essential that households be led by men, even though that was common. Women could, and did, step into this role. And in these early Christian texts, women householders (many or most of them presumably widows) were identified and affirmed in their leadership capacities, both as managers of their own household and as church leaders.

WHY NOT EQUAL MARRIAGE?

There is no getting around the fact that even when we take into account "exceptions" to the household code "rules," these passages in the New

---

[25]It is worth mentioning a certain Chloe (1 Cor 1:11) who may be another example, though Paul's reference to her is ambiguous in regard to her leadership status. For more on Chloe, see Lucy Peppiatt, *Rediscovering Scripture's Vision for Women: Fresh Perspectives on Disputed Texts* (Downers Grove, IL: IVP Academic, 2019), 127-29. We have also discussed Lydia in chapter six.

[26]Ignatius, *To Polycarp* 8.2.

[27]Ignatius, *To the Smyrnaeans* 13.2. For a longer discussion of Ignatius's references to these women, see Katherine Bain, *Women's Socioeconomic Status and Religious Leadership in Asia Minor in the First Two Centuries C.E.* (Minneapolis: Fortress, 2014), 50, 86, 94. See also Carolyn Osiek and Margaret Y. MacDonald, with Janet H. Tulloch, *A Woman's Place: House Churches in Earliest Christianity* (Minneapolis: Fortress, 2006), 6, 13, 156-58, 214, 236.

Testament still make many of us feel uncomfortable, including me. Why didn't Paul or Peter profess and affirm equal marriage? Yes, we can point to "mutual submission texts" like Ephesians 5:21, but in the end Ephesians still calls for wifely submission. How does this cast a radical Christian vision for marriage and philogyny (respect for women)?

The first thing I would say is that we tend to judge the New Testament household codes against our twenty-first-century ideas and ideals. But I think our *first* job is to compare them to popular marriage expectations, laws, traditions, norms, and dynamics in the New Testament writers' *own* time. We will then see how these writers were moving toward a more gracious, mutual, and loving spirit in the household. David Garland observes how we moderns want to rip the household codes out of our Bibles and throw them away because they are offensive. Garland recognizes that the codes reflect ancient realities (like slavery) that Christians today are called to repudiate. But there is still value in these texts. "If we read Scripture sympathetically, using a hermeneutic of trust as opposed to suspicion, we can see how Christ's lordship subtly deconstructs the old habits of domination and exploitation."[28]

Second, the early Christians were simply not in a position to make public statements directly challenging the Roman social order, and to be honest, that wasn't the approach they took to spreading their faith and values.[29] Rather, they desired to see Christians transform relationships from the bottom up and the inside out. While Paul did, for example, pass on the Aristotelian construct of patriarchal authority (as the default), he wanted to see such a spirit of goodness, generosity, humility, and respect permeate every relationship that there was no buck-stops-here or man-has-the-final-authority mentality.

I am not sure Paul (or Peter, or anyone in ancient society) could conceive of "equal marriage" the way we do now. There was such an omnipresent fog of sexism and misogyny in the Roman world that viewed women as weak, dumb, promiscuous, vindictive, and emotionally

---

[28]David Garland, *Colossians, Philemon*, NIV Application Commentary (Grand Rapids, MI: Zondervan Academic, 2009), 254.

[29]Dunn, "Household Rules," 61.

incontinent. Paul was above the worst of these biases, I believe. As far as we know from the New Testament texts we have, he says only positive things about named women (like Phoebe, Junia, and Priscilla). But I can only assume he, too, walked around with an inherited understanding of the male-led patriarchal household, because that was all he knew. While he could not imagine a post-civil-rights-era conception of equal marriage, I think Paul wanted to see radical mutuality within existing relational systems, a christological sublimation of the status quo. Suzanne Watts Henderson aptly puts it this way:

> The Colossians Code [reflects] a deliberate effort to apply the logic of the cross to the household standards of the day. In particular, the writer takes the prevailing cultural worldview—that of a fixed household hierarchy—and refracts it through the authority of a Lord who transforms human authority. Any deference on the part of wives, children, and slaves stems from neither social pressure nor self-protection, but rather from deference to the Lord of all. . . . Christ's lordship constitutes the "eschatological activity of God" at work to transform the power structure that characterized first-century Greco-Roman household relationships.[30]

Watts identifies the transformative potential of Paul's Christology and theology of the gospel at work in human relationships, but we must admit that this does not completely resolve the disappointment we feel when reading ancient "submission texts" that don't seem to reject oppression of women. There is a way, I think, that Christians today can appreciate the "gospel-progressive" values embedded within the household codes, while also recognizing from our vantage point that this could not be—and must not be—the liberative endpoint. It is simply that the New Testament writers did not have the capacity to *imagine* that ultimate good end, let alone articulate it in their own time. I sometimes compare this to treating cancer with chemotherapy (my daughter had cancer in her toddler years; she is cancer-free now). Chemotherapy is

---

[30]Suzanne Watts Henderson, "Taking Liberties with the Text: The Colossian Household Code as Hermeneutical Paradigm," *Interpretation* 60, no. 4 (2006): 420-32, at 425.

horrible, it has a toxic effect on the body, but it is one of the main ways that we treat cancer. I hope and pray for something better than chemotherapy, but I can't imagine what that is. And I don't know when or if that will ever happen. I wonder whether that is how Paul saw the standard of the patriarchal household rule. Perhaps he could not imagine (from his limited vantage point) something better than this standard, but nevertheless longed for more than, or better than, what existed. In the meantime, he wanted to see it become the best version of itself (or perhaps just the least toxic).

I also think that if we could transport Paul into the twenty-first century and explain how we got to equal marriage theologically and politically, he would need to process it for a bit but would come to see it as a natural outworking of the liberative nature of the gospel. This is a good place, I think, to talk about Galatians 3:28, which helps us understand Paul's theology of social anthropology.[31] Paul writes to the Galatians:

> Now that this faith has come, we are no longer under a guardian.
>
> So in Christ Jesus you are all children of God through faith, for all of you who were baptized into Christ have clothed yourselves with Christ. There is neither Jew nor Gentile, neither slave nor free, nor is there male and female, for you are all one in Christ Jesus. If you belong to Christ, then you are Abraham's seed, and heirs according to the promise. (Gal 3:25-29)

Throughout, this letter focuses on how the Jewish law does and does not operate as part of God's redemptive plan. The law functioned as a *paidagōgos*, a "guardian" (Gal 3:24-25). The *paidagōgos* was a household slave in the ancient world who supervised a young child. They would accompany the child to school, teach them some basic manners of civilized life, help keep them safe when traveling, and sometimes discipline them if they were rebellious. It is difficult to find the exact right English term for *paidagōgos* as we translate Paul's metaphor today, when we don't have an analogous figure. (We might get close with

---

[31]For a helpful "state of the discussion" of Gal 3:28 (1990–2014), see D. Francois Tolmie, "Tendencies in the Interpretation of Galatians 3:28 Since 1990," *Acta Theologica* 19 (2014): 105-29.

something like "strict nanny" or "governess.") The point is that prior to the coming of the Messiah, the people of God had the law, but it was an era when they could not experience all the benefits and freedoms of "adulthood." For example, my older daughter is fifteen. She has her learner's permit to drive. So she can experience driving and *some* of its benefits. But she has to have an adult in the car, and she cannot drive around with her friends until she is sixteen. While she appreciates having the permit (definitely better than *no* permit!), she is more excited about turning sixteen, when the restrictions will be gone (bye-bye, Dad!).[32]

In Galatians 3:25-29, Paul expresses the personal and unifying freedom that comes with Christ. Those who are baptized into Christ become one with him and share his "sonship" status in the family. When Paul says, "There is neither" (Jew/Greek, slave/free, male/female), he is not saying these aspects of identity are completely erased. He is not saying that Jews are no longer Jews, or that males are no longer males. In this particular context, he is talking about the ways in which ethnic, status, and gender factors give someone more or less privilege and value in the ancient family. For example, slaves were an instrumental part of the Roman household, but *as* slaves they could not marry (legally/formally) and had no right to an inheritance. Women could receive one-time goods through an inheritance, but they could not possess all the rights and privileges of a (male) paterfamilias. But in Christ, all believers share in Jesus' unique sonship, no matter their identity or status.[33] Through Christ, every Christian has the same claim to the promised inheritance to Abraham's children.

So what does this mean for women when it comes to family, church, and society? Is Galatians 3:28 a manifesto on Christian civil liberty? Not

---

[32]See my longer discussion of the background of Galatians and specifically how I interpret *paidagōgos* and Gal 3:28 in Nijay K. Gupta, *Galatians*, Story of God Bible Commentary (Grand Rapids, MI: Zondervan Academic, 2023).

[33]For a more robust discussion of these dynamics in Galatians, see Esau McCaulley, *Sharing in the Son's Inheritance: Davidic Messianism and Paul's Worldwide Interpretation of the Abrahamic Land Promise in Galatians* (London: T&T Clark, 2020). For a helpful analysis in terms of a theological social economics, see John M. G. Barclay, *Paul and the Gift* (Grand Rapids, MI: Eerdmans, 2015), 396-97.

really. Paul wasn't thinking about things like the abolition of slavery, or women's rights to vote and hold public office. But Paul's view of participation in the unique and singular sonship of Christ did lead him to think afresh about how we value persons on the basis of certain factors like sex, ethnicity, and legal status. These ways of marginalizing one another are obliterated by the work of Christ.[34] Did this perspective affect and influence how Paul interacted with women? I believe it did. It was common in Paul's time for men to believe that women were lazy, dull, manipulative, weak-willed, and gullible.[35] Paul treated women as strong, productive, trustworthy, and wise co-leaders in ministry. I believe it is more than acceptable to say that what Paul wrote in Galatians 3:28 sowed seeds of respect and equality that blossomed long after his lifetime into the civil rights movements that we cherish and whose benefits we enjoy.

THE DANGERS OF UNIVERSALIZING THE HOUSEHOLD CODES AND "SUBMISSION" IMPERATIVES

The New Testament household codes were given as instructions for first-century churches by the apostles, and they became part of the New Testament. Therefore, Christians treat them as part of God's Word. But that doesn't necessarily mean that they are universal teachings for all Christians everywhere, in all times. It would be foolish to treat the whole Bible in that way.[36] Some passages, like Jesus' Sermon on the Mount teachings, lend themselves to broad instruction about wise living according to kingdom values. But in other places in the New Testament it is clear the

---

[34]See the helpful methodological and theological discussion in Stephen Motyer, "The Relationship Between Paul's Gospel of 'All One in Christ Jesus' (Galatians 3:28) and the 'Household Codes,'" *Vox Evangelica* 19 (1989): 33-48.

[35]See the important and illuminating study by Mary Beard, *Women and Power: A Manifesto* (New York: Random House, 2019); also Inhee C. Berg, "Female Gender Marginality in the Imperial Roman World: Affinity Between Women and Slaves in Their Shared Stereotypes and Penetrability," *Gender Studies* 18 (2019): 1-26.

[36]See my discussion on biblical interpretation in *A Beginner's Guide to New Testament Studies* (Grand Rapids, MI: Baker Academic, 2019); for a more advanced discussion, see Gary T. Meadors, ed., *Four Views on Moving Beyond the Bible to Theology* (Grand Rapids, MI: Zondervan Academic, 2009): contributors include Walter Kaiser, Daniel Doriani, Kevin Vanhoozer, N. T. Wright, with concluding reflections by Mark Strauss, Al Wolters, and Christopher J. H. Wright.

command or advice doesn't apply to everyone—like when Paul tells
Timothy to drink less water and more wine (1 Tim 5:23). That doesn't
work for all stomach bugs! Discernment is required to decide whether a
command in Scripture applies at all times.[37] So, what about the household
codes? One might argue that they should be universalized because they
appear throughout the New Testament and contain justifications like "as
is fitting in the Lord" (Col 3:18). But the problem is that if we rigidly apply
the "submission" dynamics of the household codes as required doctrine
and practice for today, how can we not also smuggle in justification of
slavery? Are they universal as well? Why would we adhere strictly to one
(the husband-wife relationship) and not the other (slavery)? If we see,
then, that the New Testament household codes were *formally* most relevant to the situation of the earliest Christians trying to live out faith in
Jesus Christ in *their* world, how do we seek to be formed by them now
in our world?

Henderson offers some helpful reflections. First, she argues, the codes
are all about the lordship of Christ over all relationships: "The Code calls
all parties to manifest their loyalty to Christ through their interaction
with each other. This 'new life in Christ' transforms those relationships,
whatever their outward form, in a manner that reflects the love that
'binds everything together in perfect harmony' (Col 3:14)."[38] Henderson
recommends abiding by the "strategy" rather than the "strictures" of
these texts. She also observes that, in the case of Colossians, the author
was combating false teaching that creates division and enmity. Colossians, as a whole, aims to stitch families together in harmony. A "Christianized" household code was meant to be a step in the direction of unity
and peace. So Henderson asks, "Do our homes promote division, discord,
and condemnation by 'promoting self-imposed piety' (Col 2:23), that
reflects the brokenness of our world? Or, alternatively, do they serve as
the staging place for the renewal of that 'old self with its practices'
(Col 3:9), bearing living witness to the reconciling marks of 'compassion,

---

[37]See N. Clayton Croy, *Prima Scriptura: An Introduction to New Testament Interpretation* (Grand Rapids, MI: Baker Academic, 2011).
[38]Henderson, "Taking Liberties," 430.

kindness, humility, meekness, and patience' (Col 3:12)?"[39] A final point Henderson makes is that the code probably did carry an apologetic function, presenting Christians as thoughtful participants in society. The best that Christians could do in the time of the apostles was accept the hierarchical social conventions and then try to infuse them with christological love and grace. But we don't live in a (legal) patriarchal world built on slave labor.[40] Hearing and obeying the New Testament household codes *as Christian Scripture* today should not mean turning the clock back to first-century patriarchy—that's a step in the *wrong* direction. Christians today will *not* faithfully attract the outside world now by subjugating women or slaves: "The non-negotiable concern of this writer remains clear: to establish households that embody the 'new life in Christ' in a manner that captivates, rather than repels, the residents of the surrounding world."[41]

THE HOUSEHOLD CODES AND THE WOMEN LEADERS OF THE EARLY CHURCHES

In modern discussions, debates continue as to how Christian women and men ought to relate in house, church, and society. But I see no reason why the household codes would have prevented women from serving in ministry. What we *do* know is that women could and did serve in powerful roles in ministry leadership. Despite the patriarchal culture of the Roman world, there were still prominent and powerful women in business and public affairs. Not only did the early churches not stand against that, but they preached the gospel to such women and were clearly comfortable putting Christian communities into their hands (e.g., Nympha). Of course, male leadership inside and outside the church was normative, but as we have seen throughout this book, women were everywhere and did just about everything. This is true for early churches as well. Put another way, the fact of the New Testament household codes

---

[39]Henderson, "Taking Liberties," 431.

[40]I don't take Henderson to mean here that cultural patriarchy or "sweatshop labor" problems are not real, only that we have rightly done away with legal slavery and many discriminatory laws that underprivilege women, people of color, and immigrants.

[41]Henderson, "Taking Liberties," 431-32.

did not prevent women from exercising influence and leadership. At the end of the day, it appears Paul was a pragmatist when it came to ministry. He did not vet his list of gifted individuals to screen out women and promote men. Whoever had Spirit-given capacity and availability for leadership, man or woman, he supported and commended.

Postscript

What Paul's most famous prohibition text in 1 Timothy 2 and the household codes show us is not a unilateral prohibition of women teaching or acting with independent leadership and authority in the church. Rather, these texts are about harmony and unity in the church, and also about offering a respectable witness to the wider world. We ought not to take these commands as universal Christian laws, any more than we ought to have slaves today just because some of the early Christians had slaves and called them to obey.

We ended with these prohibition and submission texts because they deserve to be addressed, but I chose not to begin with them because I think it is important to see how the New Testament presents actual women who paved the way for the church and who became leaders alongside men in the early Christian communities.

For readers eager to go deeper into some of the topics discussed in this book, below I offer a suggested reading list.

Barr, Beth Allison. *The Making of Biblical Womanhood: How the Subjugation of Women Became Gospel Truth*. Grand Rapids, MI: Brazos, 2021.

Bauckham, Richard. *Gospel Women: Studies of the Named Women in the Gospels*. Grand Rapids, MI: Eerdmans, 2002.

Bond, Helen, and Joan Taylor. *Women Remembered: Jesus' Female Disciples*. London: Hodder & Stoughton, 2022.

Clark-Soles, Jaime. *Women in the Bible*. Interpretation: Resources for the Use of Scripture in the Church. Louisville, KY: Westminster John Knox, 2020.

Cohick, Lynn H. *Women in the World of the Earliest Christians: Illuminating Ancient Ways of Life*. Grand Rapids, MI: Baker Academic, 2009.

Hemelrijk, Emily. *Hidden Lives, Public Personae: Women and Civic Life in the Roman West*. Oxford: Oxford University Press, 2015.

Hylen, Susan. *Women in the New Testament World*. Oxford: Oxford University Press, 2019.

Lee, Dorothy. *The Ministry of Women in the New Testament: Reclaiming the Biblical Vision for Church Leadership*. Grand Rapids, MI: Baker Academic, 2021.

Mathews, Alice. *Gender Roles and the People of God: Rethinking What We Were Taught About Men and Women in the Church*. Grand Rapids, MI: Zondervan, 2017.

Osiek, Carolyn, and Margaret Y. MacDonald, with Janet H. Tulloch. *A Woman's Place: House Churches in Earliest Christianity*. Minneapolis: Fortress, 2006.

Peppiatt, Lucy. *Rediscovering Scripture's Vision for Women: Fresh Perspectives on Disputed Texts*. Downers Grove, IL: IVP Academic, 2019.

Pierce, Ronald W., Cynthia Long Westfall, and Christa L. McKirland. *Discovering Biblical Equality: Biblical, Theological, Cultural & Practical Perspectives*. 3rd ed. Downers Grove, IL: IVP Academic, 2021.

Tidball, Derek, and Dianne Tidball. *The Message of Women*. Downers Grove, IL: InterVarsity Press, 2012.

Westfall, Cynthia Long. *Paul and Gender: Reclaiming the Apostle's Vision for Men and Women in Christ*. Grand Rapids, MI: Baker Academic, 2016.

General Index

Scripture Index